W9-BUN-468

Storm Tide

Storm
Tide

Marge Piercy and Ira Wood

Fawcett Columbine
The Ballantine Publishing Group
New York

A Fawcett Columbine Book
Published by The Ballantine Publishing Group

Copyright © 1998 by Middlemarsh, Inc.

http://www.randomhouse. com

Library of Congress Cataloging-in-Publication Data
Piercy, Marge.
Storm tide : a novel / by Marge Piercy & Ira Wood. —1st ed.
p.   cm.
ISBN 0-499-00166-0 (alk. paper)
I. Wood, Ira.   II. Title.
PS3566.I4S77   1998
813'.54—dc21   97-48414

Manufactured in the United States of America

First Edition: June 1998

10   9   8   7   6   5   4   3   2   1

Storm Tide

DAVID

 When the winter was over and my nightmares had passed, when someone else's mistakes had become the subject of local gossip, I set out for the island. I made my way in increments, although the town was all of eighteen miles square. To the bluff overlooking the tidal flats. Down the broken black road to the water's edge. To the bridge where her car was found, overturned like a turtle and buried in mud.

The color of bleached bones, the shape of a crooked spine, the Squeer Island bridge was a product of willful neglect. Every ten years some town official proposed a new bridge and promptly fell into a hole full of lawyers. The beaches were private, the summer people moneyed, the year-rounders reclusive. No one wanted the sandy ways paved or the hedgerows cut back. Your deed bought more than seclusion on Squeer Island; here life as you knew it ceased to exist.

There had been a family named Squeer, but only Stumpy was left. If you asked how the island got its name, people would say, " 'Cause it's queer over there," and they didn't mean homosexual. They meant queer things happened. Peculiar things. Uncommon for a small town.

During high tide there was no access by land. The road to town flooded. Ducks paddled over the bridge. Fish darted through the guard-rails. The summer people stocked their shelves with vodka and paper-backs and waited uneasily for the tide to recede. The residents lived for its return.

I left my car on the island side of the bridge. I slogged along the mud banks of the creek, driving fiddler crabs in front of me like herds of frightened crustacean sheep. The grasses were four feet high at the edge of the bank, an inch wide, sharp as razors. They mentioned lacerations across the palms; one in her right eyeball. I closed one eye. I wondered what it was like to sink in this bottomless liquid clay, this mud the fishermen called black mayonnaise. What did it feel like to die this way? They said her hair was encrusted with seaweed and crabs, that an eel had eaten into the armpit. They say she must have struggled to free herself, that as she grabbed at the grass her efforts only increased the suction of the mud. They still call it an accidental death.

* * *

Saltash, Massachusetts, was founded in 1672 and named for a village in Cornwall, England. Summer population: twenty thousand. Winter population: divide by ten. The economy is eighty percent tourism; the leading economic indicator: the number of pickups idling outside Barstow's Convenience at seven A.M. Like any quaint, postcard-perfect Cape Cod town, there are hundreds of stories to be ashamed of here. Only conscience dictates that I start with my own.

If you lived in Saltash, you'd know that I grew up here and had been famous for something—although you probably wouldn't remember what. You might have heard that I left town at eighteen, after having signed a contract for a small fortune, and returned twelve years later. You'd know that I live in a small white half Cape on Round Pond Road and drive a red pickup; that I run a landscaping business with my sister, which (no one forgets to mention) she owns. You might have voted for me for selectman. Everyone I talked to told me they did. (For the record, I received 578 votes.) You would say I wasn't the type to make promises or suck up to people; you might say I kept to myself. You would excuse me for my private life; 578 people obviously did. According to my backers (twelve old men who fancied themselves Saltash's political kingmakers) I had been drawn in by the Squeer Island crowd—a local epithet implying strange sexual practices and not far from the truth. "Seduced" was the explanation whispered most.

It happened in September, the night of the new moon. A storm was tracking our way. Judith warned me that we were facing one of the highest tides of the year. If I couldn't get over the bridge in time, I wouldn't get through at all. "Gordon expects you. He really wants you there," she said, just so I knew it wasn't her who did.

More than anyone I've ever known, Judith loved rituals. She loved to cook for people. They didn't have to be important people or the best of friends. A festive, well-set table surrounded by guests who weren't watching their weight would do: people who arrived on time and had interests other than themselves and remembered to thank her for her trouble. But tonight was special. There were over thirty guests at the table of Gordon Stone and Judith Silver. It was special because it was Rosh Hashanah, and Judith had instituted the celebrating of the Jewish holidays when she became Gordon's fourth wife thirteen years before I met her. Special because Gordon was dying of lung cancer, and he was saying goodbye.

He looked like a living skeleton. His color was grayish-blue and he could not sit up, but reclined, lying on a couch with heaped-up pillows that had been dragged to the table. Judith was wearing a short red shift tonight and her fine skin and dark hair shone. Her necklace and ear-rings were silver. Judith did not like gold. She once told me silver was a more human metal because it aged, it changed.

Judith had prepared traditional foods. Buckwheat groats with mush-room gravy and bow-tie noodles, roast chicken, potato kugel, gefilte fish, apples dipped in honey. Those friends who weren't Jewish—including two of Gordon's adult children whose mother wasn't—hummed the songs we taught them and bowed their heads as we blessed the wine, and followed everything we did with the curious respect of anthropolo-gists at an Mbundu marriage ceremony in Angola. What they might have missed, however, was the fact that Judith wouldn't be caught alone in the same room with me, removing herself whenever I tried to pull her aside to talk.

No one on the island asked about Judith and Gordon and me. What was common knowledge was never uttered. What mattered was that Gordon had spent an entire summer vacation helping Stumpy Squeer rebuild his house after a fire; that Judith had had a troubling intuition about a high school girl's painful cramps and drove her through a snow-storm to a good Boston hospital in time to be treated for a tubal preg-nancy. There were feuds and there were grudges. But judgments among the year-rounders were limited to practical problems: Whose dog had ripped through whose garden? Who rented to noisy college kids in July?

By the second course, the lights began to flicker. The surf was halfway up the dune. Judith had arranged housing for almost everyone, except of course for me. But after the summer of silence, I was deter-mined to talk to her and, finally, finally caught her alone in the kitchen.

"What do you want with me, David?" She turned her back. "Talk to Crystal. You're going to marry her."

"I don't want to marry Crystal. Can we sit down and talk about this?"

"Not here. Not now. I have thirty people to settle in for the night. If you absolutely insist on talking, wait for me in my shack."

Judith's "shack" was an electronic cottage, part sanctum, part home office. It was fitted out with a computer, two printers, copier, scanner, and fax—as well as the double bed where we had made love many times. I lay back against the headboard, waiting, rehearsing my speech while the three cats who had been locked up there for the evening jumped from the dresser to my stomach and off again, taking out their anger on me. Sand pitted the glass and blew in through gaps in the jambs. You found sand in your shoes after nights like this, a film of sand like dust. Every shelf in the cottage shook. Wind lifted the shingles and smacked the roof. The joists shivered and sawdust trickled over the bed like snow. An hour passed. Water ran in sheets down the windows and poured from the downspout. Judith did not come.

When I heard the sound of a car horn, I knew something was wrong. One long drone, as if the driver was leaning on the wheel, and as it got closer, short blasts of pure panic. I ran for the main house, ran hard through the muddy courtyard in the pelting rain.

What I need to say is that I'm telling all this to get it straight, to reduce a tragedy to its parts and somehow understand. Call it an autopsy. A dissection of something that had once been alive; a determination as to the cause of death.

DAVID

2 I was born with a talent, a peculiar accident of reflex and bone, like an eidetic memory, or the facility to play an instrument by ear, an aptitude as curious as it was admired. I was a phenomenon, a teenage celebrity, for by some fluke of chromosomal alchemy that in no way resembled the physiology of my parents, I could throw a baseball faster, harder and with more accuracy than any other boy in my school, my county, my state. I became the focus of my family, the obsession of the local media and the hope of an entire town.

My abilities revealed themselves accidentally. We were not, except for my uncle Georgie, a family inclined toward sports: My father had been a manufacturer of women's dresses who had lost two businesses on Seventh Avenue before going into debt to buy a curtain factory on Cape Cod. Because of the size of the town and the simplicity of the product, my father assumed he could master the transition with ease. But just as his stitchers had sewn half the collars backwards on a big Christmas order of red velvet dresses for Macy's and his best salesman defected, taking the buyers with him, the crises presented themselves in Massachusetts as frequently as they had in Manhattan. My father had no time for games. Baseball, like poker and local women, were the bad habits of his younger brother Georgie, who worked for my father. Georgie—never George to my father; never "my brother" but "my kid brother"—had followed us north. In charge of maintenance and shipping, he partied with the workers his age and the local fishermen as if were native born. Up at five A.M., never home at night before eight, my father lived exactly as he had in New York, preoccupied with the business, while Georgie dated girls from town and drank beer in the oyster shacks, cast for bluefish and sea bass on the back shore and learned to bait his hooks by the light of the moon.

My father's factory was the largest business in Saltash and the least solvent. As payroll day came around, my parents' arguments began, the recriminations and slamming doors, the curses. My mom took private piano students and worked when she could as a substitute teacher, but every Sunday night my parents sat at the dining room table, staring into the account books, willing the figures to change with the same concentration and futility as if trying to make the furniture levitate.

My sister Holly was too young for the carping to upset her, but I got out of the house whenever I could. What I didn't hear couldn't bother me. My world was the old wooden bridge at the mouth of the Tamar River (long since replaced by a cement dike). When the tide was low, a steep sandy beach full of shells and crabs and acres of stones glistened in the sunlight. When the tide was coming in, waves rolled under the bridge or crashed against the causeway. During spring and fall, the alewives migrated underneath and I tried to catch them in an old wire net. The fact that I was different came up occasionally, as when a girl refused to kiss me in a game of spin the bottle or when I was held down and stripped by some older kids who wanted to see a circumcised prick. But the incidents were generally benign. (Soon after we moved to Saltash—I was in first grade—the teacher gave me a generic picture to color, a horse instead of a Santa Claus because, as she announced to the class, Jews don't believe in Christmas.) And the truth is, we were different. We spoke more quickly and with accents that turned heads in the street; we didn't eat shellfish, the one product native to the town, and nobody had ever heard of our holidays. We were stocky, with coarse dark hair and light eyes. My mother asked for books that shocked the librarian. If isolation bothered me, I wasn't conscious of it, until the day I snapped.

I was sitting on the old wooden bridge with Corkie Pugh, watching a quahog dragger slowly crisscross the harbor. Corkie was an overfed, freckle-faced boy with a lisp and an inclination to sadism. Corkie so enjoyed dismembering small animals and embarrassing his sister in public that even I, who had no friendships to speak of, shied away from him. But because his sister took piano lessons from my mom, I was stuck with him. Corkie's mother usually stayed for coffee after the lesson, and if my mom hadn't made what she called any "real" friends in Saltash, Lucinda Pugh was the woman she saw most often.

Nobody believed this, but there was no precipitating animosity that day, no shouting. We were tossing rocks at an empty beer can in the sand, watching it jump, when Corkie, as easily as he told me how he watched his sister on the toilet through a hole he had drilled in the bathroom wall, said simply, "Your parenth are gettin' a divorth, y'know."

"No, sir."

"Yes, thir. Your mom tol' mine."

I hopped down. Walked off. Kicked a few stones. Flipped one flat stone side-arm over the water's gray-green surface and watched it hop, once, twice, a third time. Then with no thought whatsoever, I began to hurl stones at Corkie, as quickly as I could pick them up, fast and hard. I had aimed at targets before, but never with such delight in my accuracy, pinging his elbow, his knee, his left buttock as he ran off threatening me with reform school. I wasn't aware of being angry or frustrated. I had no words with which to explain myself. It was as if everything I needed to say could be expressed through the violent articulation of my arm. I walked home without lifting my eyes from the ground. I blew out our garage windows, one after another at thirty feet. I took aim at my mother's car, smashing the taillights, rattling the hubcaps. I was shaking when they stopped me. I dropped to the ground. I was a human gun, an eleven-year-old catapult of accuracy and rage.

I was taken before the school psychologist and the chief of police, but only Georgie seemed to know what to do with me. He set up beer bottles on a tree trunk and bet me a nickel each I couldn't hit them. I did. He took me to the town dump, gave me rocks and pointed: that rusty old alternator. Plink! The fender of the abandoned truck. The headlamp socket. One Friday after work, Georgie gathered some of the factory guys at the loading dock and took bets on what I could hit. A can at forty feet. A stop sign at fifty. A pinecone on a dead branch. With his winnings he bought me a baseball glove.

Saltash was a town with a grade school, three churches, and a movie theater open on weekends only. Saturday night after the show, teenagers raced cars down Hill Street from the town's only grocery to the harbor, whipped around and started uphill again. The stores closed at six and the churches banned bingo. A Little League pitcher who allowed nine runs all season and could strike out half the junior high school team was something to watch. I took us to the state finals three years running. The local paper printed my stats every week in a sidebar on the sports page headed: SALTASH'S DAVEY GREENE. I started pitching for the high school team in ninth grade. In tenth the bird dogs arrived, retired baseball junkies who traveled all over New England searching out talent, notifying the big league scouts who showed up the following year smoking cigars, sitting in their own aluminum lawn chairs instead of the bleachers and logging every pitch I made on their clipboards.

After school, after work, after the season (he never missed a day), Georgie worked out with me. The next Sandy Koufax, he called me. The little Jew that could. Georgie was a veteran who in his army pictures looked like Elvis Presley: pompadour, pouty eyelids, lips in a smirk. I had once heard my parents whispering about a woman and child in Korea. Georgie lived in an apartment built in the loft of the barn behind my parents' house. His window shades were always drawn. He kept Miles Davis albums in milk crates and his mattress on the bedroom floor. One day, when I reached for a baseball that rolled under the couch, I found his girlfriend's black lace bra. Georgie used to meet me every day at the town field for practice. He had a piece of foam rubber he stuffed into his catcher's mitt so his palm wouldn't sting from my fastball. He taught me how Whitey Ford held a runner on first base, how Bob Feller stared into a batter's eyes with contempt. He taught me how to raise my leg and stretch like Warren Spahn so that my delivery was as swift as the recoil of a bow.

In my junior year, I didn't lose a game. My parents and I were invited to ride in the backseat of a yellow convertible in the Fourth of July parade. My mother was suddenly David Greene's mom to every merchant in town. My father mail-ordered a new baseball glove and a pair of white leather baseball shoes from Herman's Wonderful World of Sports. We were invited to the annual Lynch family barbecue.

Georgie said I had the closest thing to a perfect fastball he had ever seen. He had watched Koufax pitch and Larry Sherry and said I had their speed, their power. He convinced my father that he should be given time off from work at the factory to be my coach. It was an investment, Georgie insisted, because when I graduated, I would get a bonus to sign with a professional team.

Georgie went out drinking with the scouts. He was being wooed by the Cubbies, the Pirates, the Mets, who competed to earn my family's trust. He told me stories about athletes who had been swindled out of every dollar they ever made. Every time my fastball cracked into the catcher's mitt, every time I struck out a batter, I glanced at Georgie in the stands. In my senior year, twelve major league teams had scouts at every game. I was working on a string of shutouts. I was throwing at close to eighty miles an hour, putting batters down in five pitches. As the string grew to four, reporters from the big city newspapers interviewed me in my living room at home. When no team scored off me in six games, the front office men arrived. "You're the man," Georgie whispered, rubbing my shoulder. I didn't think about blowing the string because I had never blown it, because I was the only kid in school who didn't have to take gym. (I could hurt myself.) The only kid from Saltash who had ever been asked to speak in front of the Masons (who recruited my father, their first Jew). The batters had heard of me and swung nervously, trying to kill my pitches, or cowered when I hurled a warning shot near their heads. They weren't facing a pitcher but a legend, a seventeen-year-old who had never fixed himself a meal—"What if you burned yourself?" my mother said—whose arm had been kissed by God.

I signed with the Chicago Cubs for the largest bonus ever paid to a kid from my state. I was assigned to play in Wytheville, in the Appalachian League. I was given a going-away party by the entire town. There were fireworks at the pier. Local restaurants served free franks and potato salad. The bandstand was decorated with streamers and a sign was strung across Commercial Street, DAVEY GREENE SALTASH'S PITCHING MACHINE.

Out of the million and a half guys who graduated high school, I was one of only five hundred signed to a professional contract—and every single one of them was a local legend. I was facing the best athletes in America. Like every other rookie, I had good days and bad. Only, I'd never had bad days before. I was shaken by the crack of bat meeting ball, the sight of the coaches' narrowed eyes on the hitters, not on me, the jeers of the home team crowd when I walked a man after twelve pitches. I felt every hit off me as a whiplash across my back, a stinging pain that left me waiting for another. One night, after walking the streets of some town whose name I couldn't even remember, I called Georgie from a phone booth, pleading for help. "What's the matter with me?"

"Nothing's the matter."

"But I stink."

"Did the coaches say that?"

"No."

"'Course not, 'cause they know it takes time. How long did it take Koufax to find himself?"

"Six years, but—"

"But nothing. What did he lead the league in in 'fifty-eight?"

"Wild pitches."

"Fucking right. He was a maniac out of control. Remember that. You gotta have patience. You've got the best stuff I've ever seen. You're Davey Greene, the Pitching Machine."

But my best was only good, not great. In this league they waited out my pitches. They understood the physics of the game, the slow rising trajectory as the ball picked up steam; they didn't try to crush the pitch before it crossed the plate. At first Georgie was right, the coaches weren't concerned. They'd seen a thousand kids like me. I was just another rookie getting his lumps.

But I wasn't. I was the pitching machine. The kid who got his father invited to be a Mason, who gave his parents a reason not to get divorced. Other guys played cards after the games or picked up girls. I commandeered a catcher and pitched. The harder I worked, the more I tired my arm, but I didn't know what else to do. On my best days, I'd pitch three or four decent innings then walk four men, hit a batter, send a pitch into the dirt before I was pulled. I went back to Saltash in October with a record of two wins, nine losses.

I worked indoors with Georgie all winter, determined to make my reputation come spring. The club liked what they saw and sent me up two notches, to Winston-Salem in the Carolina League, where we took chartered buses to our away games instead of school buses and stayed in motel rooms two to a room instead of four. But as soon as I got behind on the count, I began to panic, to lose control, to throw harder, and harder still, until my arm ached. The coaches assured me that fastball pitchers took time to develop, that more important than strength, every movement of the arms, the kick, the follow-through, had to be in sync. I had to grow into my pitch, they told me. It would take years.

But I couldn't wait years. I needed the applause of the crowd like I needed air. I needed the envy of my teammates, my coach's arm around my shoulder as we walked to the clubhouse, the special wink that set me off from the other players, the fear in the batter's eyes.

When I was sent down to Peoria, my manager swore the club still had confidence in me, that I was a second-year rookie who needed to grow into my pitch, my body; to mature, he kept saying. But all I felt was shame. The Peoria Chiefs were a Single A club; the dung heap of baseball. I imagined my old teammates laughing at me; the Corkie Pughs back in Saltash waiting for me to return a failure. I could not keep on losing.

Working with an old reliever who had spent nine years with the Cubbies, I learned how to throw change of speed pitches, curveballs, sliders. I wouldn't give up. I could still win. I dropped my fastball like an unfaithful lover. Instead of overpowering batters, I would psych them out, use strategy. When I finally won a game, I slept the night through for the first time in a year.

Georgie was disappointed I'd abandoned the fastball; he said I'd had a pure talent for it. But Georgie was a small-town shipping clerk, I told myself. Fine with a high school pitcher, ignorant about the reality of the majors.

The following season I was assigned to the Double A Pittsfield Cubs. We trained in Florida with the big club, played our games on the same field. We stayed in single rooms in a hotel with room service. I took my meals in the same restaurants as Billy Buckner, Bruce Sutter, and Dick Tidrow. But what I'd hoped was a minor problem of timing began to recur. My leg twisted when I started my wind up, my shoulder dropped too soon. My hips and feet could not coordinate. All my old moves, my fastball moves, returned. Ten years of memory encoded in my muscles superimposed itself on my newly learned style.

At away games, the crowds cheered in ecstatic disbelief. At home, the fans booed. I no longer had a fastball or a change of speed. My arm was a slingshot with a mind of its own. My manager winced as he watched me wind up. The simplest rhythms were beyond me. The more I concentrated, the more deliberate my movements became, and the more awkward. I was like a man who had forgotten how to walk.

On the morning after blowing a fourteen inning tie with a wild pitch, I found my name on the barracks pink sheet, unconditionally released. I stuffed my suitcase and talked to no one, drove off in a cloud of shame and stopped at the exit with nowhere to go. I'd been selected to do one thing in this world and failed. In a way, the talent had never belonged to me, but to Georgie; to my father and mother. Without the Pitching Machine, there was no Davey Greene. The sports pages were my mirror: without them I didn't have a face.

On those rare occasions when I attempted to make sense of my baseball career, I wrote it off to being young. I'd destroyed my talent by not staying with it; swapped something difficult for the easy way out. But time would tell that this was a deeper flaw, a thin crack in strong cedar that would widen with age. Fifteen years later I was to repeat the mistake, and ruin more lives than my own.

DAVID

3

I remember my first night in Judith's office. I remember watching her middle finger trace the rim of her wine-glass around and around lightly, the way we seemed to be circling each other. It was mid-January and the world outside was brittle as glass. After dark, the streets along the waterfront seemed to radiate a frozen phosphor of road salt and snow. She had invited me over to talk politics, but her questions were all about me.

Most people listened to my story with thinly disguised pleasure. Everyone loves the tale of a hero fallen on hard times. Not Judith. "You must have been so lonely," she said, as if she knew how it felt to lose something you loved.

She had begun by asking me a simple question about growing up in Saltash, and I blurted out the story of my life. "In all those years of baseball, I had never held a real job or written a check or cooked myself a meal. I felt like a released convict."

She held back a smile. "With a sixty thousand dollar bonus."

"By the time I was thirty-two, I had blown every cent, ruined my marriage, lost my son and failed at the one thing I ever wanted to do with my life."

"Precocious, weren't you? Takes most men till forty." She avoided causing me embarrassment by averting her eyes. She fussed with her necklace, resettled herself like a bird on its perch, momentarily fluttering. There was something birdlike about Judith. She was small. She moved quickly. Her almost-black eyes were watchful, alert to trouble. She stopped to think before she laughed. Something most people would regard as funny seemed to cause her concern, as if worried the joke might be on her. She looked my age but acted much older. She wore wool and fine leather; I doubt she owned a pair of sweatpants. She was never Judy, always Judith.

I assumed she came from an affluent family because of her elegance, but the past she told me in snippets was of a hardworking immigrant mother, of growing up in a slum. Most women I knew complained of their mothers. Judith spoke of hers with deep affection and respect.

The wind had picked up. A sheaf of ice slid off the roof to the parking lot below. When I was a kid, this old building near the wharf had been a boathouse and after that a feed store; something called the

Rainbow People's Gallery when the first hippies moved to town, then abandoned for years. Judith had renovated it into an office suite downstairs and one enormous loft-style apartment above, in which we sat, overlooking the harbor, frozen solid since New Year's and dry as a salt flat in the clear light of the moon. Everything in the apartment was the color of fire; the stuffed chairs burnt orange, the walls vermilion, the shaggy wool rug a slash of yellows and reds. I remember three sources of light: a table lamp, a gas fire in the grate, and Judith's face, which seemed to absorb them both and cast a glow of its own.

She was known as one of the best lawyers on the Cape. It was tough luck if she wouldn't represent you; disaster if she was on the other side. She had argued zoning cases before the Supreme Judicial Court and had a loyal clientele among those involved in the drug trade, but the specialty that gave her a demonic aura with the men in town was divorce law and custody cases. She had the reputation of getting a good deal for discarded wives.

I felt large in Judith's presence, which was strange. Despite wide shoulders and a blocky frame, I was small for a pitcher. At five-foot-ten, my nickname was Little Chief. I have some Tartar from my mother's side, causing a slightly Asian cast to my eyes. I have long black hair. In summer, when my skin bronzed, my pitching coach for the Winston-Salem Spirits said I looked like a fair-eyed Indian.

"You're suddenly quiet," she said. "Something the matter?"

"Maybe I'm feeling kind of unsure."

"About what?" She wasn't going to make this easy.

"About what we're doing. How we got here like this."

"You drove here in your big red truck."

"I think you know what I mean."

"We're becoming better friends, David. I assume we are."

For a professional athlete, even at my level, there had always been women. But no one like Judith Silver. No one who studied foreign languages for pleasure or was quoted every week in the paper. No one who was happily married to a man with cancer.

I had first met Judith through my sister Holly. Holly always told people she was my business partner, but it was her husband Marty's money behind the nursery. I didn't know a thing about the landscaping business when I moved back to Saltash. I had no skills, no savings; only an ex-wife in Florida and a child I was permitted to see twice a year.

My brother-in-law Marty was a syndicated humorist whose work hit too close to home to make me laugh. My sister was training as a geneticist when she married him. Next to science, she'd always loved the outdoors. She told people that she bought McCullough's Nursery and Garden Center to keep herself from becoming a mad housewife. Nobody who knew her husband laughed. Marty's twice-weekly column appeared in over a hundred newspapers nationwide. He wrote frequently for GQ and two of his books had been best-sellers. His shtick was a nervous dad's response to a society out of control: there wasn't a man alive better qualified.

Marty lived with an almost paralyzing fear of everyday life. When the family had a home in the Boston area, he was afraid of schoolyard abductions. He demanded Holly drop their girls at their classroom every morning and pick them up in the afternoon. He carefully examined all toys with moving parts and insisted that Holly soak the family's fruits and vegetables no less than twenty minutes in a soapy solution before serving. After the random murder of a law professor in their neighborhood, Marty moved the family to Saltash. Doing lectures, promotions and television, he was on the road part of every week. He installed a fax machine in the girls' bedroom and corrected their homework assignments from hotels around the country. He bought Holly a cellular phone for her birthday so he could reach her anywhere, day or night.

I was out of baseball before Marty met my sister, but it pleased him that I had been a professional athlete. It meant his children would have strong genes. "We're Jewish," he said. "We need all the help we can get." Although I had grown up in a rural Christian area where I never felt more than a grudging tolerance of my religion, it would be accurate to say that my most intimate contact with anti-Semitism came from my brother-in-law, who sincerely hated himself.

I arrived at their kitchen door one night to ask Holly to sign some checks, when Marty summoned me to the dining room. "Sit down, David. Have you eaten? You have to eat. Hol? I asked your brother to stay. He can't eat if he doesn't have a plate."

Besides the girls—Kara, eight, and Allison, six and a half—there were two other people at the table. The man was much older than Marty and Holly. He had a long rectangular face, folds of skin like melting candle wax beneath glittering dark blue eyes. His voice was resonant and he had been holding court until I entered the room, interrupting himself with bouts of a frightening cough. The woman I guessed to be around my age was dark-haired and petite, a reserved Audrey Hepburn to his big-voiced John Huston. They were introduced to me as Gordon, a former professor of Marty's, and Judith.

"I'm sorry," I said. "I can't stay."

Marty insisted, "Have a little something, have a lot of something. Take a doggie bag, back up your truck. Your sister made enough to feed an army. It's her Jewish obsession with food."

"An obsession?" I noticed a tremor in the older man's hand. "Or a survival technique?"

"Here he goes," Marty said excitedly. "I want to start my tape recorder whenever he opens his mouth."

"Before the expulsion from ancient Israel, the Jews were an agrarian people. On sacred holidays, they congregated outside the Temple to offer a ritual portion of their harvest as thanksgiving. When the Temple was destroyed and the Jews dispersed, the rabbis decreed that each family's dinner table represent the altar of the Temple. Food became more than something to eat. It was a ritual connection to history."

"And that," Marty raised his index finger, "is how we became the Chosen. Eleven million people chosen to eat too much."

"Why can't you stay?" Holly said.

"Just need your signature." I held up the check register.

"For your nursery?" Judith seemed interested for the first time.

"You can call it that," Marty said. "I call it my wife's plan to save me from writer's block. She spends everything I make so I have to work harder."

"Don't believe him," Gordon said. "Sounds like a column to me."

"Herr Professor, on the money again." Marty touched his face to the table, as if bowing. When he raised his head, there was a bit of mashed potato on the tip of his nose and the girls burst into uncontrollable giggles. "It'll run next Monday," Marty said.

"Folks." I backed away. "Pleasure to meet you. Holly, sign this, please. And this." I was out of there.

Holly had bought the nursery at auction after the McCullough family lost it to the bank. The place had a reputation for skinny trees at Christmas and spring seedlings that died as soon as they left the greenhouse, but Holly turned it around. In the nursery Holly effervesced confidence. Around Marty she seemed subdued. That had been the case since they were dating. But at work she was my kid sister again: full of energy and attitude, brown hair braided down her back, her face darkly tanned. She set up a farmer's market to sell apples and fall produce. She lured customers in with a Thanksgiving turkey raffle. As I was standing up the twenty-foot Scotch pine that arrived from Canada every December, she wondered why we couldn't have a menorah and told me to build one, a big silver and gold painted job made of plywood. Holly and I were on our own turf again; we sang oldies in the greenhouse and traded dirty jokes with the McCullough brothers, whom she'd kept on as a landscaping crew. She teased me mercilessly about my sex life.

Two weeks before Christmas, Judith drove up. At five-foot-three, she seemed to peer over the steering wheel of her Jeep. She jumped out in Ferragamo boots, her purse tucked under her arm like a riding crop, and marched through the store back to where I was kneeling by the side of the little pond in the greenhouse. "Where do you keep your Chanukah candles?"

Just the week before, I had released eight more goldfish, large orange carp I'd brought back from Boston. "We don't carry candles."

"But you put up that big menorah out there. No dreydles? No chocolate coins?"

Cheek to the cold black surface of the artificial pond, I peered between the lily pads. "Sorry."

"I had high hopes for you people."

"Christmas trees, wreathes, poinsettias, lights . . ." Even with a flashlight I couldn't see a thing. The goldfish were gone. Not a trace.

She mumbled something and strolled through the greenhouse, then the yard. "David!" she called a few minutes later. I was surprised she remembered my name. "You have broom crowberry. I've been looking for that."

Actually, so had I. I got them from a supplier in New Bedford just the day before, a special order for a good customer and not for sale.

"I'll take both of them," she said.

I assessed her calfskin gloves, her cashmere coat, the scent of lemon and leather when she opened her purse for her checkbook. Judith was miniature perfection. Tiny nose. Pale skin, almost peach. I was trying to guess her age as I led her to the desk. Why was she with the old guy? "I'll have to order them for you," I said.

She wasn't pleased and her attention turned out the window. For a moment, knowing her reputation, I wondered if I could be sued for not selling her the plants. "That's beautiful," she said. "With the lights and all. It's the first time I've ever seen a menorah publicly displayed out here. Believe it or not, it means something to people."

"It was my sister's idea."

"Good for her. I'm tired of passing baby Jesus and the wise men on the highway. I don't begrudge the church their icons but I guess I've always wanted some equal time."

"It's not the church. The town puts it up every year."

"No," she said. "They can't do that. It's a rule of law. There's been a Supreme Court decision."

"They store it in the town garage, they repaint it, they put it up on town time and on town land."

She wanted names and dates, the facts, as if doing whatever they pleased on town time was something new. The guys in the Department of Roads, Bridges and Waterways always served the town while dividing any extras for themselves. One sold firewood cut by his crew, while some used the town equipment to clear new roads for private developments. They did whatever the town boss let them. Judith stared at me. "You know an awful lot about this town."

"It's a short story, really. Just two words."

"Johnny Lynch," she said.

"Love it or leave it, he's Mr. Saltash."

"I don't know too many people who love it."

"That's because you're from away," I said.

She didn't back off. "Aren't you?"

"I'm from here and I'm not," I said.

"You're an interesting man, David Greene. I hope you'll call me." She looked me over one last time. "About the plants."

"Hello. Who is this? What do you want?" were the precise words Gordon used upon answering the telephone.

Had I not convinced myself that my intentions were profit-oriented, I would have had my sister make the call. "You must be Gordon Silver. Your wife stopped into my nursery last week and ordered some broom crowberry."

"There is no Gordon *Silver*. Who the hell is this?"

I introduced myself. "We met at my brother-in-law Marty's."

"You're talking to Gordon Stone. Didn't Marty tell you who I was?" I only knew what her sign read: Judith Silver, Attorney at Law. I apologized.

"Did you go to college?"

I didn't know what business it was of his, but I wasn't going to be put down. "Yes, sir. As a matter of fact."

"Where?"

I knew this game. Your class status in three words or less. I wasn't playing.

He demanded: "What did you read in sociology?"

"Sir, I don't remember. If this is a bad time—"

"You're damned right it is, when supposed college graduates can't even remember the author of a book assigned in almost every college in this country for well over a decade. Why did you call me, then? Why waste my time?"

That evening, just before closing, Judith called. "Hello, David."

In my most professional voice: "I called to tell you your order arrived."

"Thank you. I have to apologize for Gordon. I hope you weren't insulted. From what I understand, he was less than gracious on the phone."

"Well, maybe we should forget it. Maybe it's too late for this season."

"No, David. It's a very good time. The ground here isn't frozen yet."

It wasn't that I didn't think about Judith. The steam escaping her lips in the yard. The way her eyes held mine, like a cat's: eyelids slowly lowering to withhold what seemed offered only a moment before. But she was married to what sounded like a nasty and possessive man. What was the point?

On New Year's Eve, I made an obligatory stop at the party of a good customer. Perched on top of a sand dune overlooking the Atlantic, the house was barely livable in winter. Blowing sand pitted the mammoth windows and shrouded the work I had done on the gardens—which would guarantee another fine contract when the owners returned in spring. I did not intend to stay. This wasn't my crowd.

For as long as Saltash has attracted summer visitors, it has had a tax-paying population of painters and writers, ex-commies and anarchists, and dating back at least to the early 1950s a colony of old Time-Life people. They had retired to vacation homes bought decades ago or spent long summers here, sometimes eight months long, May through December, before going south for the winter or returning to an apartment in New York. I did landscape work for a Professor Emeritus from Yale; an ex-commissar in the Abraham Lincoln Brigade; a researcher who claimed to have written much of John Hersey's war reportage. Some of them had been around for my glory days in Little League. They were friendly, but they weren't my friends. They were articulate and glib, fond of whiskey and wisecracks I didn't always understand. The truth is, they liked having a local guy to talk to, but I wasn't quick enough to interest them in conversation. Moreover, this being the holidays, many of their children were at the party, ex-prep-schoolers who'd summered together since they were kids and whose conversations bragged about their accomplishments since. Backed into a pissing contest between a foreign correspondent covering China and a playwright whose agent at

William Morris said Swoozie and Olympia were dying to star in her new play, I excused my way to the buffet table for one more sandwich before going home. As I reached for the roast beef I overheard someone say, "So you and Gordon are a childless couple?"

"Is that like a burpless cucumber?" Judith smiled, but her stare was as sharp as cut glass.

"But you don't have any children?"

"We thought about it," Judith said. "But decided on a sex life instead. Actually we have five children and six grandchildren. Hello, David." Judith turned her back on the other woman. "I'm glad you're here. I want to ask you something."

She was wearing a black velvet dress, a slender string of natural pearls like baby teeth across her bare upper breast. I followed her to a dimly lit corner near the huge bay windows, and in the glass reflection, instinctively tried to catch sight of her husband.

"I couldn't really ask you on the phone," she said, so softly I had to lean close to hear. "I was afraid you'd say no. Promise you won't say no until you think about it."

I was about to touch her. I was about to make a fool of myself, when she said: "There are a number of people in town who say you'd make a good selectman."

Talk about a cold shower. "Me?" Ridiculous. I wasn't sure how long she'd been living in this town, but people like me didn't run for selectman. Businessmen, professionals, developers: always older, often retired, and until only recently, very connected to Johnny Lynch. "I don't think so."

"Why not? You know a lot of people and everybody knows you. You're the closest this town ever had to a hero, David Greene." I liked hearing her say my name, I liked the attention; *her* attention. As I was about to respond, she touched her finger to my lip. "Remember, you promised," she said. "You can't say no until you think about it."

Saltash was a town built on a hill. From High Street in town center, every road sloped down to the harbor, a deepwater basin with a sizable fishing fleet and some of the best yachting on the Cape. The Tamar flowed into the bay just east of town. Once a swift moving river with a vast floodplain, it was now a muddy stream, bounded by a marsh of cattail and bramble where Johnny had been slowly filling it in. Separating the harbor from the river was Johnny Lynch's dike—maybe ten feet high, fifty long—and whether you favored tearing it down or keeping it determined who your friends were and who ignored you on the street.

Little Saltash was a town at war. Economics was a part of it, but not the core. Retired bankers linked arms with shellfish scratchers; electricians and roofers attended meetings with the president of the golf course; on both sides were rich and poor. At the heart was a tall and courtly man who wore bow ties and a gray felt fedora; who had read stories to the kindergarten children on the fourth Friday of every month and saw to it that no one born in this town went without shelter or a meal. Johnny Lynch had discovered Saltash on a fishing trip the summer of his last year at Suffolk University Law School. He set up an office on High Street and attracted clients by writing their wills for free. Nor did he ever send a bill for helping people fill out their tax forms. They received nothing in the mail but a postcard, asking that they remember him at the polls. John Mosley Lynch won his first seat on the Board of Selectmen by two votes and ran unopposed for the next twenty-four years. He made sure widows kept their houses and residents received building permits while he quietly searched the tax collector's files after the Town Hall closed. Over time he bought hundreds of properties lost to back taxes. He was elected chairman of the Board of Selectmen and moderator of town meetings. He created a rescue squad. He lobbied his State House friends for the funds to construct a pier and dredge a basin for yachts—and filled in a productive salt marsh with the muck that was removed, building a hundred vacation homes in a development he called Neptune's Garden. Johnny Lynch drifted into a dying fishing village and created a new economy based on tourism and a thriving tax base of second home owners.

But the people who bought those homes had a different agenda. They liked Johnny—most of them had been to his house for drinks— but they didn't think he should handpick the police chief, the fire chief and the Board of Health. They said the builders he had chosen for the new grade school had worked so badly the roof leaked and the walls were cracking. They were opposed to men on the town payroll laying out roads on Johnny's subdivisions on town time, using town equipment. They hated him for the concrete dike he'd forced through a town meeting to replace the old wooden bridge washed away in a hurricane. They remembered the acres of dead shellfish after the dike was completed, the stench that carried for miles, the shellfishermen who wandered around their ruined beds in a state of shock, kicking mounds of dried-up oysters they'd raised from tiny seed. They resented the loss of the most productive estuary in the region, which had once given the town hundreds of species of finfish and mollusks. They mourned the loss of habitat for migrating birds, endangered reptiles, marine and terrestrial mammals—all to keep a golf course from flooding.

The retired population, educated and well-to-do, had made it through the Great Depression and World War II and weren't about to be gaveled to silence by Johnny Lynch. They carried copies of Robert's Rules of Order to town meetings. They understood that protecting the environment meant protecting their property values. It was the retired population that voted in new zoning regulations: one new home per acre instead of four; that supported Audubon and tied Johnny up in court. They had time on their hands and they used it to organize. After twenty-four years they voted Johnny Lynch out of office—but he still controlled three of five seats on the Board of Selectmen at least until the upcoming election.

The Monday after the party, I received four phone calls before noon. From the Committee for Civic Responsibility: "Hello, David. Why don't you come to one of our meetings to talk." From a local reporter: "Is it true you're running for selectman?" From my sister: "What the fuck would you want to do that for?" From Judith: "Have you made up your mind?"

Judith and I spoke every day, on the phone or over coffee. We discussed strategy, the three candidates who had already declared for the one seat up for grabs, some of the issues. But not the real one, not until that night in her office.

"This is insane," I said, watching the fire in her gas grate. "I'm not the kind of person who does this."

"Maybe that's why a lot of people want you to do it."

"What lot of people?"

"Everyone we polled," she said.

The word "poll" made me laugh. We were talking about Saltash, a town with a pharmacy that had to special-order any drug stronger than aspirin, with no place after Labor Day to buy a pair of socks.

"People think you're hardworking and honest, David. They think you listen to them when they talk. They think you're very bright."

"By Saltash standards."

"By any standards. Including my own," Judith said, quashing any doubts I had about why I was considering this at all.

At first I thought it might be revenge. Taking power, sitting in judgment. I thought it might be the idea of becoming an important person again. Even making my mother proud. But it was Judith. It was her attention, my name on her lips.

It was being invited upstairs on a freezing winter night, sitting in a wing chair by her fire. It was books all over the walls and photographs of her in a white sundress in Mexico and Arles. It was her chin in her palm as she waited me out, her eyes lingering on my shoulders and hands. "So what have you been thinking?" she said finally.

"About running?"

She laughed. "Is there something else?"

"I think you know there is."

"And would you like that to happen?"

Neither of us spoke for a long time. "Judith, you have a husband. And from what people say, Gordon is a very nice man."

"You didn't answer my question."

"Yes," I said. "I'd like it to happen. If I didn't feel I was taking you away from someone who's weak, who can't defend himself, who—"

Judith closed her eyes. She held up her palm: stop. When I did, she said this: "David, you can never take me away from Gordon." We both heard the chill in her voice. "There are no models for the way Gordon and I live. We do not fit a mold. We do not ever try to hurt each other. We don't have affairs. We do have close friendships. Do you understand?"

I did not. I said I did because I could not imagine refusing this gift.

"It'll be all right," she said, kneeling on the rug in front of me, laying her cheek on my lap.

She undressed me slowly. She moved her fingertips from my neck to my breast bone to my nipples. She sighed when I touched her. She grabbed my wrists to govern the speed and pressure of my hands. She wanted it to last, she whispered. It had to last all night and all week until the next time. When I touched her between the legs, she arched back reflexively. She seemed to quiver. When I entered her, she gave a short cry. The first time I made love to Judith, I thought I had hurt her, but she explained that great pleasure could almost be a kind of pain. We lay awake in each other's arms, barely moving—estivating, she called it, nearly asleep but fully aware—making it last. "Trust me," she said. "Don't you trust me? Why so glum?"

Because even then I knew, it would not be all right. Even as I traced my fingertips down the bridge of her nose, to her mouth, to her breasts. Even as my cheek touched her naked belly, I knew it was wrong.

Judith

Judith had a birthday party the day before, with twelve candles on the chocolate cake. Her mother had given her a new flowered rayon skirt. Her other father, Sandy, had given her a necklace with a golden rose on it. Yirina, her mother, had her call Sandy "Daddy," which was okay with Judith. Sandy's full name was Sanford. He told her New York Jews of his generation all had names like Sanford and Sherwin and Marvin and Walcott. They wanted to be WASPs he said, but of course as soon as Jews used those names, the WASPs dropped them. Sandy had hair like his name, and he was suntanned even in April, her birth month, because he was a painter for real and a housepainter for money. All week he worked, but he spent weekends with them.

Now today, her real birthday, they were having another birthday party with Dr. Silver. She was very careful with Dr. Silver. Her mother's American name was Jerri Silver. She was not married to Dr. Silver, who had another legal family, two daughters and a wife named Sharon, but when Mother had been buying the papers that would let her enter the U.S. as an immigrant, with Dr. Silver's secret sponsorship, she had taken his name. Mother had thought he would marry her, pregnant with his son.

"If you had been born a boy," Yirina said oftener than Judith liked, "he would have married me. All that American wife has given him is two daughters, no better than you." But then ten minutes later Yirina would kiss her and take her on her lap and tell her how precious she was. Judith had only not to cry, not to speak and to wait, and her mother's love would return.

"We're lucky he acknowledges you, think of that, child."

"He doesn't acknowledge me. I have two sisters I've never seen. I know about them but they don't know I exist."

"So it must be," Yirina said. Dr. Silver visited them every Wednesday night and he gave Yirina money. They always needed money. Mother had various jobs. She had met Sandy when she was playing cocktail piano in a restaurant-bar right off Prospect Park. But they had got rid of her a couple of years ago. Mother said she was getting too old for that work, but Judith did not believe it. "You're beautiful," she told Yirina. As with so much else about her mother, it was impossible to know her age, which varied up to fifteen years depending to whom she was speaking and her mood. According to Yirina, she had escaped Czechoslovakia in 1938 when she was fifteen, eighteen, twenty, and once, twenty-three.

Yirina had baked both cakes and decorated them. She had sent Judith into Prospect Park where the daffodils were in bloom, to cut some and hide them in a bag pinned into her old coat that no longer properly buttoned. They looked lovely in the vases Yirina had brought with her from Mexico. Yirina had taken out the good tablecloth she always washed by hand, with fine embroidery of birds and flowers. Yirina had had it since her years in Turkey, during The War. Judith's mother could always make a feast. She could make a celebration out of a chicken, a couple of candles and a bottle of cheap Chianti. She could make a celebration out of a sunny afternoon and tuna fish sandwiches in Prospect Park. For Judith's father, Dr. Silver, she was wearing her best red dress of real silk and the diamond necklace that went in and out of the pawnshop several times a year. It was very important that they please Dr. Silver. Judith wondered if she ever really pleased him. Was he happy she existed? Did he wish she had never been born? She was always covertly staring at his square face, impeccably shaven, and trying to read his feelings for her.

Once again Judith unwrapped the flowered skirt that her mother had wrapped in the same paper, carefully opened the night before. Dr. Silver was a stout man of medium height, a bit stooped. His hair was all white, even the hair that bristled from his nose and ears. His eyes were a pale luminous blue, but Judith had dark eyes like her mother. Sometimes she tried to find herself in her father. She had her mother's dark hair, her mother's pale skin with an olive tint. Dr. Silver was ruddy. She was small like her mother, small for her age. Her mother could pretend she was ten for several years longer, when they occasionally went to the movies. But she had her father's hands, what Yirina proudly called "a surgeon's hands." Long-fingered but quite strong. She had his long narrow feet. Her mother's feet were small but wide. Her mother wore size 5C, a size they looked for in sale bins or rummage sales at the nearby churches of Brooklyn.

"I've brought you something I noticed you need, Judith," Dr. Silver said. "I hope it's the right size."

"I'm sure it is," Yirina said. She had been on the phone with the doctor's secretary, for Judith had listened, pressed against the wall. The doctor's secretary, a formidable woman called Cindy, was the only person in the doctor's world who knew Judith existed, except for Dr. Silver's lawyer. When Judith was little, Cindy would give her lollipops on the rare occasions Judith and Yirina went to Dr. Silver's office. Now that she was older, Cindy gave her magazines from the office. Judith studied them for clues on how an American woman was supposed to be. Cindy did the doctor's shopping for him, for his wife, Yirina, and all three daughters, the legitimate and the illegitimate. That was a word Judith brooded over. People spoke of the legitimate theater. And children. She was a bastard. When Yirina lost her temper, she called her daughter that. To which Judith, if she was furious, would yell back, "Whose fault is that?"

But it was her fault for being born a girl, apparently. Dr. Silver sat at the head of the table, his hands in his lap. They had eaten the cinnamon-flavored chicken. (Her mother cooked Czech; her mother cooked Turkish; her mother cooked Mexican; her mother cooked American. Yirina said proudly that she knew a hundred ways to cook chicken.) They had eaten the lemon poppyseed cake, a particular favorite of Dr. Silver's. When he was in the little three-room apartment, everything swirled around him sitting stiffly until he retired into the bedroom with Yirina and Judith was told to watch television on the set he had bought them five years before. They did not watch it much. Judith had homework every night, which she did passionately. Dr. Silver gave her a dollar for every A she got and fifty cents for every B. She managed to bring in almost all A's. A good report card could feed them for several days. But she also wanted to prove to him she was worthy, of value. She hoped that her grades were better than the grades of his other daughters.

She opened the package carefully, automatically saving the paper and the ribbon. It would all be used again. Sometimes the ribbons turned up in her clothing or Yirina's. Inside was a red spring coat. "It's beautiful!" she said. "Can I put it on?"

It was truly beautiful, and a little big, but she would not say that. She knew Yirina had wanted it that way so that it would last longer. She paraded around the table, as Yirina told her to do. "Doesn't she have fine posture?"

"Like a little princess," Dr. Silver said. "Judith, I hope you are improving your grades in math."

"I like science better," she said. "But I'm working on the math."

She was named after Dr. Silver's grandmother, who had died the year she was born. Who had never known about her. She was a secret child. She kissed Dr. Silver dutifully. She could feel his slight embarrassment. They were both awkward at affection with each other. She felt he liked her but could not love her. Often she wondered if he loved his other daughters. She fantasized sometimes that they all shared some holiday, Passover or an American holiday like Thanksgiving. "I'm going to visit my half-sister Lisa this afternoon," she would say. They would all become friends. She would have a real family as others did, instead of only her mother, old photos and Yirina's shape-shifting memories. If they only could meet her, she knew they would like her. She would please them. She would.

Then it was time for Dr. Silver and Yirina to retire into the bedroom and for Judith to turn on the TV loud until, about an hour later, they emerged. She hated those times but she gave no sign of her feelings, because she understood this was how Yirina kept Dr. Silver coming back. She minded less with Sandy, because he spent the night and she slept on the daybed. Other nights she and her mother shared the double bed. Sandy was almost like a real husband.

They had a small apartment on the top floor of a narrow brownstone in a neighborhood just turning Black. Most of her classmates were Jewish, like her, but not like her. Most had two parents. At school she said her parents were divorced, but that her father came to see her once a week. That was acceptable. She learned what she could say about her family life. She did not bring friends home. She was careful whom she trusted. Dr. Silver paid for her Hebrew lessons at a local synagogue; it was understood she would have a bat mitzvah next year, although Dr. Silver would not be there. Sandy would, if he was still with her mother then. Judith had learned not to take such continuity for granted. But Yirina said of herself, "At least I know how to please a man. That's important, Judith. If he pleases you, that's nice, but it's icing on the cake, you understand me?"

"I won't need to please a man," Judith said, when Yirina was going on about speaking softly and laughing in a pleasant refined manner. "I will work and make money."

"I don't work?" Yirina laughed dramatically, tossing her head with the black hair all teased up in a new style. "I just sit on my fanny all day. Who would have known from the way my back aches?"

"If I go to college—"

"We must get Dr. Silver to help you go. We must!" Yirina's mood changed abruptly. She was wearing her house smock, sitting at the sewing machine with material all over the kitchen. She was making drapes for a lady in the next block. Yirina did alterations and made draperies and slipcovers. She had signs up at all the dry cleaners. "My own mother tried to tell me I should go to college. She was a doctor, Judith, back when there were few women doctors. She had an office on Listopadu." Whenever Yirina used a Czech word, a name from Prague where she had grown up, her face changed. It softened. A nostalgic glow came upon her. "She tried to make me get an education, Judith, but I wouldn't listen. I was a pretty girl, and I thought that was all I needed. I went to university, but my classes meant nothing to me. Only boys mattered. Never be like that, Judith. *They* can take everything from you, your money, your home, every possession, your name, but an education, Judith, you can take that with you wherever you go." Then she leaned forward, staring at Judith, as if to see into her bones. "You must speak properly, not the way they do around here. They talk like hoodlums. You must speak like an educated person. I have an accent. But you have no reason to have one."

Judith usually remembered to speak a different way at school with other kids than at home. Sometimes she forgot.

A week after Judith's bat mitzvah, paid for by Dr. Silver, but attended by Sandy, there was a phone call from Cindy. "Jerri," Cindy said. She always spoke so loud that Judith, sitting next to her mother, could hear both sides of the conversation. Yirina, who had excellent hearing, held the phone away from her ear while Cindy was bellowing. "Jerri, it's Dr. Silver. He's had a heart attack. He's in the hospital."

Dr. Silver never recovered consciousness. Cindy said they should not go to the funeral, but Yirina disobeyed. Yirina got Sandy to drive them (it did not matter anymore if he went with them, since Dr. Silver could no longer ask who he was) to the cemetery, way out on Long Island where they had never been. It was a cemetery in a wilderness of cemeteries. They stood well back. Judith stared at her sisters. They were older. The widow was blond and so was one of the daughters. They were dressed in suits and hats.

She got a much better look at them a couple of days later, when they were called in by Dr. Silver's lawyer, Mr. Vetter, along with the rest of the family. He seemed ironically amused as he introduced them, without explanation. "Jerri Silver," the widow Sharon Silver repeated. "Are you a cousin?"

Yirina shook her head no. She volunteered no information. Judith stared at her sisters. Lisa was pretty, dressed in a pink pants suit with bell bottoms. She must be eighteen, maybe nineteen. Brenda was pregnant. Her husband was addressed as Doctor. They all kept looking at Yirina and Judith. Judith felt frightened. Yirina was wearing black, one of the dresses she used to put on when she was playing piano in the cocktail lounge. She held Judith tightly by the hand and sat upright in one of the chairs.

"I don't understand why they're here," the widow said. "What are they, some obscure relatives?"

"It will all be clear when I read the will," Mr. Vetter said suavely, poking his glasses higher up the bridge of his nose. "Should I commence, then?"

This man was the first lawyer Judith had ever met face-to-face. Judith did not have any desire to be a doctor, although Yirina spoke of it as the highest calling. She hated hospitals and sickbeds and pain. But it looked powerful to be a lawyer. You told people what was what. The law stood behind you. People waited on your words. She felt as if Mr. Vetter did not despise them, but was somehow on their side. He was a slight man, balding with a patch of dark hair over either ear, but he seemed to radiate power and confidence. He had a strong carrying voice like an actor or a rabbi.

Dr. Silver left most of his considerable estate to his wife and his daughters, with a trust for his coming grandchildren. But he also left a trust for Judith, to be applied only to her education. It was not to be touched except for that purpose. If she failed to attend college by age twenty-five, it was to revert to his other daughters. She was so referred to. She was finally spoken for as a daughter. They were his other daughters. Judith began to weep, not from grief or joy, but from the overwhelming sense of no longer being invisible. She hardly listened when the lawyer read the bequest of five thousand dollars to Yirina, to be paid in two installments a year apart. She hardly registered the screams of the widow and the daughters, their ranting, their insults.

"You're telling me my husband was having an affair for the last fourteen years? That's not possible. This is a lie!"

The blond daughter, Lisa, began to sob. "Our daddy wouldn't do something that low! You're trying to tell us that . . . that shabby creature is our sister! She doesn't look anything like us! And her mother can't even speak English."

"I speak six languages," Yirina said coldly. "English, Czech, German, Turkish, Spanish and Yiddish. I also read and write them. If you never have to change countries in your life, you should thank Adonai, rather than insult those who have had to begin again and again."

"I don't know who you are or what kind of hold you had on my husband, but you will not get a penny!" the widow said, shaking her lacquered finger at Yirina. "I see no resemblance between this gawky child and my dear husband."

Mr. Vetter stood. "Dr. Silver has acknowledged his daughter. He wishes to leave her a small remembrance. That was his wish and I doubt if you will find a court in New York to overturn this will, ladies. After all, he left you almost everything."

Yirina stepped forward and smiled at the lawyer. "Thank you, sir. You've been very understanding to a woman who has survived many troubles. Dr. Silver meant a great deal to me. I'm sorry his widow and his other daughters resent his acknowledgment of his second family. But I appreciate your gentlemanly treatment of me and our daughter."

"Five thousand dollars," Yirina said after they left. "He wasn't so generous. I thought he might give me a little house or a trust fund or some stocks. He promised to take care of me. Well, it's better than nothing."

For Judith, the will meant she would go to college; and it meant she was visible, no more a shameful secret. She no longer believed her sisters would be her friends, for they had treated her as if she were a rabid dog. But she still felt better. Mr. Vetter was her new hero.

JUDITH

5 Judith went to NYU on scholarship, majoring in political science and commuting from Brooklyn by subway. In her junior year she had a part-time job typing for a professor. Often she did not get home until ten at night, after studying at the library, working for Professor Jamison, sometimes seeing her boyfriend Mark or working on her column for the school paper.

Mark had an apartment with two other guys in what was beginning to be called the East Village, which sounded better to parents than calling it the Lower East Side. His apartment was dirty and run-down, with what passed for a bath in the kitchen. There was only one bedroom, with bunk beds. The guys took turns sleeping on the fold-out couch at one end of the big room, the kitchen. It was hard to get privacy, but obviously that was the only place they had to make love. They had managed it six times. Judith found it awkward, never knowing if the roommates would walk in, hearing the neighbors through the open barred window. The guys had been robbed once, of the TV and stereo parents had provided. This was the beginning of spring vacation, so both roommates were gone tonight. Mark had decided to stay around, to have time alone with her and to work on a term paper.

They were both earnest skillful students, adept at taking exams and dealing with professors' demands and foibles. She was the more driven, viewing being a student as a job. He did not have to work as hard, since his parents were putting him through. They lived in Fairlawn, New Jersey, where his father owned a men's clothing store. Mark had many clothes and his roommates were always borrowing them. It was part of his capital at college. She thought Mark extremely handsome: he was a full head taller than she was, slender, with a curly dark golden beard that made him look far older than twenty-one. Mark had light brown hair, a shade or two darker than his beard, and medium brown eyes she thought soulful and commanding. He had a fine singing voice. His roommates called him the Lounge Lizard because of his habit of singing show tunes in the tub. He was her first lover: she found everything about him extraordinary.

But when she came home, Yirina was a cold shower. Yirina did not think much of Mark, although she did not dislike him. She simply viewed him as a puppy, with friendly contempt. "He's just a boy," she said to Judith. "You have twice his brains. Don't tie yourself down. He'll do as a boyfriend, but anything more? He's a pastime. You'll forget him."

Sandy had long gone, marrying a woman whose house he had painted, a woman with a steady income and two children. Yirina played out a five-year affair with Dr. Silver's lawyer, but that too was over. She was working in a dry cleaner's, which gave her terrible headaches, but what choice of jobs did she have? She had finally begun to look her age, whatever that was. "I'm tired is all, darling. I'm so tired." They lived in the same apartment. The neighborhood was eighty percent Black now, a lot of Haitians. All summer police helicopters hung over the rooftops, setting their nerves on edge. There was a drug scene on the corner, but Yirina had always got on with her Black neighbors. Many people knew her from the cleaners, owned by a Haitian couple. Yirina's legs kept swelling. "It's from standing so much," she said. "My feet could explode!"

Yirina was nostalgic these days. She did not have many mementos or photographs from her previous lives, but what she had, she cherished more than ever. Often she took down the leather-bound album with its black pages and showed Judith the two photos she had of her parents, the photo of her brother graduating from the lycée, even a photo of her husband, a handsome Turk. In one photo, Yirina, fresh-faced in a flow-ered dress, was standing in the curve of his arm holding a baby.

"Who is that?" Judith asked.

Yirina's face crumpled. "Don't ask me that."

She wondered if somewhere in Turkey she had a half brother. Her half sisters were both married with children. They pretended she did not exist, but now they knew. They could not undo her existence or their knowledge of her. For that she was grateful. Neither of them had amounted to anything, as Yirina said. "But you, my daughter, you'll be a success! Not just a suburban house biddy."

It was the end of spring vacation and she longed to stay over at Mark's. At ten she called Yirina. There was no answer. She knew Yirina would not be going out. She was too exhausted after work. Judith was afraid her mother had been mugged. Something was wrong. She must go home. "But you can't go! You promised!" Mark insisted, pouting.

"I have to see what's wrong."

When she finally reached the apartment, the lights were on. She called Yirina, hurrying through the rooms. Her mother's purse was on the couch. Yirina lay on the bathroom floor, her face twisted, breathing hoarsely. She was unconscious. Judith could not tell if she had hit her head. She knelt over Yirina, wiping her face with a damp cloth and calling, "Mama! Yirina! Can you hear me?" Judith called an ambulance. It took half an hour to arrive. Ambulance services did not like to go into Black neighborhoods.

Yirina had suffered a massive stroke. In four days, she was dead. Judith hated sleeping in the apartment. She was depressed, lonely, given to weeping half the night. Everything reminded her of her mother, every dish, every chair, the bottles of scent and lotion on Yirina's vanity. They had never been separated. She wandered their rooms, no longer at home in a place that meant only deprivation.

A month later, over the protests of his parents, Mark and Judith were married. Only his roommates and two of her friends from school attended. They could not find a rabbi who would marry them over his parents' objections, so they were married at City Hall. Mark did not want to move to Brooklyn. They found an apartment three blocks from where he'd been living, similar in layout, a bedroom, a bathroom, a big kitchen and a tiny room overlooking the street that became Mark's study. She studied in the kitchen. She brought her desk from Brooklyn, along with the things of Yirina's that were precious to her: a teapot with marvelous curlicue blue and white designs on it, the Mexican vases, some pieces of jewelry (the diamond necklace was long since permanently pawned), some fine Czech glassware. Within a month those were broken. She could not keep Mark from using the goblets for beer and then leaving them in the sink, where other dishes inevitably ended up on top of them. She started out keeping house with zeal, studying recipes, scrubbing the floor, making curtains.

That Friday she roasted a chicken with carrots and potatoes. Mark did not come home when she expected him. An hour later she gave up. Weeping quietly, she lit the Shabbat candles and sat down to supper. When he came in at nine, she was furious.

"Well, who asked you to make a stupid fancy supper? I had a hamburger at the Cedars with guys from my class. Jeez, what is this stuff? We aren't living in Fairlawn. What's got into you? Who needs all this bourgeois fussing?"

She did not do well on her midterms. That frightened her. She stopped cleaning daily and then stopped cleaning weekly. The dirty clothes piled up and the dirty dishes began to swarm with roaches. She studied at the library. Now that she wasn't trying to keep house, she had time. Mark expected her to be there when he got home, and he expected to have sex with her. Weekends they went to movies, danced in a bar, bicycled in Central Park. They went to a lecture on the constitutional implications of Watergate; she went alone to hear Gloria Steinem. She worked for her professor whenever he wanted her to type papers.

Their lives went on as before they were married, except that they fought more. She got her grades back up by finals and finished well. She admitted to herself she was bitterly lonely without Yirina, and that Mark did not make an adequate replacement for her mother. He was a kid, as Yirina had warned her. She did not feel married. He was not her image of a husband. She had never had a father, but she had many fantasies. They were not fulfilled by an adolescent whose idea of a great evening was watching a Knicks game in a bar while eating potato chips or nachos and drinking beer.

They both got summer jobs in New York and went on living in their dirty apartment. In the fall, they were seniors with a full load of classes. They ate most meals in the school cafeteria or in hangouts around the Village. She could not remember why she had married Mark; she was sure he had no clue why he had married her. She felt ashamed. When she met some women who were meeting for consciousness-raising, she joined them every Wednesday night. It was a month before she confessed she was married. She felt it was a fake marriage, a failed improvisation, each of them playing in different stories. His parents finally had them to dinner, but it was painful. Mark disappeared with his brother after supper. She was left to make conversation.

She had never told Mark about her family; she had given him the official story, and by the time they were married, it was too late to tell him the truth. She felt her face turning to brittle lacquer as she answered his mother's questions about her dead father. It was hard to explain why her father had not left her mother better off, considering he was a doctor; she invented an unscrupulous uncle who had obliterated their inheritance in bad investments. Whatever she said sounded hollow to her, and relieved none of their anxieties. She could not cough up a normal family for them. She sat on the beige sofa balancing a cup and a china plate with a slice of cherry cheesecake on it and lied and lied. Finally, unable to eat and half nauseous, she dropped the cheesecake into her lap.

Without telling Mark, she applied to law schools. She went to see Mr. Vetter. He kept repeating how bad he felt about Yirina's death. "She was a lovely woman, an old-fashioned woman. They don't make them like that anymore." For the five years he had his affair with Yirina, he had helped financially. He had been far more generous than Dr. Silver.

"Will my father's trust cover graduate school?"

"The way it's set up, it should. The investments yield a good return. Why do you want to go to graduate school? You're married now."

"I don't know if that's going to last," she said frankly. Mr. Vetter was the first person outside her family to understand her situation, and she was always truthful with him—it was a pleasure. "I want to be a lawyer."

"I suppose you could practice domestic law," he said doubtfully. "Some women do well with that. Or estates and trusts."

"I've wanted to be a lawyer since the first time I came to this office—do you remember?"

He grimaced. "How could I forget such high drama? Well, you have an orderly mind and you're argumentative. Perhaps you can do research or title searches. Divorce law is untidy, but it can be lucrative. . . . Where have you applied? And does your husband know?"

"We haven't discussed life after graduation."

She was accepted to three law schools. The money from the trust would cover only tuition and some expenses. Then, finally, a letter came from Michigan, offering her a scholarship that made the deal sweet. Mark was interviewing with corporations. She was almost terrified. She could go to law school. She could do what she wanted if she dared. If she could admit she had been an idiot and married someone with whom she could share little.

She precipitated the final confrontation by leaving her correspondence with Michigan on the kitchen table when she went off to school. She knew he would see it when he drank his coffee and ate his muffin.

"You bitch!" he screamed when she came home at four. He had cut his late afternoon class to confront her. She refused to be baited. She had done her crying. "You used me!"

"How?" she asked. But he was probably right. She had been lonely and he wanted to screw her. He paid the rent. "I would have made you a good wife if you'd really wanted a wife."

He calmed down by suppertime and they went out to share an Italian meal. "It was a stupid thing to get married," he said. "I'm never doing it again."

"Sure you will. But in a few years, when you really want a home and family."

"Do you think you'll ever get married again?" He studied her face and her hands on the table.

She did not want to hurt his feelings further. "I don't know," she said. "I can't imagine it."

"You really going to be some shyster?"

"I shall fight for the right and the underdog," she said, and got a smile out of him. For a moment they almost liked each other.

That night they had sex as usual. She did not want to, but far more, she did not want to make a scene. She just wanted to detach, quietly. In her head she was figuring out her finances.

There was no property, no alimony, no children, nothing but a few books and records to divide. Mark took his clothes and ski equipment; she packed up her surviving mementos from Yirina. Awkwardly they stepped around each other. He was off to a job in New Jersey. She was bound for Ann Arbor to look for an apartment and a summer job. In the midst of their boxes and trash, they shook hands politely.

She went down the steps first. One of her friends from the women's group was going to store her things until she found a place. She would sleep on her friend's couch tonight and leave for Detroit by bus.

She had to return for the divorce, but it was hardly worth bus fare. Mr. Vetter had arranged for an inexpensive lawyer to file her papers. It was over in ten minutes. She took back her maiden name. The divorce left her feeling vaguely unclean. She seemed no more likely to be a wife permanently than her mother had been. Her marriage was a pile of dirty dishes she had fled.

DAVID

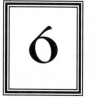

The chief of police salted his fries, knocking the bottom of the white plastic shaker against the heel of his hand. He ate more than any man his size I'd ever known. You were more likely to find Abel Smalley at the Binnacle Cafe than in his office, and in a better mood as well. He spread tartar sauce on a fried fish and melted cheddar sandwich, dropped two pats of butter in his corn chowder and shook his head with a soft but regretful smile, "That's a Department of Roads, Bridges and Waterways issue."

"It's an issue of safety," I said. "The assholes plowed all the snow to the corner and left it there in a mountain ten feet high. My mother can't see around it to leave her driveway until she's in the middle of the street."

Despite the trend in small communities to recruit professionals, Abel was Saltash's first and only chief of police, for decades our only full-time cop. He knew everyone's bad habits and every teenager by name. It was Abel's strategy to ignore trouble until it was impossible, then cover the dirt like a cat. Not too deep, they said about Abel. Just so it didn't smell. "Why not call Donkey Sparks about it?"

"He doesn't return my calls. Chief, you know how fast cars take that corner. Especially now, when it's icy."

He was strong and wiry, no taller than five-eight. His white hair stood up like a bristle brush and his gaze was hard, the clear ice blue of a menthol cough drop. He didn't wear a uniform or a firearm and rarely took a case to court. Years ago, when the local lumberyard caught fire, Abel paid a call on the last worker laid off. No investigation ensued, no charges were filed. The young man enlisted in the army the following week. When Abel received complaints about a gang of kids smoking pot on the town green, he slowly crossed Main Street and invited them to lunch at this same window table. He treated them all to burgers and made his position plain: There were twelve thousand acres in Saltash, and they'd be wise to party on one that wasn't in front of Town Hall. "You plow snow yourself," he said. "Why don't you just remove it?"

"I'm not paid to plow for the town." I had signed up but I'd never been called.

So that was it. When Abel smiled, his eyes narrowed to slits, straight as a ruler. Two years ago a homeless family was discovered squatting in a large vacation home in the woods. The local newspaper carried it as a headline story: CITY PROBLEMS IN SMALL TOWN. A neighbor sent a copy to the owner of the home, a psychiatrist from New Haven, who faxed Abel he'd be up to survey the damage and press charges. By the time he arrived, the homeless family was gone. No one could say where, except the town accountant, who quietly processed a bill for five Greyhound bus tickets to Atlanta, under police budget line item number 762000, Travel/Seminars & Training. If Abel could, he'd put me on a bus. He asked, "You call the town manager?"

"Twice."

"And?"

"And I wouldn't be wasting your time if I wasn't worried about my mother being blindsided one night when she leaves to rehearse the choir."

"I'll drive by this afternoon." He unwrapped a fresh package of Lucky Strikes. "But I'm the wrong person to see." The right person was Johnny Lynch, who'd appointed Abel and every other department head in Saltash. Johnny liked my mother and would probably help if she asked, but he'd been in Florida since his last heart attack. "You gotta go through channels. That's the way things work in this town."

"Thanks, Chief. I know very well how things work in this town."

The Saltash Committee for Civic Responsibility met around a glass-topped liquor cart every other Wednesday night in the parlor of a white Victorian captain's house overlooking the harbor. Twelve regulars, old New Deal Democrats, most approaching eighty, dozed off with drinks in their hands but woke up sputtering fury at the mention of Johnny Lynch. They talked about the need for young blood and looked me over like a steak. They reminded me they made generous campaign contributions and were good for 250 votes. Judith called them the *Alter Kockers* Against Johnny.

"Old cocks?"

"Didn't your parents speak Yiddish? Old shits."

Judith and I had our own line about most groups in town, and nicknames (should I decide to run) for my potential opponents: Blossom End-Rot, Bird Man, Captain Ahab. We met when we could after work, after dark, and the mere sound of tires on my oyster shell driveway, like the tip of her tongue on my nipple, gave me goose bumps. The first time she came over, she stayed the night. There was a new moon tide the next morning that would have kept her from getting to court if she returned to the island. I stopped her in the hallway and kissed her eyes, her lips, her fingers. She whispered, "David, David, David," her cheek against my chest, then took a step back and requested a hanger for her coat.

She walked though the living room, then the kitchen, disappointed. "You haven't made supper?"

It was past eight o'clock. I'd had a sandwich after work. "I can't cook."

"You can't fry an egg?"

"Is that what you want right now? An egg?"

"With a little Parmesan cheese, fresh bread and a decent red wine, why not—as long as you don't burn it."

So saying, she lugged a shopping bag to the kitchen. A bottle of wine. Fresh bread. Parmesan cheese. "You have eggs, don't you?" (I did.) Apricot preserves. Olive oil. Coffee.

"You didn't think I had coffee?"

In weeks to come she'd arrive with casseroles from home, flower bouquets, a reading lamp, fragrant soaps. Beginning with that first night's coat hanger, she commandeered half my hall closet and a dresser drawer for her underthings. She opened the wine with her own corkscrew—the truth is, I was a beer drinker and didn't have one—pulled a wire whisk from the bottom of the bag and started an omelet.

"Not talking?" she said over her shoulder. "What was your day like? What did you do?"

As far as I was concerned we could talk on the telephone but had a very small window of time when she didn't have to go home to her husband, prepare for court, or beat the tide over the bridge back to Squeer Island. I missed her and I wanted to touch her, and I suppose I was hurt that she didn't want me. She didn't say a word as she ate, just watched me as if amused and waited me out.

"I met somebody in the post office who wanted to know my position on school taxes. I don't think she was pleased."

"Why? What did you say?"

"I told her what I thought."

"Wrong. You're supposed to ask her what *she* thinks." Judith cut a slice of bread then dipped it in olive oil and cheese. "You want to leave people with the opinion that you both think the same way."

"Maybe we don't."

"You want the best education for the fairest price, right? Same as the woman in the post office, same as everybody. Just ask her how she believes you can go from here to there." She drew an arrow on my tabletop in bread crumbs. "Nod a lot. Tell her you hear what she's saying."

"Isn't that deceptive?"

"Not if you're listening."

"Judith. I'm not sure about this. I'm no politician."

"That's your strong point. Stand up." She did. "Let's practice."

"Where are you going?"

She dropped her plate in the sink. "To get my mail."

"What do I do?"

"Come up and ask me for my vote."

"Get serious."

"Then I won't vote for you. What are you waiting for? Stand up! I'm going to leave you behind with the junk mail. I don't have all day."

"Hello. I'm David Greene."

"Mmmm." A tip of tongue peaked through her lips.

"What does that mean?"

"I'm summing you up. Most women will." She cocked her head. "Honest face. *Great* shoulders. Very intense eyes. I'm listening."

"Can I have your vote?"

"Just like that? Don't you know women like to talk for a while first?"

"Well, ma'am. I've been thinking that things have been the same around here for a long time. I was thinking you might be ready for some new blood."

"I like that. Very visceral."

"What's *visceral?*"

"You are," she said. I lifted my fingers to her breast. She grabbed my hand. She was fast. Strong. "What are your goals?"

"I'm supposed to ask you that."

She studied my face. She wasn't smiling now. She spoke slowly, forming every word. "I want to be with you, David Greene. I want us to be happy." The game was over. She whispered, "Let's make love now," and led me to my bedroom as if it was her own. She was wearing a little cream-colored camisole through which her nipples stood up hard and brown. She was mine for the night, all night until morning, and I kept myself from sleeping even after we'd made love a second time, after she succumbed to sleep. The scent our bodies made together, the lingering stickiness of her sex on my face: I wanted it to last.

The moonlight overlaying the furniture and our clothes on the floor; her panties where she stepped out of them like a puddle; all mine for one night.

Late the next afternoon, she phoned me from court. Her case wouldn't finish until tomorrow. She would have to work late at the office but she was going to sleep there. Would I like to join her?

The following day at work, my sister seemed preoccupied. I went my own way all morning. By noon she was shoving things around her desk, avoiding me in wide conspicuous arcs.

"Is there something the matter, Holly?"

"Why, David, have you done anything wrong?"

Only one thing I could think of. "Does this have to do with Judith?"

"Are you fucking anyone else?"

"How did you know?"

"David, your own mother knows. She heard it at the beauty shop."

I started to laugh. I was thirty-seven years old. "Am I supposed to care?"

"I think it's a pretty cruel thing you're doing, don't you? Screwing a sick man's wife. Or did you think you could keep it a secret? If so, you shouldn't have parked your bright red truck with the name of my business on it outside her office all night."

"*Your* business." Holly had always treated me as a full partner although I'd had no money to buy in.

She sighed, "Mine and Marty's."

"Is that what this is about? Did he go out for his morning *New York Times* and hear the gossip at the Binnacle? Did he blame you?"

"He's protective of Gordon," she said. "He thinks what you're doing to Gordon is wrong. And so do I. And if you were thinking about anything but getting laid, so would you."

Judith didn't talk a lot about Gordon, but he was a presence, always; a looming figure, like the portrait of a great progenitor. She never acted guilty about sleeping with me, never complained about their marriage. I assumed myself to be a pleasant secret; that however brightly Judith glowed in my dim life, I was only a flicker of warmth in hers. My sister, like her husband and a legion of former students and ex-colleagues, saw the man as a living legend.

Gordon Stone's compound had been notorious for dancing that lasted until daybreak when people coupled off in the dunes or lay in heaps around the fire to sleep. Holly will still talk about the night Gordon's guests, men and women both, came to blows over politics, then tore off their clothes and ran naked into the bay. She'll tell you that

Johnny Lynch wrote the town's antinoise, anticamping, and antinudity bylaws as a response to Gordon's annual summer solstice celebrations; that people still remember the FBI men snooping around and the marijuana bust—a small-scale military operation at four-thirty A.M. that sent one of the summer neighbors to the hospital with a heart attack. Since then, Gordon's botanical projects were legal: He collected hearty succulents, yucca and cactus from all over the world, so that the compound looked like a patch of high desert in the New England sand dunes.

Long before Judith arrived in his life, Gordon had laid out a courtyard with a mosaic of stones and beach glass. He had no vision of a compound when he began, Holly said, but followed his whims. The idea of espaliered peach trees spurred him to build a wall blocking the north wind. The wall reminded him of a cottage in Taos—so he built one. Unable to house all the students like Marty who used to descend on him in summer and the colleagues who managed to appear without their wives, Gordon built a second main house larger than the first. He used massive beams from an abandoned mill in New Bedford which he floated across the inlet because the Squeer Island bridge couldn't bear the weight of big trucks.

Gordon had been fired from three colleges and written fourteen books. (Marty had all of them on a shelf in his study; signed first editions.) He had marched with Martin Luther King in Selma. When he was still healthy, Holly said, you might see him skirting the roof rim of some new building going up—shirtless, a hammer in his hand, a butt in his lips. Or he might be sitting on his deck, naked, in front of his typewriter, inhaling as if ideas could be dragged out of a Marlboro. Holly said that Gordon was still with Judith only because she was wife number four. Like a greyhound, he had needed to sprint for the better part of his life before he was tranquil enough to live with. He was over fifty when they married; she was in her twenties.

Gordon had a reputation as a satyr, an American Picasso—tyrant, genius, egomaniac—an undisciplined savant who could not write in solitude but threw enormous parties in which he talked himself into an intellectual frenzy before stealing off to a shack with a bottle of scotch to pour out his book. Gordon was rumored to have lived with three women at once, and every night to choose the one with whom he shared his bed. Holly knew only that Judith had broken into his life like an ax through a window in a room full of gas. "Judith is not a warm person," Holly said, before leaving me to contemplate my behavior. "But she's been good to Gordon. At least until now."

Later that evening, I called Judith at her office to tell her we'd made the headlines in Donna Marie's Beauty Salon.

I was ready to concede we had to cool it for a while. Instead she said, "Come out to the house Saturday, can you?" Her voice trailed off as she checked the tide chart. "About one? Gordon's been asking to meet you."

DAVID

7 The first thing I noticed was the pistol in Gordon Stone's hand. He approached my car with a steady smile. Although Judith hadn't warned me to expect something like this, I knew I deserved it. Half the town was talking about his wife and me.

Judith protected Gordon. Once I'd asked her: "Do you sleep with your husband?"

She grimaced. "Could you sleep with somebody who snores like a bull moose?"

"But do you sleep in the same bed?"

"How can I sleep if he keeps me awake?"

"Judith, do you have sex with him?"

"Does the idea make you jealous?"

I didn't think I had the right to be jealous. "Do you know that whenever you don't want to answer my questions you ask me another one instead?"

She seemed intrigued. "Does that annoy you?"

"You've just done it again."

It had more to do with how I judged myself than anything I actually knew about Gordon, but I assumed that Judith had turned to me out of desperation. I invented an image of her husband as a man who depended on a regimen of drugs that erased his pain as well as his ability to satisfy his wife. I told myself they lived like dear friends, that affection had replaced passion. I simply had to picture Gordon as more intellect than flesh. I could not imagine him watching her dress, for instance. I refused to believe that any husband, however frail and disinterested, could bear to watch my Judith step into her black silk panties in the morning and know she would slide them to her knees for another man.

I had left my house that afternoon as late as I dared and drove at a coward's pace down the road to the island, only recently emerging from the last high tide. The salt marsh grass was silver in the sun, the creek swollen and meandering. To me, heaven would smell like a salt marsh, fresh and yeasty and sweet with life—a little like a woman. I rolled my window all the way down and inhaled. As my front wheels hit the first loose plank of the bridge, a great blue heron rose from the creek, the scythelike shadow of its wings guiding me like a bat to Nosferatu's castle.

Just beyond the first dune, the road made an abrupt left turn in front of Stumpy Squeer's new house. About a quarter mile up a dirt road I made out the letters on an old driftwood oar, STONE–SILVER. I was hearing loud cracks, five or six in succession, pistol fire. Two men were plinking cans arranged on a picnic table. As I drove into the parking area, the taller man stopped shooting and turned. He was broad from the back but willowy, craning slightly forward at the waist as if nursing a pain in the belly. A baseball cap cast all but his mouth in shade. He moved in a slow straight line to my truck. "David Greene?" Gordon spoke my name like a bailiff in a court of law. I climbed slowly out of the truck. Judith appeared on the deck of the house just above us. Gordon said, "If you're going to be coming to this house, do not be late for lunch again. I am famished. Damned woman wouldn't serve until you got here." He switched the gun to his left hand and extended his right to shake mine.

"That's a nine-millimeter automatic, isn't it?"

He seemed impressed. "A Smith & Wesson. Do you shoot?"

"A little." Before my uncle Georgie married and moved to Hawaii, it was something for us to do together that didn't involve talking.

"Got another shooter here, Stumpy."

Stumpy Squeer was a Saltash legend. Some said he never left the island, but actually he rowed across the harbor to town every couple of weeks for provisions. Stumpy was short and thick, fifty more or less, with barrel-like haunches that made him seem to roll forward as he walked.

Judith stood on the steps. "Let's go, you guys. Gordon? David! Lunch!"

"Will you join us, Stumpy?" Gordon's voice was deep and courtly.

Stumpy shook his head no. People said that he had stopped growing at eleven, on the night his father shot his mother in the face. She had just returned from a party where she danced with another man. Her blood seeped through the floorboards on Stumpy, sleeping in the bedroom below.

"Going to get back to your book?" Gordon asked him. "Stumpy's been working on one for three years now."

"Four," Stumpy said.

"Really?" I loved the idea. Stumpy Squeer, hermit scholar. "What are you writing about?"

"Not writin'. Been readin' it," he said. "Almost finished too."

Judith called again. "I said, let's go!"

The house was situated at the base of a tall clay sea scarp protecting it from the beach on the other side. Gordon climbed the outer stairs with effort. The Smith & Wesson seemed to weigh him down. I wanted

to take it, or even grab his elbow to help him make the climb, but I wasn't
about to embarrass him.

The deck wrapped around the house and offered a quick view of the
compound, six wooden structures of differing colors and sizes and
styles, some with porches, one with a cupola, one painted pink, all built
in a protected bowl between the dunes. Gordon seemed to stagger as
he led me through the kitchen door. Although the afternoon tempera-
ture hovered just above freezing, I noticed a few drops of sweat rolling
into his collar.

Judith took the gun, ejected the clip, then disappeared with him into
one of the back rooms. As my eyes adjusted, I took in a large kitchen of
hardwood and tile, mostly in shades of brown and yellow. Baskets were
suspended from hooks on the ceiling. Bowls everywhere overflowed
with fruit, with dried herbs, with balls of yarn; some filled only with
other bowls. Where there weren't windows there were bookshelves and
hundreds of cookbooks with broken spines. Judith had referred to this
as the Big House. Through an archway and three steps down, a baby
grand stood in front of a truly fantastical hearth. As much a sculpture as
a fireplace, the bricks flowed and changed directions like brush strokes
in an Impressionist landscape.

"Gordon calls it his wailing wall." Judith caught me running my fin-
gers along the grooves between the brick. "Because he groaned and
complained the whole time it took him to build it."

She had to call him several times. When he appeared, he was older
than the man I had met outside. His skin was gray and his chest looked
hollow. Gordon felt stronger or weaker during the day, sometimes ener-
getic, sometimes enervated to near exhaustion. Mornings were good
(I was to find out), while by late afternoon his strength ebbed. Judith
served a beet and cabbage soup with bread and salad. Gordon stared
into his bowl, chewing without interest.

I imagined the man's shame in my presence, the rage he must feel.
Although I found the silence intolerable, I couldn't think of a thing to
break it. "How's the campaign going?" Judith said finally.

"What campaign?" Only after I spoke did I realize that I'd probably
blown the only thing we all had in common. "Well, I was asked to speak
to the Saltash Friendship Association."

Gordon lifted his eyes from his bowl. "The old Johnny Lynch
clubhouse."

I'd never heard that one before. "I thought it used to be a church."

Gordon seemed livelier. "A church, and then a grange hall and
fishermen's co-op and a social club. Used to be a dance there every Sat-
urday night." His eyes narrowed mischievously, "That's where Stumpy's

mother was spied in the arms of another man. But for years and years, Johnny's group met there for cocktails before the Board of Selectmen meetings. Johnny used to get to Town Hall so drunk that the minutes of the meetings made no sense. The secretary couldn't understand half what he said, and when she asked him, he couldn't remember."

"Did people know?"

"Everybody knew. But they didn't care. Because he was the nicest, funniest, friendliest guy in the world. They loved Johnny Lynch. Hell, *I* loved Johnny Lynch. He handled all my mortgages and wrote my wills and never charged me a dime—until I spoke against him one night at town meeting. Then I got a bill for fifteen years' worth of work! Johnny never made his money from the law. It was my vote he wanted, and my loyalty. He had to be a town official, you see, that was his access to government contracts, to the pot of gold." Gordon looked at the table as if a mistake had been made. "Judith, where's the wine? Don't we have some cold white wine?"

"For lunch?" she asked, but was quickly on her feet, searching the refrigerator.

"Understand," Gordon said, "and I should never tell this to a politician, but people don't care what you do. It's what you do *for them*. Johnny Lynch took care of people. He saw that every nitwit who couldn't find a trade drove a truck for the town. If you couldn't make your taxes, Johnny had a word with the tax collector. He intervened when you were in trouble with the bank."

"He was Chairman of the Board," I said.

Gordon seemed impressed that I knew. "He took care of your wife if you went to the army."

"That's never been proven." Judith set the glasses and the bottle on the table.

Gordon winked. "Johnny had friends on the Selective Service Board. One of his girlfriends was married to a boy who'd left her. Summer of 'sixty-nine. 'Seventy?" he asked Judith, who shrugged, working on the cork. "When the boy showed up in Saltash again and started making trouble, what do you think happened?"

"He got drafted?"

"Johnny Lynch was King David in this town. And do you know why? Because people wanted a king."

When the wine was gone and the sun filled the space between the clouds like a pink neon fire, Gordon led me outside, literally by the sleeve. "Help me with something, will you?" Four rolls of roofing paper, four pallets of asphalt shingles, were piled at the foot of the drive. Gordon asked me to carry them up the dune. As I lifted the first, he turned his back to the house and slipped a pipe and a pouch of tobacco from his jacket pocket. "Ever do any construction?"

"Some," I said. I had worked for my father-in-law in Florida. Not a period in my life I cared to talk about.

"After you played baseball." He watched my reaction. "Davey Greene, the Pitching Machine. I used to take my son to watch you play." He led me up the slope. "Wind lifts these damned shingles like feathers. Finish one roof, start another. One a year, every year. Used to do it by myself, if you can believe that." He stopped outside a cottage with a peaked roof.

I managed one roll on each shoulder, all four up the dune in two trips. I couldn't carry more than one pallet of shingles at a time. On my last trip up, number six, I was laboring like an old mule. Gordon was waiting for me, smoking his pipe, staring at the purple silhouette of the peaked roof. "Don't mention to Judith I was smoking. She won't let me buy cigarettes, but she doesn't know I have a pipe. So are you going to do it?" There was no question what he meant.

"I don't know."

"There's a line drawn right down the middle of this town."

"If this is about the dike, it's not as simple as that. People stand on both sides," I said.

"And where do you stand? With Johnny Lynch?"

I didn't like him trying to push me. "Why don't you run?"

"I'm an old man."

"So is Johnny."

"But he's desperate now, don't you see? He's fighting for all he's worth. Johnny's been in and out of court for years. He never invested his money. Why bother? Saltash was a money farm. He could always grow more. Now all he's got left are those lots in the river valley. As long as the dike stays closed and the land stays dry, he can build. To make sure it does, he needs the Board of Selectmen. He's got two votes, we've got two. You're the tie breaker."

"That's a lot to drop on my shoulders."

"From what I hear, you've got some pair of shoulders."

What did Judith say about me when they were alone? How much did he know?

"Will you do it?"

Was he making me some kind of deal in exchange for his wife? "Why me?"

"You're bright. Fair-minded. You're perceived as neutral."

"Tell me something, Gordon, have you people asked anybody else?"

"Oh, yes. Maybe twenty people."

"And they said no."

"Every one."

Judith insisted on showing me around. Putting on a goose down parka, she led me down a lowland path through the pines. "He liked you!" She skipped ahead like an excited little girl and drew me into the forest. As the sun disappeared, the scent of pine sap overwhelmed. I walked faster and faster to catch up. "I thought it would work out," she said over her shoulder.

I liked him too, which didn't make screwing his wife any easier.

About fifty yards ahead, I made out a clearing, a gap where the trees opened to the twilight. As we neared it, Judith began to run. She stopped abruptly at the gate to her garden. It was an enormous square, protected by a wood and wire fence. On top of each fence post was a painted wooden finial, some red and white, some yellow, green and red, or orange striped with black like tigers. There were bamboo tripods for growing pole beans, the withered vines now frozen like brown lace; all kinds of structures made out of bicycle spokes and hammered fenders, torn nets salvaged from the sea, a huge scarecrow with a rusted muffler torso and arms of copper pipe. There wasn't a plant left growing and yet it was alive, a frozen circus on the edge of a marsh.

Judith took my hand and led me to a small A-frame beyond the garden, with a double bed inside, a desk, a computer and files. "I work here. I fixed it up when Gordon got sick." The room smelled of her perfume and cedar; it was still warm from an earlier fire. She touched her finger to my cheek. I moved toward the door.

"You don't want to be with me now?" she asked.

"But he's at the house. Suppose he follows us."

"He's taking a nap. He doesn't object."

"I can't believe he doesn't care."

"He loves me, David. He wishes me happiness."

I was not proud of myself. I thought a better person would resist. But as she kissed my eyes, I found her zipper. As she sought my lips, I cupped her buttocks and carried her to the bed. As her husband slept, I licked her sex like an eager puppy.

"It's going to be all right," she whispered. "We won't be like anything you've ever done before. Can you understand that? Can you give up how you think people are supposed to love? How they're supposed to live? Because we're not going to be what people expect. We're not going to live that way." Judith clung to me with a strength that belied her size. "But I'll promise you something. If we're honest with each other and if we have patience and respect, we'll live more happily than anyone you've ever known."

I wanted to believe Judith. I would have conceded anything she asked. But what I thought I was agreeing to, a kind of consensual adultery, fell wide of the mark. I didn't understand what Judith and Gordon had in mind because it was unthinkable.

JUDITH

8 Law school was like camping in a wind tunnel. After the first two weeks, Judith hardly knew who she was. She was no longer Yirina's daughter, she was no longer the child of shame and romantic mystery, whose mother had three different passports in different names hidden in her underwear drawer, kept although they had long expired. Nor was she the adult she had felt herself to be after her divorce. She was a tired cranky frightened child, assigned seats, given hours and hours of unintelligible fudge to learn in minute detail, at the mercy of tyrannical professors, sleeping at first six hours a night, then five, then three and then hardly at all. She felt ugly and drawn thin as paper. Her skin looked sour and blotchy. Her hair was usually dirty. She lived on food that Yirina would not have considered fit for consumption, pizza and bad Chinese takeout. She ate cafeteria food and fast food. She no longer spoke like a human being. When she opened her mouth, legalese came out. All she thought of were torts and contracts, opinions and citations. Her passion was pleasing professors who despised their women students; she loved only her grades. She had no culture. She had no heart. She had only a headache that never went away and fatigue that drained color from the sky.

She lived for the approval of cold distant daddies, the professors who taught enormous classes. The first time she was in the hot seat, called upon to discuss the fine points of a case, her throat closed and her voice emerged squeaking like a mouse in mortal danger. Who was she? She was her grade point average. She was her first brief. She was what her professors pronounced her. What was she doing inside the baroque castle of the law? Like K., she was guilty already. Like K., she would be punished no matter what she did. How could she, the child of illegality and secrecy, make her way in the law? But its very power attracted her. She wanted to live in that castle of power. She wanted to bring that power to those who most needed its help.

Yirina had always been powerless. Judith did not want to be. She saw her classmates in the second year gravitating toward the corporate law firms. That was where money and prestige were. By the time she interviewed for a job for the summer between her second and third years, she looked much like all the other savvy law school women. She wore a gray suit. She had bought that and a navy one at a discount barn in

New York. She had good earrings from Yirina. She put herself together and got a job for the summer in a Boston law firm already looking over students for associates. Prestigious large firms were beginning to court women, under pressure from antidiscrimination legislation. Her grades were as high as any woman in her class. She interned at Tremont, Smith and Cordovan, where there were forty-two partners and a hundred-odd associates. It was an unusual firm, in that there were two women partners. Both were divorced and neither had children. They worked twelve to fourteen hours a day.

All the associates seemed to put in at least a sixteen-hour day. Not infrequently they worked all night, they worked weekends. They dressed well, they made good money, but there was no intimacy in their lives. If they were married, they probably made love twice a month. If a woman had children, sometimes she became part-time; then the others spoke of her as if she had died. "Adrienne was a good lawyer," they said elegiacally. "Too bad."

For what did these people destroy themselves, burn up their years? Money. Not power. She did not see any women with power. Even the two women partners were less powerful than any of the male partners. They were not rainmakers; they did not count. One had created a valuable niche for herself as a specialist in pension funds. Little that happened here seemed useful. She found most of the partners nasty and overbearing.

The summer was no vacation, as much as she loved Boston, and she did. It was less tropical in the summer than New York and somehow more manageable. She had little time to play tourist but knew she wanted to live there. After a couple of years in the Midwest, it felt sunnier, saltier, brisker. She worked as fiercely as she had in school, but in addition, she had to look presentable every day. She had to shine. That summer job between the second and third years was supposed to be the forerunner of the job she would take when she graduated. By the time the summer was over, she knew that she was not going to follow the high path. She would not go into corporate law.

She decided on family law, as Mr. Vetter had long ago recommended, but she was also drawn to criminal law. She could easily identify with people on the fringes of society, with the illegitimate, the poor, even the violent. She went after a job with Legal Aid.

The veteran lawyer who interviewed her asked before the interview was five minutes old, "Do you think you can handle child abuse? Domestic violence? The seamy side of the city the way you can't imagine it."

"I want to do this work. I think it's important."

"Do you have any idea what you'll really be doing? It's not Perry Mason. It's sleaze. You're dealing with the riffraff of the city so they can go back on the streets. You're dealing with crazy old ladies and crack mothers and kids who think cockroaches are decoration. You get all of five minutes to prepare a case and you'll be handling sixty cases at a time."

"I can do it," she said. "I grew up in Bedford-Stuyvesant. Those riffraff were my neighbors. They're human to me and I can talk to them. I can learn quickly."

She was hired, although her interviewer told her he didn't expect her to last eighteen months.

After graduation from law school, Judith received the last of her bequest from her father, Dr. Julian Silver, one thousand dollars upon finishing her schooling successfully. "I thought we might consider that your schooling was successful," Mr. Vetter said. "On the law review. Honors. Your father would be proud of you."

"Would he? I never understood him. I was always a little afraid of him."

"His own daughters were never what he imagined they would be. You are. You're beautiful as your mother and bright and capable. I think you'll go far."

She did, immediately. As a present to herself, she took a charter flight to Europe with two friends from law school, Hannah and Stephanie. Hannah was the real beauty, blond, willowy and well-connected. Her father was a state senator. She would be interning in Washington. Stephanie was going into a big firm in Chicago. She was tall, a little gawky but extremely hard-driving. Judith could not imagine what she would be like on vacation. Hannah, Stephanie and Judith had gone through law school in a study group with two other women off already to their new jobs, dividing up assignments before exams, trying to carry each other through the grind.

Judith was desperate to be done with schooling. She had been deferring her life. She needed a vacation and she needed to see Europe, finally. She had always felt only partly American, with her mother so European, so multilingual. She had a heritage she barely understood, like the legacy of a diary in a language of which she knew just an occasional word. She had only a vague notion of her quest, what she must find to complete herself. She should be studying to pass the Massachusetts bar, but she would do that when she returned.

I did what I set out to do, she thought to herself: I conquered. But there's no I left. She had five weeks. She had to be back in Boston by July first to move into the apartment she had rented, to get ready for the bar exam and to begin her new job at poor pay and long hours in Dorchester.

The charter flight put them down in Amsterdam, which was pleasant. She got by on her bad German which was really Yiddish, scanty, rich in curses but poor in daily phrases like "Where is the women's toilet?" They went on to Paris. There, a sublet and a temporary job had been arranged for Hannah. Stephanie and Judith lived in a cheap Latin Quarter hotel, famous for a nineteenth-century French poet Judith had never read. Every day they walked miles. Stephanie was eager to notch every museum, but Judith found she liked best to wander the neighborhoods. To sit in cafés staring at passersby. She felt like someone in a movie, a young woman vacationing in Paris, waiting no doubt for romance. But she did not fall in love with a Frenchman. She fell in love with a village.

It was in the mountains of Provence. Stephanie and she were staying at a small inn set in vineyards belonging to the inn family. The inn had only six guest rooms. In the middle distance were cliffs studded with juniper and pine. The local houses seemed to sprout from rock. Red rocks, beige rocks, gray rocks, black rocks. The sound of goat bells came into her bedroom. Bougainvillea grew up the side wall, spilling its luminescent blossoms everywhere. Doves cooed under the red tile roof.

She was in the middle of a large self-involved family. The wine served was grown in the surrounding vineyards. The food was cooked by Madame, mistress of the house. One of the daughters was pregnant and lay out by the pool like a beached whale, sunning her belly. They were always laughing together, the married and unmarried sisters and a sister-in-law. They all looked somewhat alike, about the size and coloring of Judith, with dark brown eyes and black hair. She had grown up hearing many languages, and she picked them up quickly. Unlike Stephanie, she was not afraid to use her French. The sisters normally ignored the guests as if they were made of glass, but gradually they found her acceptable. They began to include her in their gossip and their games. They had names for all the men who came by. They strolled in the vineyard. They shelled beans. They picked flowers and decorated the inn. They mended, they knitted, they read, they talked, they swam in the pool.

Judith and Stephanie had been supposed to move on in three days. Stephanie did. Judith canceled the rest of her reservations and persuaded the family to let her stay. Gradually she began to do small tasks. Her rent was reduced. She spent the next three weeks as part guest and part servant and almost family, not a daughter certainly, but almost a cousin.

Partly it was a fantasy, a big family in place of the isolation in which she had grown up. A female-dominated family full of singing and laughter and in-jokes, full of grooming and flirting. She was studying something at least as interesting as anything she had learned in law school. What Judith saw that caused her to stay was that these were people who knew truly how to live in a daily, ordinary way. They were rich in small pleasures.

Madame could turn any scrap fish or tough old hen into a sumptuous repast. They worked hard but they also had much time simply to sit and talk, to sip wine and enjoy. There was a casual grace to their lives that was partly the beauty of the sunburnt landscape, partly the closeness to peasant life but with enough money to provide little luxuries, partly the climate and the habits of the place. She did not idealize them. They had no idea she was a Jew, and she was careful not to tell them. She was a spy in the house of comfort. They were parochial people who despised the tourists and vacationers they catered to. Madame would not let any of them near the stove when they were menstruating, since she held as an article of faith that a menstruating woman would curdle milk and spoil wine. Madame believed in sympathetic magic and tried to cure most ailments with herbs and what seemed to Judith voodoo. Gradually Judith learned to cook most of Madame's dishes, from watching, from making notes. She understood that the cooking style of Madame was not so much a matter of recipes as of overriding formulae. Nothing was measured; nothing was ever quite the same twice. But there were general rules and she learned them. She knew what to do with a firm fleshed fish and how to make a marinade or a sauce from olive oil, tomatoes, a few herbs and a little wine or vinegar or lemon.

Stephanie called her from Florence. "I hate traveling alone. Italian men are driving me crazy! What are you doing there? It's not even the beach."

"I'm resting," she said. "I'm exhausted. I never want to move again."

She could not explain her pleasure in scraping carrots and washing rice, watering the kitchen garden, picking caterpillars off the roses: hardly Stephanie's idea of a vacation. Hannah would think she had lost her mind. Yet Judith was almost, almost happy. She had not been happy since Yirina died. Stephanie and Hannah were two women who had been part of her study group all through law school. She was as close to them as she was to anyone, a slightly frightening thought because now they seemed to have nothing in common.

She still did not know who she was, but she had found a part of herself that had been lost, the part that had flavor and a body and tastes and knew, as Yirina would say, how to enjoy an orchard in a flower pot.

She observed how these women dressed, how they laughed, how they held their bodies. Her particular mentor was the sister-in-law, Yvonne, who was a little the outsider too, married to the older son. The younger son was off in Toulouse in hotel school. Soon he would be working in Switzerland for a couple of years. Yvonne cut Judith's hair and restyled it, critiqued her wardrobe, showed her tricks of coddling the skin with strawberries and milk. It astonished Judith how comfortable she felt with the Barbière family. This was not her life, just a pause for healing and rest. Yet she felt more at home here than she ever had with Mark or her various roommates. It was not that she felt truly intimate, for they did not know her and did not even ask the sort of questions that might have led them to understand. She told them her mother was Czech. Czech refugees were not uncommon. They assumed her mother had left her country to escape the Communist regime. For years she had let people make what assumptions they chose about her background.

The younger son was home for a weekend, on his way to Switzerland. He flirted with her. "You're so beautiful," he told her. "You're like a perfectly ripe peach, delicate and suave."

Like all the family, he was handsome. They seemed to radiate a sensual health that was attractive and unrefined, like the coat of a well-groomed, glossy and well-fed horse. He kissed her under the arbor. She did not let it go further. She had had only one affair since her marriage. Men her own age seemed callow to her, a regiment of Marks; she did not believe in getting involved with her professors, although two pursued her mildly. She had had a romance with an older man the summer between her first and second years, where she was interning. He said he was separated from his wife; it turned out he meant, by several miles, from the suburb where he lived. She let it go on in a desultory manner until she returned to school. It was mildly educational and sexually all right. She had backed into it and could not extract herself gracefully.

The son left. An Italian on vacation kissed her under the same arbor. He left and she stayed on. She asked Yvonne if she was beautiful, since Mr. Vetter and the son Armand had both said she was. Yvonne cocked her head. "*Bien sûr,*" Yvonne said, "you're pretty enough . . . *assez jolie.*" She had not classic features, Yvonne explained. Her chin was a trifle sharp. She was short of stature. Her nose was a little long, perhaps. "But," Yvonne said, waving her finger, "what does that matter? You must have confidence that you are quite pretty enough for any man you want. That's what matters. That you feel you are desirable and that you act desirable. A woman does not have to be a classic beauty to get exactly what she wants, little Judith. She just has to act as if she is one."

Finally the pregnant daughter went to the hospital and the tempo of the house increased and withdrew from her. Judith understood it was time to leave. She phoned Stephanie in Athens and said she would meet her in Paris. Her French had vastly improved, even though French vacationers told her she had a Provençal accent. "You must get rid of that!" they said, but she did not want to.

She had a week before she was due in Amsterdam to catch her flight home. She stayed with Hannah in her small flat. She had not spent as much money as she had expected to. She spent it now on clothes, on accessories—exotic panty hose, a stylish bag. She experienced a frantic desire to shop, to bring home souvenirs of what she felt she had learned. I want to live well, she thought to herself. I will work hard but I want something different. I want a graceful life. A life that satisfies the senses and the brain. Yirina would have understood perfectly. She knew she would not be able to put any of her desires into effect for years, since she must establish herself as an attorney. She would be working at least sixty hours a week. But she knew what she wanted, and she would not forget. Eventually, eventually, she would reach that pleasant shore.

JUDITH

Judith thought that the mother or perhaps both parents might come in with her client, but the family group that trekked into her office was larger and noisier than she had expected. There were four other adults and a child. She had one of the smaller offices at Birch and Fogarty, a Boston law firm she had joined after two and a half years at Legal Aid, and she had to borrow chairs from the other associates.

Her eyes went first to her client, looking surly and messy. When it came to court, she would have to make him clean up his act, or the judge would punish him. He was a kid from an affluent respectable family, and he had to look like one, not a bad imitation of a ghetto runner. "In this office, you will remove your hat," she said firmly, not smiling, gesturing at the greasy wool cap he had pulled down almost to his eyes.

"What for?"

"To get used to looking like someone the judge should take pity on. They don't like drug cases. It's going to be a battle to make sure you don't do time. The sooner you get used to taking my advice, the better our odds are."

Larry Stone was pouting, oozing self-pity. He was tall like his father, but looked rather water-softened, slumping in the chair. His attitude was just as it had been the first time she sat down with him, petulant and put upon. Being caught was something he shouldn't have to endure.

"Larry can't go to jail!" That was his mother, now Mrs. Caldwell, talking. She was a well-kept woman with short crisp blond hair and nails that matched her pale blue designer suit. Judith was sure her gold was twenty-four karat and her earrings were real pearls. Her current husband said nothing. He looked extremely bored, glancing at his Rolex every two minutes. He was a Texan in a beige suit who resented every second he spent in her modest office.

Her eyes kept being drawn against her will to her client's father, Gordon Stone. Years ago when she was an undergraduate, she had gone to hear him speak. He was still an impressive presence. So far he was mostly listening, yet the room seemed to revolve around him. He was a tall lean man with dark hard blue eyes, fierce, hawklike, but his mouth was full and sensual. He had what people called good bones, meaning

his face would photograph well and his features had an edge, a defini-
tion she had to call attractive, charismatic. While she was talking, she
caught herself trying to figure out his age. Fifty maybe? No, he had to
be older.

She lectured on the seriousness of Larry being caught selling mari-
juana at B.U. He had done a sloppy job of it and someone who did not
like him had reported him to the campus police. It was probable that if
Gordon had a better history with the college administration, the matter
would have been quietly dropped. But Gordon Stone had always been
too famous for his own good, controversial, often being quoted on top-
ics the administration would have preferred he ignore, and he had been
fired from B.U. before being hired by Brandeis.

"Larry has to say he's very, very sorry, right?" That was Natasha,
eleven and bright. She seemed to be trying to take care of her half
brother, who did not even look at her when she spoke. Natasha was a
forthright child with whom Judith had immediately fallen a little in
love. She could be my child, Judith thought, although of course that
was not literally true: she was only sixteen years older than Natasha.
But Natasha was the child she could wish for.

"The more persuasively he can apologize and the humbler he seems,
the better we're likely to do in court," Judith said.

Larry made a retching sound. "This is just sickening."

"My darling, I feel for you," his mother, Mrs. Caldwell, said. "This is
so unfair. They're treating him like a criminal." She glared at Gordon
Stone. "I know you could have hushed this up, if you'd tried a little
harder."

The current Mrs. Stone, the third one—Judith consulted her notes
to discover she was named Fern—sighed heavily. "This is all such a
trivial matter clogged in process and meaningless words." Fern had been
gazing out the window, as if she could pass through it and escape. She
was wearing wide silk pants, an overblouse and various shawls, scarves,
draperies. She was so vague and unkempt it was only the third time Ju-
dith glanced at her that she noticed how beautiful Fern was. Her hair
was long and red-blond; Judith realized where the term strawberry-blond
came from. Fern's eyes were large and pale brown against her ivory skin.
Her face was oval and her features classic. Vaguely Judith remembered
that Larry had described her as an ex–soap opera queen; but then Larry
was sarcastic about everyone in his family. Fern did not seek to be the
center of attention, as Judith would have expected from an actress. She
basically seemed to want quiet. Judith thought of the White Queen in
Through the Looking Glass. This was a gentle ineffectual woman who

appeared to generate centrifugal force that caused her to leak scarves, tissues, sighs.

Gordon sat up and glared. "Why don't you go back to the ashram, Fern. You aren't doing us any good—as usual."

"It isn't an ashram." She wrapped her arms in her shawl. "The center is based on the teachings of Bodhisatva Selena MacDowell, also called—"

"Please, Fern, shut up and leave if you want to."

Smiling slightly for the first time, Fern gathered up her fringed cloth bag and several shawls. "I'm used to operating on a higher plane."

"Mother!" Natasha yelled. "Larry may go to jail. Wake up." She planted herself in front of her mother, frowning.

"It's not the place that defines us, but we define our place. Selena wrote that. . . ." Fern floated out, abandoning them all.

Gordon grinned. "My wife has grown a little weary of the world, defined as me and the family."

"Including me," Natasha said, tugging at her hair.

"No, darling," Gordon said, "nobody ever tires of you. It's the rest of us who bring her down."

Judith tapped on the desk. "Now if we could discuss our strategy in Larry's impending trial, there might be some chance you won't have to traipse off to prison to visit him."

Judith did in fact get Larry a sentence of community service and two years' probation. He barely thanked her, but Gordon paid her bill in full and promptly. He was the family member she had the most contact with, besides her client. He was the one who argued with Larry to obey her. He was the one who listened carefully to her plans. He picked out Larry's clothes for court, with her approval. When she had to consult the family, it was Gordon she called, and she now called him Gordon. She admitted she liked having an excuse to talk with him. Their conversations rarely stayed on the case. She was almost sorry when the trial process ended with her successful plea bargain. She would miss their discussions of the events of the day, politics, the judicial process.

Therefore she was surprised but delighted to be invited out to what Gordon called the Compound for July Fourth. She had no other good invitations and she was curious about him. She threw some clothes in an overnight bag and drove out, following the photocopied directions. They were so precise she assumed Gordon had written them. After a series of turns, she found herself crossing a humpbacked rickety wooden bridge to the island where Gordon had a summer home.

She had imagined a glassy modern house on various levels, nicely landscaped. There was such a house, but there were five other buildings, four of wood and one of stucco, so different one from the other and bizarrely constructed, she assumed Gordon, perhaps with the help of some of his sons and daughters (she knew he had five children ranging in ages from nine years older than her to sixteen years younger), had thrown them up by whim. All this random architecture was built in the lee of a bayside sand dune obviously blowing away. No one had landscaped. Piles of discarded objects lay about, not trash, not bottles and cans, but abandoned projects—a fence that separated nothing from nothing, a shed without a roof, a half-built tower, a flagstone path that led halfway across the courtyard, various pieces of abstract sculpture of rusting metal. She learned that the second wife, Mrs. Caldwell, had dabbled in sculpture.

Gordon greeted her with a kiss on the cheek and a little more body language in the hug than she had expected. "Where's Fern?" she asked, looking around. She saw many people picnicking, sunbathing, sitting in the shade—including a baby in a playpen—but no Fern.

"Fern has filed papers. I told you, she's tired of the noise. I think she imagined that things would quiet down over the years, but they never have." He waved his hands vaguely at the scene. Children in a loose posse were chasing a black Labrador. Another kid was throwing a ball hard against one of the houses. Voices were raised in song somewhere, several radios were playing not only competing stations but wildly incompatible music, opera and rock duking it out in the ears of everyone. Two teenagers were having a fierce argument. Someone had started a fire that was smoking badly. No one was tending it.

She found Natasha in the kitchen trying to make lunch, near tears because she had burnt the tomato soup.

Judith put down her bag on a kitchen chair and took over. She tried to send Natasha off to amuse herself, but the girl begged to stay. "I want to help. I have to learn how to do all this!"

"Won't you go with your mother?"

"To that stupid place where people walk slowly like zombies and sit on the ground with stuck-up smiles? No thank you. I'd rather be with Daddy. Besides, I'm hoping he gets married again real soon."

Gordon had come quietly into the kitchen. She could feel him behind them. She realized she had begun to be aware of him physically. She did not want to turn, but finally she had to.

He was propped against the doorjamb, amused. "You're making order out of chaos. A rare talent. Everyone here seems to have the opposite knack."

"Is that why Fern gave up?"

"Let's talk about that another time." He was wearing a tee and shorts. His body was lean and tightly muscled, a much harder body than his son had. As if he could read her thoughts, she felt her face heat. She turned back to the stove.

It was twilight. A group of them had decided to stroll on the beach. She started off walking with a young woman whose thesis advisor Gordon had been. They talked about the Reagan administration. Gordon appeared at her elbow. Gradually she found herself walking with him instead. He was full of questions. They sat on the beach as the last lavender light drained from the sky, the waves whooshing in over the pebbles to their bare feet.

"So, where do you come from, Miss Judith, lawyer? Not New York or Boston. You have no obvious accent."

"I grew up in Brooklyn."

"So much for my ear. Where in Brooklyn?"

"The corner of Bedford-Stuyvesant that touches Flatbush Avenue and Prospect Park. I am the illegitimate child of a doctor whose name I bear and a mother who was born in Prague, married and divorced in Turkey—I think—and may have had a son there I know nothing about. She met my father in Mexico."

"Why didn't he marry your mother?"

"He was married already. To a very middle-class lady. He had two daughters, both older than me."

She did not know when she decided to tell the truth. She did not know why. Perhaps she felt it did not matter or perhaps she felt it mattered very much. She found herself compelled. His attention was like a drug that loosened her mouth. Suddenly she wanted to be who she was. She had developed a proficiency for obfuscating her past; but now she just wanted to speak of herself. She decided to take that enormous chance for the first time in her life. Her husband, Mark, had known less about her after a year of marriage than this man knew right now.

They spent the evening talking, until the breeze grew cool and she was chilled. Walking back to the compound, he put his arm around her. He led her to a room she assumed was his. She resisted the pressure of his arm and stood flatfooted in the hall. "I don't have casual sex," she said, planting her feet. "It doesn't appeal to me."

"Who says this is casual?"

"I've only been with two men, and one of them I was married to."

He frowned, tilting on the balls of his feet, regarding her. "I must say, I'm disappointed. A lack of curiosity I didn't expect in you."

She turned away. "There are other things to be curious about."

He stepped back. "You're too young for me. Of course."

"I'm not too young for you!" she snapped. "I'm more mature and more capable than either of your wives I've seen so far."

He began to laugh helplessly, sliding down the doorjamb. She gave him a hand and drew him to his feet. He opened the door to his bedroom and bowed her in. She went.

What she had considered satisfactory sex before that night was if the man was not unclean or piggy and did not hurt her, and if she had an orgasm from time to time. Perhaps Gordon was simply more sensual than any man she had been with, perhaps he was simply more patient, perhaps he was simply more experienced with the bodies and needs of women. Whatever it was, she lost control as she never had. By the time he entered her, she was moaning like an animal, grabbing at him, lurching to meet him. When she came, it shook her. She lay afterwards with the feeling of having been dropped from a great height. She fell asleep almost at once.

Natasha was up before her in the morning, waiting impatiently in the kitchen. "You stayed with Daddy. Do you like him?"

"Yes, I like him a lot. You know too damned much for your age, Natasha."

"I have to. I'm the house mother, haven't you noticed? Daddy says Fern started turning things over to me by the time I was seven! I want a stepmother, but I want some choice."

"It's a little early to talk about that."

"It's never too early," Natasha said firmly. "We can't let you get away."

She decided that what she saw around her was a paradise gone to weeds. Sunburned children chased puppies nobody had bothered to housebreak; students camped out on the beach among great mounds of garbage bags and green-headed flies. Gordon had begun building a tower to distance himself from the chaos. He simply could not manage the logistics any longer. He needed help, obviously, and she began slowly to make order.

She did not leave the next day. She did not leave until the morning she was due in court. By the time she drove into the city through the hot gritty morning in rush-hour traffic, she knew she was obsessed with him. That night she called Hannah in Washington. They often spoke at ten at night, about the time they usually got home to their respective tiny apartments from their respective overheated demanding jobs.

"Do you love him?" Hannah asked.

"I don't know . . ." Judith clutched the receiver hard. "I never thought I was capable of falling in love."

"When you look at him, does he make you feel weak?" Hannah asked.

"No! He makes me feel strong." She was going to marry him. She knew it then. Yirina would have loved him too.

DAVID

10

"Let's play home movies," Judith said, curled up with me before the fire. "Tell me about your marriage. I was married before too. I was twenty when I got married and twenty-one when I got divorced."

The image that came to me as she talked was a cartoon of a pimply faced boy from New Jersey; then I added a beard to the pimply faced boy. Ridiculous. But Judith was more interested in questioning me.

"I married the boss's daughter. I was twenty-three, I had forty thousand dollars left of my bonus, every possibility in the world, and I couldn't think of one. I was drifting around Florida, where I felt comfortable because everybody seemed to come from someplace else." I lay on my side staring at the flames in the gas grate. The room was almost tropical. She had turned the heat high when we made love.

One night in the lounge of a seafood restaurant under the bridge to Singer Island, I met a guy who'd seen me pitch. He'd played baseball himself. "But never professionally," he said. Few people knew enough to refer to minor leaguers as professional.

"Jewish kid, aren't you?" Wynn Hardy was the kind of man who thought he could say anything he liked. He was taller than me, lean except for the beer belly he steered like the hood ornament of an expensive car. His lips were always set in a half smile, so everything he said could be taken as a provocation or a joke. "It's a compliment, son. Means you're probably smarter than the average asshole I hire, that you don't stay out drinking till four in the morning when you have to be at work at eight." Wynn described a forty-acre property he'd just bought, only recently an orange grove, six miles from the coast, twenty miles north of Palm Beach. He was putting up a hundred Spanish-style ranches with white plaster arches and wrought-iron grillwork. He offered me a job and I took it.

"I liked working construction," I told Judith. "The same as I like nursery work." I liked swinging a hammer, using the power in my shoulders and upper arms. Most of Wynn's crew were Dominican and Cuban. When it came to keeping records of deliveries and dealing with inspectors, I was important.

"So what was she like, the boss's daughter?" Judith leaned over me, her eyes alight with curiosity. "Did she have a name?"

"Vicki. She loved horses." Had she won the lottery or married a rich man, she might have spent all her time preparing for competition. But she had to work, which left her only mornings, from dawn until about eight, evenings and weekends to exercise her horses and muck out the stables. Vicki Hardy was as strong as most men her size. Her butt was pure muscle and something of a family joke. Her doctor, Wynn Hardy's best friend, once said that giving her a booster shot was like trying to penetrate an orange with a drinking straw.

"What did she look like?"

"She was lean and mean, sort of a boy's body. Blond hair." Short, because she couldn't find the time to fuss with it; bleached by the sun a pale white-yellow. Her eyes were light blue, almost turquoise, and contrasted with her skin, the color of a scuffed penny, to give her face the impression of a tomboy with dirty cheeks. Because she was employed by her father's company, she didn't have to dress for work, but drove from the stable to the office in blue jeans, boots and one of a drawer full of faded chambray shirts from which she carefully removed the sleeves at the shoulder seam with a razor blade. She smelled of leather and cloves and the horses she loved.

Vicki drove out to the site every Thursday afternoon with our paychecks. When she brought me mine, we talked. She told me she'd dropped out of community college. What she really loved was business, her dad's business, making it grow, and her riding. "Nothing else in the world interests me. . . ."

Vicki was twenty and lived with her parents. I always asked about her horses because I liked to watch the sun-gold goddess gush like a little girl. Gallant Prince was a seven-year-old quarterhorse and Arab cross. Sheena was a chestnut mare, with a star and wide-set eyes; her filly's name was Dottie because she was dun color with dapples. At least one weekend a month, Vicki went off to cross-country competitions. I knew nothing about horses and felt like Sancho Panza when I clambered up on one. But I had been a competitor.

"It's almost like I hate it and I love it," Vicki said. "All week and for a month beforehand, all I think about is the course. And then just as our number is called, just as I'm trying to settle Gallant down, I get so nervous I want to cry and run away."

"Sometimes before a game, my stomach would clench so tight I'd get the dry heaves."

She laughed. "I *wish* mine were dry."

"But I felt so alive at that moment. That nothing else in my whole life had ever been or ever would be as intense."

She said shyly, "Do you want to go with me to Bradenton for a show?"

"Where do you stay?"

"We'll get a motel room," she said.

The Monday after Vicki and I returned from Bradenton, I was afraid to face her father, but Wynn dropped his arm on my shoulder and asked me out to the house. From then on I was a regular Sunday guest. Unlike my own family, the Hardys didn't carp at each other, complain about their neighbors or things that might have been, parties they weren't invited to. They *gave* parties, every Sunday for bridge and barbecue around the pool. I got to know Vicki's brothers and their girlfriends; aunts, cousins, all the family friends. I was so in love with the Hardys and grateful for their acceptance that it hadn't occurred to me I might be exactly what they were looking for.

Vicki was still exotic to me. She made love the way she rode, with a fierce, faraway look in her eyes and tough silent concentration. She liked to be fucked hard, ridden high, and thrust herself to meet me with alarming strength. We never spoke in bed. Watching her mouth roll open, her head sway side to side and the shimmer of her tiny breasts, I imagined her riding me in her mind, across fields of new-mown alfalfa. Sex wasn't easy for Vicki, but a matter of concentration and muscle control. Not unlike riding. Or for that matter, pitching. It was usually after sex that I wondered, Who does she think about when she's alone? What does she want? I was afraid of the answer so I didn't ask the question. I was too in love with my place in the family.

"After we got married, Wynn sent me to school. I worked days, took business courses at night. Weekends Vicki and I would go to one of her meets or just hang around the Hardys' pool."

Judith frowned. For a moment I had a sense of the litigator in her. "The woman you describe sounds damaged. As if some early trauma had damped her down and made her cut her losses."

I stared. I could only say, "Nobody mentioned it until we were married and a friend of her mother's started telling me how good she thought I was for 'poor Vicki.' "

Wynn Hardy had caught his daughter with a boy named Mauricio, the son of a Cuban who worked for Wynn laying tile. They were just fifteen and went to school together. Wynn drove to the beach one day and found Vicki topless. He threatened if he ever saw them together again, he'd kill both of them. He sent her to a private school. She phoned her mother in tears every night.

Then Vicki stopped calling. The school called instead. The kids were caught in a bus station in Tampa, waiting for a connection to New Orleans. When Mauricio was returned to his home, his father and two uncles who worked for Wynn had been let go. Wynn never lifted a hand to the boy. His own father beat him half to death.

"What happened to Vicki?"

"Wynn got her an abortion. And her first horse."

We received a three and a half acre lot from Vicki's parents for a wedding present, large enough for a stable and a paddock. I used my bonus money for the down payment on the house, but the truth is, we wouldn't have had a house at all if Wynn hadn't built it. Soon he was talking about kids. We weren't avoiding having kids, we weren't using protection; we just doubted it could happen. Vicki menstruated with comical irregularity. I had a year to go for my degree when Vicki went to the family doctor for digestive problems. It turned out she was in her third month.

Wynn, Mrs. Hardy and I ganged up on Vicki to try to get her to stop riding. She stopped jumping, but that was all. It was a difficult pregnancy. She hated the changes in her body; she hated feeling fat. One Saturday she came back from the stables and her water broke. My son was born prematurely just after midnight Sunday morning. The birth was terrifying. Vicki was home from the hospital after two nights. The baby stayed three weeks. I'd been married to Vicki Hardy for five years and hadn't the faintest idea how she would respond to motherhood. I was secretly afraid she'd just go off riding every day and leave the baby to the maid the Hardys had hired.

My first quarrel with Wynn was over naming the baby. My father had died a few years before, and while I didn't expect them to like the name Sam, I wanted something that started with the letter S, as was the custom among Ashkenazi Jews. Steven or Seth or Stan—I would have been happy with any small honor to my father's name, but the Hardys wanted Wynn the Third. I didn't believe it.

"He'll be called Terry," Vicki said. "Tertius. It means 'the third' in Latin. That's what we do in my family."

"But not in mine, Vicki."

"Why are you doing this to me?" She brought her hands up to hide her face. Arguments with her father could make her physically ill. "Why do you always think about yourself?"

I began losing my son before he was out of the premie ward.

Vicki took a leave of absence. I was at work all day and still finishing up school in the evenings. Vicki spent any time she wasn't with the horses at the Hardy house. Terry was fussed over by his grandparents, by his nursemaid, by his mother and all the family friends. He was a small baby, but by the time he was crawling, he was growing every week. His hair was yellow at first, but gradually began to darken. His eyes were mine; his other features and his long lean body seemed to come from Wynn. He stood up at around eleven months and began to walk soon after that.

"I remember the day I began to feel superfluous," I told Judith, "like a pitcher about to be cut. It was a Sunday at the Hardys' pool. Terry was a year and a half and running around like a little colt. He tripped over a hose and fell on the concrete, banging his knee. He began to wail. I picked him up and kissed him but he wouldn't stop crying—until Wynn lifted him out of my arms."

"What happened to the marriage? Did Mauricio return? Did she have an affair? Did you?"

"It was a matter of business."

Wynn got backing from a local savings and loan for a new development. The land was flat as a soccer field. The nearest town was fifteen miles away and the only view was the interstate. But Wynn had big plans.

He gathered the family around to name the place. Think in the grand Spanish style, he told us. He talked about an Olympic-size pool, a health club, an on-site shopping plaza and a long wide entrance road he called the Boulevard of Palms. Vicki's older brother designed glossy full-color brochures in English and Spanish. I was in charge of sales, Vicki the office, Wynn and Vicki's younger brother, construction. When La Fonda del Sol was featured in the Sunday real estate section, Wynn used the headline in all our ads: DEVELOPED BY THE HARDY FAMILY. Early interest was tremendous. Our clients were largely Spanish speakers buying their first homes outside the Miami area. Wynn had planned 130 four-bedroom homes with red tile roofs. Construction went on six days a week. The development was sixty percent occupied when the complaints began. Where was the swimming pool? The health club complex? Where was the on-site shopping center they had read about in the brochure? The nearest store was a half-hour drive. Trucks stirred up clouds of dust on streets that had yet to be paved; there wasn't a tree planted on the Boulevard of Palms. Residents appeared at my desk every day, and all I could do was beg their patience and their trust, while I was losing my own.

There were things I didn't like about the way Wynn did business. He had a Spanish-speaking salesman but wrote up all the contracts in English. He never told people they'd have to bear the cost of being connected to the local sewer system. Vicki said I didn't understand his financial pressures, the headaches that kept him up at night. But I couldn't keep quiet any longer.

"Wynn, I have a problem," I said one night over a beer.

"You have a problem? Find a place at the back of the line, son, there's a lot of people ahead of you."

"I thought we could talk about some of the promises we made."

"And what promises might they be?" he said tiredly.

"The pool. The health club."

"I know all about it."

"Then what are we waiting for? We made a deal."

"You made a deal? Your name is on that piece of paper with the bank? Do me a favor. Until you have the union and the inspectors and the bank on your fucking back, just sit in your little air-conditioned office, do what you're paid to do and keep your mouth shut."

"Maybe I can't do that." I hadn't meant it as a threat, but these were good people. No, they didn't speak native English but they worked hard for their money, the way my own father had worked, twelve or fourteen hours a day, and it was wrong to make them come begging for the things they'd paid for. "It just doesn't sit right with me."

"And I'm supposed to give a fuck?" Wynn's eyes burned blue fire. "If I was you, I'd watch my own backyard."

"What's that supposed to mean?"

"It means if what I hear about my daughter and her friends down at the stable is true, if I ever see another grandchild it'll probably be brown."

My hand closed around a bottle of beer. I knew Wynn Hardy and I knew his game, insults instead of answers, but he always aimed for the heart and he'd cut me, hard and deep. Vicki and I hadn't made love six times since our son's birth. I felt like one of those horses who stand at stud. I felt, rightly or not, I had been used to produce the next generation of the Hardy family and that everything I had, including my son, belonged to them and not to me.

That night I told Vicki about the unfulfilled contracts, the violations of federal law. I wasn't going to force another family to suffer the same mistake mine had, sinking farther into the hole to salvage what they'd invested. It took my father years to admit he'd been a fool to take on a dying business in a rotten building, but he would have been the first to tell you that it cost him his marriage and everything he had ever been able to save. Finally I think it cost him his life.

"We're leaving here," I said. "It's time to strike out on our own."

"I can't do that, David. Terry loves his family. I can't yank him away from Mom and Dad. And the foal is just at the training level. She's supposed to take her first test next month."

"We can't stay here, Vicki. Trust me. We'll make a better life."

"But I like it the way it is." I had never heard that sharp edge on her voice. "I love my family. I thought you were one of us. If my father needs you to stick by him, I don't see why you can't. What's the matter with you, David? Why do you always put yourself first?" That night she packed Terry off to her parents' and never came back.

When I went to see him, he hardly seemed to know me. When I brought him a toy or a book, he didn't need it. He had plenty. Anything I gave him disappeared into the Hardy family and seemed to dissolve. When I tried to take him someplace for a few hours, he cried.

They wanted full custody. I gave Vicki the house (after all, Wynn had built it), and in return she asked minimal child support. I was supposed to have visiting privileges, two weekends a month, but Terry hated it. I was this stranger who came to drag him off to the movies or the beach or McDonald's, away from his grandparents' pool, his cousins, his golden retriever. I was working construction, living in a furnished room on the Gulf coast, and every time I brought him home to my place, he seemed to stare at me with Wynn's own contempt. When Vicki remarried, I moved back up north. I send my monthly check and visit twice a year and try not to think of him every time I see a kid his age.

"Most of us don't seem to get it right the first time," Judith said, taking my face between her palms. "But it might be possible to do something about your custody arrangements. . . . How old is your son now?"

"He was nine last month." I dug in my wallet. "Every year they send a photo after his birthday with a card he signs thanking me."

"Who did you cut out of the photo?"

"Wynn, Vicki and her two new kids."

"Ah . . ." She was silent, staring at the card-sized image of a tanned and healthy little boy beneath a palm tree. Under a shock of dark brown hair, his pale eyes stared into the camera with a big grin—not at me, at whoever was taking the picture. He had broad shoulders and chubby red cheeks; the son I wasn't allowed to name.

"I do a lot of custody law. . . . If you want things changed, we can talk to someone I trust down there. . . ."

"What do I have to give him, Judith?"

She looked at me the way no one else ever had. "I'd say a lot."

"When I get hopeful, I imagine him striking out on his own to find me when he gets to be seventeen or eighteen, being curious, maybe as a kind of rebellion. But none of the Hardy kids ever left home. It's a fantasy."

"Maybe not," she said. "It happens. Think of it this way. If your marriage had worked out, you would never have moved back here. You'll have a house again, and a wife, but more suited to you. More caring."

"I doubt it," I said.

"I don't." She kissed my lips lightly. "Are you hungry?"

JOHNNY

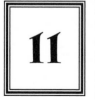

Johnny Lynch was up at four A.M. with a feeling so foreign that he had to talk to himself to understand it, coax himself down like a cat from a tree, as he'd coaxed his wife so many times. Although he was no stranger to the rush of adrenaline and the cold draft of sweat on his forehead, it wasn't until the drive into work that he could even name the problem. Fear. Back to his own office for the first time in eight weeks, at the desk he'd had custom built—thirty-two inches high to accommodate his knees—and instead of speeding down the highway, he slowed for every yellow light. He was as scared as he'd been of the nuns in school, of his father's rage when he couldn't make good grades. In order to succeed, he had purged himself of fear, learned to plunge through it, and in so doing understood that the others were more scared than he was and would fall in behind him once he cleared the way.

Johnny Lynch was sixty-eight. He'd lived twice the life of most men his age and felt half the man he used to be. The last time his dog had flushed a duck from the tall reeds behind the dike, he'd had all he could do to lift his shotgun and aim; the recoil nearly brought him to his knees. By the grace of the Lord, or maybe to provide Him with a good laugh, Johnny had survived this last bypass—if he could call the list of foods he couldn't eat, the things he couldn't do, surviving.

This was the day he had anticipated for three weeks in bed and another five in a Fort Myers resort that felt like a cemetery with palm trees. Now, three hours back in his office, the well-wishers dismissed, the mail stacked in piles of importance, he sat at his big cherry desk like the ruler of an empty kingdom. The phone didn't ring, the door didn't open. Maybe he shouldn't have demanded this afternoon's meeting with the bank. A wiser man might have waited; a lesser man wouldn't push. But finally, he was John Mosley Lynch, and he preferred bad news to silence.

He used to order his desk blotters thirty at a time. From them, Maria copied notes he scribbled while on the telephone, the numbers and contacts he gleaned, the names and the tips and reminders. Now there were few of those. He still had the real estate business, which did well despite the competition. (There hadn't been any when he began because there was no housing market in Saltash. He created it.) But the big deals were few and far between. To develop property you needed major financing now, for the endless surveys and design reviews, the regulatory hearings created to discourage all but the most determined. He had little interest in summer rentals and second home sales and left that to the girls, most of them grandmothers by now. They were demanding a new secretary, a younger girl who understood computers. As for the law practice, the indictment had all but ended that. He'd beaten the bastards, but it cost him a fortune and his reputation. Before he was indicted, even as the rumors swirled and his partners ran scared and the newspapers descended like vultures on a roadkill, there was no other lawyer worth hiring in this town. He had written the damned bylaws: zoning, health, conservation. Only after the case went to court did he find out who his friends were, who gave him their business and who turned their backs. Six years had passed, six long years of damage control. The worst of it fell on his wife, God rest her delicate soul; a finer woman had never lived.

Emily Ann was too good for this earth, and that was the cause of her troubles. This bitter world was hard on everyone's nerves, but that a woman so sensitive and pure, so good to the marrow of her bones, would succumb to its pressures was no surprise. She had everything a woman could ask, as she herself said a thousand times—a fine home, three children, a town in which she was a veritable queen—but what she needed was a world clean of petty rumors and people who lied for the sheer pleasure of causing pain. It was the indictment that claimed his wife of forty years. All those whispers about a mistress and a love nest, as if he was some Turkish pasha with a harem; those charges of sweetheart contracts and that bad business with Kevin, their second-born, Emily Ann had endured; with help from the doctors they'd gotten through her bad spells. But the indictment had been too much. Two months or three, that was all she'd ever needed to be away up in Boston; then she'd come home, how did she put it? Refreshed. But she had never come home again after he'd been hounded into court, and those who had pursued him had killed her as surely as if they'd hammered a stake straight through her heart.

For a long while he thought it was revenge he was after. He would sit in this chair, staring into the marsh as the shadows lengthened. He would watch as the tide receded and the herons returned to feed, imagining the pain he would deal his enemies. But for all that he had endured, he was not a vengeful man. To be sure, he could deliver an eye for an eye, but to waste time brooding about his enemies was only to play into their hands. Time was his real enemy.

Johnny had built this town not by thinking about it but by making the contacts that mattered, by forging alliances with the governor and the legislature. When he had first moved to Saltash, the selectmen saw Boston as the devil; one, Larsen, boasted that he had never in his life had a reason to go over the bridge—and the idiot died of a burst appendix, diagnosed by a local physician as gas. They tried to make Johnny ashamed of where he came from. Washed ashore, they called him, the mick from South Boston. But it was Boston State House money that built the highway to this town and the pier and dredged the harbor deep enough for yachts. It was all his trips to Boston, three and a half hours each way in those days, that made Saltash a place to visit and put its men to work. "John Mosley Lynch," Emily Ann used to say. "Just what do you do from seven in the morning till twelve at night?" What he'd done was build this town.

They tried to push him out. Those who'd moved into the houses he built, on the land he had cleared: in forests so thick the sunlight didn't shine, off roads no wider than wagon trails. First it was counsel to the town. Thank you very much, if you please, we'll find our legal advice elsewhere. Then selectman. Defeated after two decades on the board by fifty-four votes. They wanted him stuck in an office with three yattering women who rented summer cottages. They wanted him dead and buried.

At a quarter before twelve, apologizing lest she make him late for his one o'clock meeting, Maria brought in the new girl. Maria had worked for him for twenty-two years and knew enough about this town to run it. She was a small Portuguese girl, mother of five, and he'd watched her age over the years as if watching his own face in the mirror. Dark, sensual Maria, whose body had moved with the grace of a cat, with black curly hair and a magnificent round rump. Was she really the gray-haired matron who stood before him? She used to leave the office a half hour early and meet him at the cottage by the lake. She liked to be completely naked when he arrived. She never turned the lights on and didn't like to talk. They knew each other's secrets. Her husband, Pepe, was captain of a scallop dragger; a pot smuggler Johnny had bailed out of trouble more times than he cared to remember. His drinking was under control unless the fleet was frozen in, when he got bored and beat his wife. Johnny never told Maria about the warning he gave Pepe, that if he hit his wife again, he'd bill him for every cent he had, including the boat.

"Mr. Lynch, this is Crystal." Maria dropped the girl's résumé on the desk blotter. In twenty-two years she had never touched him in the office. "Crystal Sinclair."

This was a big girl, a head taller than Maria, substantially built, with strong wrists and a fine heavy bosom. Her white blouse was frayed at the collar and cuffs. There was a yellow stain just below the left shoulder. She needed this job. Good. He didn't want a retired woman, back to work after she'd moved down here; he wanted loyalty. Thirty-two years old, according to the résumé. Same age as his son Kevin. Well, they needed youth around here. Strange, the color of her hair, not blond or silver, but something in between. She was a pretty girl. Her smile was confident and she held his eyes. He liked that.

"Sinclair," he said. "You wouldn't have known a Dr. Sinclair?"

"I'm his daughter."

"No, sir! Well sit down, sit down. He did have two daughters," the sorry bastard. "You know we haven't had a dentist in this town since he . . . moved on." Johnny scanned the résumé with interest. It didn't surprise him that she'd been educated out West. "University of Nevada, Las Vegas. Fine school. Fine school." He didn't know a damned thing about it except they had a basketball team. He'd never been to Las Vegas. Never had the time or interest to gamble. There was something (he didn't want to stare) coquettish? made up? about her. The dark lipstick. The perfume. The tight skirt. Nothing that put him off, exactly. It just wasn't Saltash. "I see you've worked in a law office before."

"Well, I'm not really a legal secretary."

"But you've worked with computers. You've got WordPerfect, Word, Excel." None of it meant a thing to him. "And what brings you back here?" He watched her carefully. He listened for the stammer, the hesitation. The eyes flitting to the floor. Her gaze didn't falter. She was sharp, this one. She'd have the other girls eating out of her hand.

"I wanted a good education for my son."

"You have a boy?"

"He's just turned eight. And, well, I know we have a great school here and it would be perfect for him."

"You thought right. What's his name?"

"Laramie."

"After the western town!" What the fuck kind of thing is that to name a child? "Very nice, very nice." He noticed there was no wedding ring. As soon as he saw her address, he knew her story. Four twelve Dock Street. The closest Saltash had to a housing project. But he wasn't a man who judged people by their morals or their circumstances. Frankly, he thought their politics a better gauge of character. Do you believe in caring for the sick and the hungry or do you babble a few words on Sunday morning? That was the test. "Well, Crystal." He rose, offering his hand. "Welcome aboard."

"Then I have the job?"

"You had it before you walked in. I'm just the rubber stamp around here. Maria's the real power behind the throne."

The meeting was two towns over, fifteen miles up the highway, in the bank's main branch. He was five minutes early. Bernice Cady came out to meet him and escort him back. Bernice had polio as a child, and if her bad leg dragged slightly as she walked, she still walked as fast as anyone he knew. Her family had discouraged her from applying to college and assumed that she'd look after her widowed father the rest of her life. Johnny remembered her buck-toothed smile, her bony arms waving, full of questions, whenever he read stories to her class. When she graduated high school, she asked him for a job at the bank, and in spite of the other board members' reluctance and her father's disapproval, Johnny saw to it she became a part-time teller. The kid surprised him, landing the job full-time within a year. Then she became head teller, branch manager when the local bank merged, most recently a loan officer.

"Mr. Lynch, I'm sorry, no one's back yet. They called to say they'd be a few minutes."

They were still at lunch. Years ago this meeting would have been called for lunch and drinks in a private room in the best restaurant in town. Now, he could wait. Bernice couldn't do him any special favors, other than tell him the truth: it was going to be a hard sell. She saw him daub the bead of perspiration from his cheek and she knew what he had left in the world: the house he lived in and 120 acres behind the dike. He had a pain like a burning lump of coal in his chest, and it only got hotter when her bosses walked in. Two boys of forty, one bald with glasses, the other smelling of onions, both in navy suits, Roger and Steve with the power of money.

"We like your plans, Johnny," Roger the bald one said. "The timing is good. There hasn't been a significant development in Saltash in years."

"About twelve," he said. "Since the bottom dropped out. And there won't be another. There's not a more beautiful spot on Old Cape Cod. You have to see those hills in the light of the moon. The dew turns the color of silver."

The two boys exchanged a glance. Bernice looked away. He knew he sounded like a fool. Steve spoke, and the smell of onion was unbearable. "We're worried about the dike, Johnny. There's been a lot of talk about opening it. If that happens, your acreage is cut by seventy-five percent and the rest is soggy ground."

"That talk has been going on for years."

"But times have changed, Johnny. The town has changed. It's full of new voters."

"If the fools vote to open that dike and the river floods the basements and ruins the property values of fifty luxury homes, owned by doctors and lawyers and the kind of people I'm attracting, the town is looking at a lawsuit that can bankrupt it."

The bald man crossed his legs. "If the homes are built and sold first."

"Jesus, Mary, and Joseph, how can I build them until I have the money?" And what'll I do without the money? he thought. He had never been a man to take expensive vacations or wear extravagant clothes. He liked a new car. He liked to help his children. The bills for Kevin alone were as much as a man made at the height of his career. He'd never gambled with stocks and bonds. Land was where the money was—and he'd had to sell most of it to keep himself out of prison.

"Johnny, you know how much we want to help." He knew the smelly little bastard didn't give a shit about anything but covering his own ass. "But how can we commit to this project when we don't know the houses will be built and sold first? We can't afford to be stuck with ninety acres of soggy land."

Bernice shocked them all by speaking up. "What do we need, Roger?"

"Some guarantee that the dike will still be standing and in place until all the houses go up."

"And what guarantee could I give you?" Johnny felt hopeless.

"There's a seat open on the Board of Selectmen this May. As I understand it," Bernice said, "you have two votes for the dike standing and two committed to tearing it down."

Johnny looked straight into her eyes. "And if the swing seat voted to keep the dike in place?"

"I think that would go a long way toward convincing this committee. Roger?" she asked, and the bald man nodded. "Steve?"

Steve cleared his throat. "Yes. Well, as I said. We would like to do business with you."

When Johnny returned from lunch, something lemony, something fresh, lingered in the air around his desk. The new girl's perfume? The room felt brighter somehow. No, he hadn't gotten what he wanted. But

Johnny Lynch had never expected a thing without working for it, nor the rules to be stacked in his favor. What he asked was a shot at the prize. He felt heady. He felt a lightness in his step. Public opinion was against him. He'd have to work behind the scenes. But he liked a vigorous campaign. A good fight alerted his senses. No time to mull over the past. There was too much work to do.

JUDITH

12   Five years after Gordon and Judith were married, when she was thirty-two, Gordon retired from Brandeis and wanted to live on Squeer Island year-round. It was a hard move for Judith, for it meant giving up her chance at partnership in her Boston law firm, fought for grimly year after year. On the other hand, it meant she could approach the image that had remained in her mind since France of a more gracious, sensual life, integrated into a landscape. Saltash was beautiful, sloping down toward the busy harbor, the hills crowded with Victorian captain's houses, older Capes, mostly white, some painted pale blue or green or cobalt or barn red. Town center was a combination of white steepled churches on High Street and the incongruous but handsome redbrick Town Hall built in 1870, to replace a structure destroyed in a hurricane. The aesthetic of the place appealed to her, the famous light, the sea, the dunes, and of course the compound on the island. Here they would change their life. They would spend far more time together than had been available since they married, with her working at least twelve hours a day and often weekends, and Gordon teaching full-time and then flying around to lecture all over the country.

Judith became a partner in a two-person law firm in Saltash, with Austin Bowman, a man older than Gordon. By her fourth year living in Saltash, Gordon and she were fully involved in the effort to defeat the Johnny Lynch machine. Johnny Lynch controlled the entire town government, but they saw a chance to elect at least one selectman who would not be loyal to Johnny: a beginning, anyhow. It would take years to get a majority, they knew. One February morning, when fog lay over the ice in the Bay, her partner Austin called her shack just as she was about to head to town. "This guy Lyle," he said in his raspy voice. "I don't think he can cut it. Johnny is running his man hard and spreading rumors Lyle wants to raise property taxes. For our first real contest with Johnny, we need a stronger candidate."

Austin was close to seventy and on the verge of retirement, or so he said. He had been saying that since she joined his practice. She said, "Lyle makes a decent speech. People seem to trust Lyle."

"Some do, some don't."

"Suppose we get a reporter to interview both candidates about taxes. That will give Lyle a platform to insist he doesn't want to raise them."

"But, Judith, we need to raise taxes for a new water system."

"Austin, even if we win a seat on the board, one selectman out of five can't push that through."

Austin cleared his throat. "I want you to talk to someone. He's thinking of running, and he might be better for us to back. War hero from Vietnam. Lost a foot. Many relatives here."

She agreed to meet with the putative candidate at four-thirty. That would cut it close to get back over the bridge before high tide. The damned rickety bridge that high tides submerged had seemed amusing and romantic when they were summer people. Now that they lived on the island year-round and she had to make a living on the Cape, it was a nuisance to her—but Gordon had a real attachment to the island and its inhabitants and its customs. She had a cot in her law office so she could sleep over when the tides were not cooperating or when she must appear in court. She respected Gordon's attachments. The bridge might infuriate her, but the view from the bridge was one of life's pleasures, the bay full of islands, the great blue herons when the tide was low, the tern acrobats.

Austin did not like her sleeping in the office, considering it unprofessional. When he finally did retire, she was going to move the practice to a better office with a small apartment attached. That would make life easier. By the time she got off the phone, she had twenty minutes to dress and get herself across the bridge to her office to meet a client.

When she ran into the main house, Gordon was at the kitchen table, a cigarette in one hand and a cup of coffee in the other, the telephone clamped between his chin and his shoulder. "So the manuscript is late," he was saying. "The economy won't go into recession because of it. It's taking longer than I estimated, yes, but I'm making a more interesting and comprehensive book than if I hurried. I had a couple of bouts of bronchitis this winter, and it slowed me down." He nodded to her as she passed. Either his agent or his publisher, having fits because his book was not finished by deadline. She was perhaps excessively punctual, someone who did not like to keep anyone waiting, whose life was timed to the minute. Gordon was casual about deadlines whether they were getting to the supper table or showing up to a meeting. To him, time always seemed far more elastic than to her.

Practicing law here was a motley operation, now a drug dealer, now a divorce case, a suit against the town, restraining orders, whatever local life tossed up. She was getting a reputation as a good hard lawyer, the first choice of people in trouble around Saltash. Some of her clients she liked and some she detested, but she gave them all their money's worth, a well-prepared brief and a good fight in court. She was at her best in the courtroom. She thought well on her feet. It was nine-tenths being prepared and one-tenth pure competition. She liked to win as much as she ever had. She would never be done proving herself. Now she had ten minutes to drive the rutted sand road and cross the bridge before the tide rose.

Her biggest case at the moment was a woman suing the local pizza parlor. The woman, a vigorous fifty-year-old who liked to keep in shape, had fallen through a rotten plank on their deck. Her spine had been injured and her arm broken in three places. She had lost some control of her right hand and she had recurring numbness. The problem was that the pizza parlor had been carrying minimal insurance. The insurance company was refusing to pay, claiming the woman had been careless. The owner claimed that the suit was putting him out of business, the only pizza available in winter for five miles around.

When Judith went into town, about one person in four glared at her. "You're the grinch who stole pizza," the fish man roared at her.

Her first two years in town, she had felt invisible. Now that was all changed. She was visible, all right. She liked her client, Enid Corea, a no-nonsense woman who boarded dogs and had served until her accident as the town dog warden and crossing guard. Mrs. Corea smelled of the kennel, was a cheerful woman whose husband had died on the highway and whose children were grown and departed. She needed the money, and Judith meant to get it for her, even if the suit did close down the only pizza parlor for miles.

Since Gordon's retirement, they had created a life she wanted. Life by the sea, with a garden, with friends of all sorts, with an extended family. Most lawyers she knew had friends who were lawyers, perhaps a few other professionals or politicians. Through Gordon she had friends who were oystermen, scallopers, carpenters, plumbers, friends who taught history at Brandeis or Milan, friends who taught sociology in Berkeley or Melbourne, former freedom riders and war protesters, radical rabbis and radical priests and nuns, writers and painters and colorful drinkers who no longer did much of anything but tell tales of what they had done before they drank so much. Some of them she liked, some she tolerated, but theirs was a style of entertaining that was open at the same time that their work was jealously protected.

She saw her clients in town. They could call her at the office only, but she checked her messages compulsively. If one of her regular clients called, no matter from where, if they had been busted in Westfield or Revere, she got in the car and she went. After all, the time driving was billed at the same rate as her time in court. She made a reasonable living. She would never see the income some friends from law school made. But she earned about as much as Hannah, on the staff of a senator whose mistress she was. Hannah was still her confidante, as she was Hannah's. They saw each other perhaps once a year, but talked twice a week, after ten as they always had.

They were both impassioned about the law and totally involved while they were working, but both demanded to have a life besides. Both were involved with men much older than themselves, whom they admired as much as they loved them. The style of Hannah's life was entirely different from her own, but to Hannah too, how she lived was important. Hannah's elegance was closer to the Washington notion of the good life; Judith's had been formed, she was aware, partly by Yirina's fantasies and partly by her European travels, alone and with Gordon. She wanted a life rooted in a local landscape, rooted in the seasons and natural beauty, however little all that had to do with her profession.

Therefore she put up with the tides, with Gordon's children: the one she loved, Natasha; the two she got on with (the older sons Dan and Ben, their wives and children); and the two she had trouble with, Larry, her former client, and Sarah. She had trouble with them for different reasons. Sarah was hostile. She was a divorced mother who ran a travel agency, and she considered it an affront that Gordon should have married a woman so close to her in age. Larry tried to mooch, to lean, to leech. He had to be kept within bounds whether he was calling late at night needing money, or whether he was underfoot, feeling sorry for himself. He was an aspiring filmmaker who worked in a video store in New York—if he still had that job. Yet even the offspring who gave her trouble added to her sense of a rich web of connection. It fed a hunger she had always had. She longed for ever more connection into the community.

After the insurance lawyers (an offer finally, too small, but they had begun to waver), she had a meeting with the possible candidate Austin had touted. If they could get even one selectman elected who wasn't controlled by Johnny Lynch, issues could be raised at the weekly meetings, town government could be rendered more accountable. She was looking this guy over for Gordon and the liberals who often met at their house. If she thought he was for real, she would invite him over and they would interview him as a group, deciding whether to back him. She was the first interrogator. If they did not back him, they would back Lyle.

"What do you think about the dike?"

"The dike . . . Well, the dike is certainly a problem, yes. The dike." He was a slight man with a high-pitched voice and a tendency to stare into corners. "We should do something about it, yes."

After ten minutes she realized he was a lost cause. Public meetings would make a fool of him. He meant well, but he couldn't say what he meant quickly or clearly enough. No go. It would have to be Lyle.

"He won't do," she said to Gordon as they sat down to a supper of broiled salmon, boiled potatoes with herbs, bread from the local bakery, spring salad from the garden and pinot grigio. "We need somebody with more . . . conviction, more energy, more charisma."

"Johnny has enough charisma to pave the highway as far as the bridge," Gordon said wryly.

"I never found him charming," she said, propping her chin on a knuckle. "Are you charmed?"

"Sure I am. He's the last old-fashioned boss in Massachusetts politics. He's the real thing."

"A real crook? A real swindler? A real manipulator? That's like saying, a real pothole. They come by the dozen." She wanted to set Gordon off. After nine years of marriage, she was still fascinated by the way he thought. Many of her best moments in any day were spent arguing, discussing with him, listening to him reminisce, analyzing together.

"A true political boss offers as much as he takes, or almost as much, to be more accurate. He gives you a bargain. Support me and I'll do for you when you need it. Can't get a mortgage? Bank threatening to foreclose? Can't meet your payroll this week? Can't afford an operation for the wife? Need a scholarship for the boy? Just give me leeway to develop all the land I want the way I want to, give me leeway to run the town to my advantage, and your boy will go to a state college, your wife will be off to the county hospital, and your roof will stay over your head. That's the devil's bargain—and it is a bargain. The folks who support him aren't stupid. They want it."

After supper they strolled in the twilight that was beginning to perceptibly lengthen as May began. Gordon had to pause several times as they climbed the dune, shaken by coughing. That nasty bronchitis from February had never really let go. Warm weather would dry it up. He liked to bake in the sun, and she could rarely get him to use sun screen. She was always trying to take care of Gordon, to feed him nutritiously, which was not difficult; to monitor his health; to get him to cut down on his smoking, since she had reluctantly realized she would never get him to stop. He was convinced he would not be able to work if he didn't have a cigarette at hand. "My mind is stimulated by nicotine," he would say blithely. "Caffeine in, nicotine in, words out. That's how the machine works."

"I still think you should see Dr. Garvey about that cough. You've had it since February. And see why your arm has been bothering you."

"It doesn't bother me. Just too much wood chopping. And my cough is just a smoker's cough. We're all a little short of breath as we get on. I don't see it slowing me down."

They walked along the bay, not touching but aware of each other. The waves hissed in, the pebbles rattling. There was only a horizon of greenish light left at water level. Venus was bright already. She thought that by the time they turned for home, both of them knew that as soon as they entered the house, they would head for their bedroom and make love. People sometimes let her know that they assumed hers was a marriage blanc, since Gordon was so much older, but there was nothing blank about it. They turned to each other now almost as frequently as they had in the early days. Oftener now she was the top, the more aggressive, the more vigorous, but Gordon's desire had not diminished, nor his skill. Making love was at the center of their marriage.

DAVID

13

The better part of March passed and I'd done nothing about the election. Judith stopped asking if I'd found someone to be treasurer of my campaign, to write absentee voters or nail up signs.

One night Judith put her hands on both sides of my face and stared into my eyes. "I think I finally understand what's happening with your campaign."

"That I'm not the person you're looking for."

"That you're afraid to ask for help."

Tommy Shalhoub was an old friend and the only phone call I could bring myself to make to prove her wrong. He didn't hesitate when I asked if he'd post election signs along the highway and suggested tearing down my opponents' signs as well.

I'd known Tommy Shalhoub since grade school, when his family moved to Saltash from a Syrian neighborhood in East Boston. He was an outsider, like me, but with coarse black curly hair and olive-brown skin, often lumped with the Portuguese, the bottom of the local pecking order. They called him the Sand Nigger; I was merely the Jew. While I escaped into baseball, Tommy was happiest alone, prowling the ponds for snakes and frogs, sleeping under a blanket in the woods. Just about the time I signed a contract with the Chicago Cubs, he left high school in the eleventh grade, got caught selling pot, and enlisted in the army in lieu of prosecution.

Tommy was the only guy I knew who talked with nostalgia about the military. Upon his return to Saltash, he worked as a house framer. Whenever the opportunity arose, he searched out construction work in disaster areas. Homestead after Hurricane Andrew. North Dakota after the Red River flood. Cheap motels and road food were perks for Tommy Shalhoub. He watched Weather Channel the way most people read the help wanted ads. He was out of town for months at a time. I had chosen Tommy to call because asking for help was as easy for me as taking a knife to my flesh, and I did not expect to find him at home. I was even more surprised when he sought me out at the nursery.

Tommy arrived accompanied by the pounding bass of the tape deck in his pickup, a noise that carried above the wind and the creaking joists of the greenhouse and the water I was draining out of the artificial pond. Tommy marched across the gravel floor. His presence seemed to disturb the air, to cause a sudden vibration of molecules like the rumble of a nearing motorcycle. "Dav-eee, what ch'up to?"

"Every time I put goldfish in this damned pond, they disappear. No floating bodies, not even a skeleton. I don't understand it."

"I mean in your life. I mean tonight. Let's have some fun. I got ideas."

"The last one was Lisa." She was a bank teller in her early thirties, a former girlfriend of Tommy's with a cocaine sniffle and hips that could slide into a child's pair of jeans. I knew she was coming off a bad relationship, and she knew I was on the make. We had sex twice, the way you draw water from an old stone well, trying to get what you need without falling in.

"Yeah, Lisa, Lisa," Tommy said. "What's she doin'?"

"Looking very hard for someone to take care of her."

"Listen t'me, Davey. I gotta ask y'somethin'." Tommy wore a thin leather jacket over a V-neck tee. Thirty-five degrees outside: no muffler, no hat, a blue crucifix tattooed on the back of his right hand. "You know my girlfriend, Michelle?"

"I met her last year at a baseball game." Cape Cod league. Tommy had left us alone in the bleachers for an hour. Wouldn't say where he'd gone.

"I remember that, yeah. You explained all the rules to her. But that was a different Michelle. This one has a friend who just moved back to town."

"Tommy, I'm not looking to be fixed up."

He didn't sound surprised. "If I was seeing a certain lady lawyer, I wouldn't either."

Tommy had been married and divorced twice. For all I knew, Judith might have represented Tommy in a court case or fought him on behalf of one of his ex-wives. I wasn't about to feed him information about Judith's private life. "I don't know what you're talking about."

"Then what's the problem? This girl's name is Crystal. She used to live in town. She just moved into Michelle's with her kid. He loves baseball."

"You've got two women on your hands? Is that it?"

"Hey." He threw up his palms, no contest. "If it doesn't fit in your busy schedule . . ." Tommy brushed past me to kneel at the pond. "What the fuck is that?" A black slime-encrusted lump rose from the murky bottom, projecting its head like a snake.

"A turtle?"

"A snapper!" Tommy said as the thing opened and closed its jaws. It had obviously lived on the bottom for months, dining on goldfish. It scrabbled for purchase, preparing to lunge. Tommy clopped into the pond, sinking to his ankles, and grabbed the thing by the rim of its shell. Flailing its limbs, it pissed like an open drain while Tommy held it at arm's length, staring into its ancient eyes. I told him sure, he could have it. He strolled out like a boy of twelve enchanted with his latest find.

As Passover approached, Judith asked me to join Gordon and her, his daughter Natasha, and a few friends, for a small seder. I was surprised. "Gordon told me he wasn't into that stuff," I told her. He'd been telling me where he grew up: "Jewish Cincinnati," he'd said. "But I was never into *that stuff.*"

"He's finding his way back," Judith said. It was obvious why. I wanted to accept her invitation, but Passover was the one religious ritual we observed in my family, and it was always spent at Holly's.

Passover was early that year. It fell the day after Gordon's sixty-ninth birthday, which Judith insisted I come over to celebrate. Judith said she would be cooking for two days, today for his birthday and tomorrow for Passover.

The door was opened by a young woman who looked me up and down with open curiosity. I expected indifference or hostility, but there was something in her glance that spoke of complicity. "You're David Greene? I'm Natasha Stone."

She had red-blond hair and Gordon's eyes in a sharp pointy face. All elbows and knees and attitude, she was grinning like a hungry fox. "Come right in. Judith's finishing up the asparagus soup."

The dining room table was not set. "Do you need some help?"

"We're not eating here." She lowered her voice. "Daddy's having a bad day, so Judith set things up in his bedroom." She read my expression. "Just act like everything's normal."

Judith kissed me briefly on the mouth as I came into the kitchen. Then she handed me a tureen of hot soup.

Gordon was sitting up in his queen-sized bed with bookshelves built into the headboards, wearing a plaid nightshirt and looking gaunt. He was even thinner than the last time I had seen him, and there was a bluish cast to his face. His nose seemed to have lengthened. Across his lap, a wooden tray table squatted. Judith had set up card tables on either side of the bed so that Natasha could eat at one and Judith and I could share the other. With the meal, we drank champagne.

If I stepped back from the scene, it was bizarre, Gordon in bed and us at card tables eating roast lamb with garlic potatoes, baby string beans, and for dessert, a strawberry pie; Gordon, his wife, his wife's lover and his youngest daughter. Gordon rallied and was bawdy and cheerful, holding forth about everything from why asparagus made urine smell weird, to the history of Passover and the birthday customs of different cultures. Natasha was obviously crazy about her father and close to Judith. She kept taking me in with sideways glances, no flirtation but a powerful curiosity. After we cleared the remains of the meal, Natasha said, "I always take a birthday picture of my dad, just like he always takes one of me. He started it when I was a baby. This time, you both get in it." So Judith, in her black velvet dress, and I climbed on the bed. Natasha took several shots before she let us get up: Gordon with his arms around both of us, Judith and I lifting our glasses to her behind the lens. I couldn't remember a livelier dinner party or a better meal, and strangely, it felt natural. I was half sorry to miss Passover with them.

The next night, I was off to Marty and Holly's. No one in the family would ever say it, but the truth is, Holly married above herself. Ever since she had first brought Marty home, I sensed she was a little ashamed of us. Marty's father and mother both taught at Harvard Medical School. Their brick colonial on Commonwealth Avenue outside Boston was the kind of home that made my mother sigh. In my parents' presence, the Doctors Sterling wore the kind of patient smiles you see on politicians touring a public school. At the wedding they stayed long enough for pictures and left before the cake. Since my father's death, they no longer invited my mother for Thanksgiving dinner, and Marty himself ignored her unless she came to babysit.

My mom was referred to as "a big girl" by those who liked her, a full-figured woman. With long legs and large feet, she was taller than my father by three inches, although soft to his rigid, tight-bodied intensity. She spoke in a rich alto (in fact she conducted the local choir), and this almost manly voice, coupled with her size and a strange birthmark on her forehead, the color and shape of a spilled cup of coffee, had set her apart from others all her life. She was impatient with herself, obviously anticipating criticism before she received it, and an embarrassing flirt. She tended to treat me and Holly (and my father when he was alive) like a painting she could never quite get right. Holly was hardworking and cautious to a fault, but my mom usually found one. Marty wrote a column once, comparing my mother to a Mobil Travel Guide Inspector and his house to a hotel that couldn't get more than two diamonds. It was very funny and widely reprinted, and Holly and I hated it. Our mom wasn't easy but we resented her being exposed as a national mother-in-law joke.

At the seder, Holly's food was superb, Marty's ceremony short, and

my mother on her best behavior. She cherished her one formal invita-
tion every year (all other holidays were spent at Marty's parents), her
beautiful granddaughters, her famous son-in-law. She wore her best
blue suit. She complimented Marty's singing voice and insisted on do-
ing the dishes with Holly so the girls could watch TV.

Marty sat glumly all through dinner staring at me. As soon as the
dishes were cleared, he asked me back to his study. He did not pull out
the videotapes of himself on the Letterman show or the photographs of
his junket to Japan, but a bottle of cognac from the cabinet behind his
desk and two glasses. Marty had a strong squarish face made vulnerable
by delicate wire-framed glasses, and a tendency for his cheeks to turn a
deep and glowing pink, a litmus test of his emotions. Strangely, he was
just my size. Neck, sleeve length, chest size, shoe. Once a year he'd
drop a box of his old clothes at my feet and act insulted if I didn't plow
through it with effusive thanks. "Tell me something." Marty poured
himself cognac. I didn't care to drink with him. "The truth, what is this
election shit? You're goofing on everybody, right? You're not serious?"

"I'm thinking about running."

"Hell, maybe I'll get a column out of it. Why not? My brother-in-law,
the small-time pol. The ticket fixer. You can feed me the crazy stuff."

"I don't think so, Marty. It wouldn't be fair."

"To who? The motel owners? The restaurants? Are you kidding? My
column has a circulation of four million. They'll be booked all summer."

"Don't you think Saltash has enough problems without turning the
town into Mayberry?"

"You are serious." He studied me over the rim of his glass. "All right,
so tell me the burning issues." He put his feet up on the desk. "Win my
vote."

"Fuck you."

"Don't be so sensitive. We're family, we can't tease each other? Be-
cause we're going to be dragged into it, you know. Holly. The children."

"I don't think so."

"People say you're doing it because you like to get laid."

"That's what *people* say? Or you?"

"Me?" Marty said. "I could care less."

"You don't care that Judith and I are friends?"

"Ooh, I like that. Friends." He pitched forward and refilled his glass.
"By that definition of friendship everybody'd be humping each other all
over this great nation of ours. This is my friend. She sucks my cock.
Next time my kid says she made a friend in school, I'm going to get her
birth control."

"You are one nasty son of a bitch."

"Me? Then what do you call a person who screws a sick man's wife?"

"I've had enough." I stood.

"You're not the only one, you know. Judith has a thing for younger guys."

"What's your problem, Marty? You wanted to be one of them?"

I watched his cheeks light up. "One of them was a buddy of mine."

"I find that hard to believe."

"That her husband's an old man and she likes young meat now and then?"

"That you could have a buddy."

Marty stood, knocking his glass to the floor. Holly heard the crash and came to the office door. "You guys all right? Marty? David, where are you going?"

I told my sister I'd had a lovely evening and would see her in the morning. Marty was close behind me. "You don't believe me, David?" he called from the door. "Ask her! Ask her about Brian. Her *friend* Brian!"

Judith was usually awake before sunrise, but because it was Sunday morning, I waited a few hours to call. I sensed what Marty had told me was an exaggeration. The trouble was that it explained things too well. Why a young woman would have an affair in the face of her husband's illness. Why she might choose someone like me. I had to see Judith right away.

At nine-thirty her line was busy. I called again fifteen minutes later, and once or twice after that. I drove out to the highway to buy the Sunday paper. I tried again from a pay phone, and still unable to get through, made a decision I would regret.

The mainland was clear, but a blue band of fog clung to the treetops over the island. In the distance, soft shell clammers were bent in right angles at the waist, clawing a living from the mud as their wide-bottomed boats drifted on long anchored leads. Although there was a bitter chill on this April morning and the roads were slippery with patches of ice, you could see green shoots growing up under the dead brown stalks; you could smell spring in the funky decay of sea life, salt air and mud.

I pulled up in their drive and hit my horn. Through my own reflection in the glass door I saw Gordon tying the strings of his robe. He waved. He started slowly toward me as Judith appeared behind him. She too was wearing a robe, which she held closed with a fist over her heart. She bolted past him and whipped open the door.

"What are you doing here?" she demanded. I smelled toothpaste and soap and the same perfume she daubed between her thighs in my bedroom. "Don't you call first? Do you just barge in on people?"

"I did call. I've been calling for hours."

Gordon laughed, slowly making his way to the telephone on the kitchen wall, where he replaced the receiver on its hook. He ran water at the sink and filled a kettle. He suggested we have coffee. Judith told me to wait outside and ran upstairs to dress.

I followed her down the path to the garden, through the hollow where pine needles crackled beneath our boots, to the little cottage where we met to make love. But this time she didn't beckon me with a silent smile. This time the garden didn't look like magic, but a trap full of nets and sharp edges. She turned on me as soon as she slammed the door. "Do not ever come over here without calling again."

"Sorry I interrupted whatever it was."

"You know what it was," she said icily.

"So you do sleep with him?"

"He is my husband."

"Fine. But why didn't you *tell* me?"

It was not often that Judith would fumble for words. "Because it's . . . not a regular thing."

"I assumed he was too sick, Judith. I assumed that you didn't have that kind of relationship, that I wasn't in the middle of something."

"Most of the time he is too sick. Sometimes he feels all right. I don't always know." By now she seemed more confused than angry. "It's all new, David. Gordon hadn't been . . . able for a long time."

"How new?"

"I don't know."

"Sure you do. Since you started sleeping with me?" The way Gordon sometimes looked at us. Nothing suggestive. He didn't make innuendoes. He never leered. But I sensed that my presence, a younger man with his wife, excited him. "Does it happen after I visit you here?"

She wouldn't answer. She didn't have to.

"Hell, I'm glad he *can* make love to you."

"I doubt that."

"I am," I said. "I'm glad he's well enough."

"He's not well. Sometimes his body can remember me through the pain. Sometimes he wants to be near me. Since I met you, yes, a door has opened. Gordon senses that I'm happy. He's my friend and my family and my teacher. We talk. And we remember what it used to be like. And we try to plan how things are going to be. And this morning . . . yes." There was no fire in the woodstove. We had not turned on a lamp. A shaft of gray light poured through the skylight like a pillar between us.

"Judith, who is Brian?"

"Brian?" She looked confused. There was nothing in her expression to suggest he meant anything. She had trouble recalling his name. "He did a book with Gordon. A photographer. What's going on here?"

"I'm trying to understand what you want with me, Judith."

"I assume," she moved toward me tentatively through the cold shaft of light, "the same as you want with me."

"But Gordon—"

"Wants us all to be happy."

"You're serious."

"Yes. Yes, why not?" There was pleading in her voice. "Gordon and I have a life together. You and I have a life together. No one has to be deceived or disappointed. What is the problem?"

"Where is this supposed to go? How long can it go on?"

"What's to stop us?"

"Only the opinion of everyone around us," I said.

"Are you under the illusion that they, whoever they are, have perfect little marriages? Above criticism? No dirty secrets?"

"Not at all."

"And do you judge them for the way they look for love?"

"I couldn't care less."

"Then what is the problem? We live our own lives. We do what we want. Everybody's honest. Nobody gets hurt. What is the problem?"

Only my own sense of right and wrong.

JUDITH

Two weeks after their ninth wedding anniversary, Judith insisted Gordon go to a doctor in Boston. She was not satisfied with the chronic bronchitis diagnosis, and nothing seemed to be helping. She felt guilty because she should have managed to get him to a good doctor months before. She had nagged him, she had set up an appointment. The first appointment she made, he found an excuse to cancel. He was too busy for that nonsense. He had a cough, big deal. At his age, everybody had something. He had missed his deadline on the new book, he had three speaking engagements. He didn't need an unnecessary trek into Boston, just because she was a worrywart and a control freak and overfond of doctors. But she would not let him cancel the second appointment, when she was able to get another. She want in with him, she marched him into the office, she tried to put a good face on his grumpiness.

The doctor poked and prodded him, particularly in his neck and lymph nodes and over his chest and listened to his breathing. Then he pronounced that Gordon must go to another doctor, an oncologist. He was careful how he phrased his opinion. "To eliminate several possibilities, you need to have some tests. Then if you don't have *that problem*, which is at the moment only a possibility, we need to run more diagnostic tests back here."

Oncologist. The doctor they decided on after consulting friends and acquaintances was associated with the Dana Farber Cancer Institute. There, the word was out in the open at last. The man they saw was the surgeon of a particular team, as he put it. Dr. Edward Barrows was a year or two younger than Judith, a handsome West Indian who spoke with a lilt. He called Gordon by his first name, which made Gordon bristle. His assistant took a complete medical history, so complete that Gordon asked, "Are you sure you don't need to know the last time I cut my toenails?" They took a sample of Gordon's sputum and scheduled an X ray and a CAT scan of the chest.

They both understood the doctor was testing for cancer, but they did not talk about it. She did not want to believe Gordon had cancer; she knew Gordon rejected the idea. They both clung to the hope that Dr. Barrows would clear that possibility.

The X-ray diagnosis appeared to be inconclusive. Gordon celebrated with a bottle of champagne. She was not sure but drank it with him. It turned out Dr. Barrows wanted a tissue sample. "You mean you're going to take out a piece of me," Gordon thundered. He was reluctant, but what choice had he? The tests went on, more and more invasive. Needle aspiration. A tube inserted through an incision in the neck to test a lymph node. The tests went on for over a month, back and forth to Boston or to Hyannis, where the doctor had a satellite office.

Finally Dr. Barrows was ready to give a diagnosis. There was a tumor. Given its size and location, a combination of chemotherapy and radiation therapy was indicated to reduce it. Then they would operate, perhaps in six months if the other therapies were successful. Now they knew. The moment the doctor had told them, she realized she had suspected as much secretly, for a year. Never had she mentioned the word "cancer," but she had always been thinking it, in a locked compartment at the back of her mind which usually contained only a certainty that some yutz she was defending was actually guilty of whatever he had been accused of. Hiding that opinion from herself let her function as she must. Hiding her fear for Gordon had let her get through the months when she could not force him to a doctor. But now they both must live with the fact of cancer. Gordon took it well. "It's like going into a dogfight," he said as she drove them home. "You know you may die, but you plan not to. You figure you have your will to live and your reflexes and your knowledge of the enemy and your own plane. There's terror in facing down death, but there's also a crazy high like nothing else I've known since."

As they returned to the office where Dr. Barrows must have given similar bad news to patients every day, the next stage of the process began. "We must agree on a plan of treatment," said the doctor, and somehow his "we" grated on her all the more because he was young, because he was handsome, because he was radiantly healthy. The oncologist who dealt with radiation therapy, Dr. O'Reilly, was much older, red in the face as if he drank or had high blood pressure or had spent too much time in the sun. Judith and Gordon both liked him at once, perhaps because he seemed vulnerable. He explained how precise the machine was that burned away at the tumor, but could not penetrate it all the way.

The doctor in charge of the chemotherapy was a woman about Judith's age, slightly overweight, her hair straggling out of its do, the air of a worried mother. Dr. Sara Ripkin turned out to be the star, when they eventually came to her office. Besides her diplomas, she had a string of plaques for prizes. She worked with several of the oncologists.

"Chemotherapy is a little like cooking," she said to them, resting her elbows on her desk and her chin in her cupped hands as if her head was heavy. "You try a mix and then you see how it tastes—to the tumor, to the cancer cells. There are a great number of possible chemicals and a great many possible combinations and dosages. If at first we don't succeed, we try a different mix. We keep checking, week to week. It may seem tedious but that's the formula for success."

The first question was how much to tell the children.

"Ben's what? Forty? If he can't deal with it now, when will he be able to?" Gordon scowled.

"Forty-five," she corrected automatically. As a good wife should, she had their birthdays memorized. She bought gifts and cards and sent them to his sons and daughters, his grandchildren. Their spouses. A reminder program on her computer told her when it was time to order a gift. Mostly she mail-ordered, except for Natasha, for whom she shopped personally.

"If we tell any of them, we must tell them all," she said.

"Whatever." He looked exhausted. "Can't we just play it down? I have a touch of cancer." He reached automatically for a cigarette.

Her hand was faster. She grabbed the pack and threw it in the fireplace. "No more. The price has been too high already!"

"Isn't it a little late to worry? I might as well enjoy myself."

"It's never too late to worry. You don't want the cancer to metastasize. What I've read suggests that smoking increases the risk. No more, Gordon. You've bullied me into putting up with it for the nine years we've been married, but guess what? My tolerance ran out yesterday. No more, not one." She went to stand in front of him. "I love you, Gordon. You're precious to me. I refuse, I refuse to give you up. We're going to fight this. People have remissions. Some people are cured. And don't think you can smoke out in your shack and I won't know it. I can always smell it. Your puffing days are past."

That night she called Natasha at school. There had been a price tag on her marriage all along: Gordon had said no more children. He had demanded that pledge from her, and she had given it. But she had a daughter. She had raised Natasha from late childhood, and Natasha was far closer to her than to her biological mother, Fern. Hannah and she had often talked about the advantages and problems of being involved with men so much older than either of them. But this cost was new and far higher.

Natasha was in her senior year at Brown, planning to go on to veterinary school. When Judith told her, Natasha was silent for a full minute.

"Sometimes I hate him!" she burst out. "I've been trying to get him to stop smoking since I was seven. I've heard you trying, again and again over the years. He's so arrogant! He thought it couldn't happen to him!"

"But Natasha, getting angry at him won't help him—or you."

"But I don't want to lose my father!"

"I don't want to lose my husband. He's not dying, Natasha, he hasn't even started treatment. We have to express hope, and to do that we have to feel it. They say that attitude has a lot to do with who survives and for how long. We have to be a cheering section. And for that we have to let go of anger and despair—do you understand?"

Squamous cell carcinoma had spread from the lung to the hilar nodes. Even the name was ugly. She had never heard of a squamous cell. Being married to an invalid was a different marriage. Sometimes Judith felt pushed to the wall. Her work was unremitting, full-time law that was now, besides Gordon's pension and occasional royalties, their sole source of income; now full-time nursing as well. She wished she were a more patient woman. She wished she were a better person. She loved Gordon passionately, but now the major way to express that was through taking care of him. The chemotherapy and the radiation therapy sapped his energy and left him debilitated. He was often nauseous. She cleaned him up and cleaned up after him. Nursing did not come naturally to her. Gordon was cranky. He hated being ill. He was heroic in his own way, stoic, committed to the treatment. He had finally stopped sneaking cigarettes. What drove him crazy was not being able to work. He was simply too weak, too tired. His disease was his new career, he said wryly, but he meant it. He had to be taken to Boston twice every week and once to Hyannis. She could not meet those obligations and continue to practice law, so they found a young man to drive him back and forth on Mondays and a young woman who would do the Hyannis trip every Thursday.

Gordon actually liked having two drivers. He was used to enjoying an intense social life. His illness, at least during chemotherapy, curtailed that. He got involved in the lives and problems of Tim, the son of a fisherman serving time for bringing in marijuana, and Camilla, who had moved into her parents' summer house when she lost her job. He knew all about their loves, their family squabbles, their financial burdens, their fantasies and unlikely plans. Judith listened to his reports with as much interest as she could muster, because she was touched by his involvement and she understood what this was in lieu of: his intellectual, professional, political and social life.

Some of the drugs worked and some didn't. It seemed highly experimental. They were throwing drugs into his system to see what happened. He got very sick from some of them. The doctors monitored his white blood cells, the tumor, his blood chemistry. He was losing weight but his face was somewhat swollen, along with his neck. When he was wrapped up in a tweed jacket or sweaters, for he was often chilled, he could even look as if he had gained weight. But she saw his wasting body. She massaged him. Some days she had to dress and undress him. About two weeks after the radiation therapy stopped, his throat was so painful he could swallow nothing, not even water. His hair came out in handfuls. Soon he was bald, Gordon who had always had a full lush halo.

The doctors threw drugs into him and she threw random food in front of him. Finding food he could endure eating was a constant experiment of another sort. His sense of taste was off. Foods he had always loved tasted burnt or spoiled. Some smells disgusted him. She had to stop wearing perfume. Even her hand lotion irritated him. He was always thinking the milk had turned. He developed a taste for something called junket, an old-fashioned pudding made of rennet and flavored with raspberry. She could only find one mail-order source for the stuff. He also liked vanilla tapioca pudding and chicken soup. Childhood foods, perhaps. She would do anything to make him less miserable. Discomfort, the doctors called it, you'll be experiencing some discomfort. They never said pain. Agony. Terror. He was on the chemotherapy for a week and then off for three weeks. Then just as his weakness was lessening, another cycle began.

She slept badly. Insomnia had never been a problem of hers. In law school she had been constantly exhausted, but that was because she only had three hours to waste in bed every night. Now she lay down beside him but rarely slept. She was secretly relieved when he suggested they have separate bedrooms. He found it painful when she bumped against him or curled into his side during the night. Still, it seemed an ominous change, to move out of the bedroom they had shared. It was a long winter and a slow spring. Fern arrived for a week and tried to teach Gordon visualization. At first he was forbearing and went along with her exercises. It made sense to Judith that the mind should be able to infiltrate the immune systems, but it was too New Age for Gordon. Why had he ever married Fern? Fern was not a difficult guest. She was used to living in group situations, and did not spread out through the house and always cleaned up after herself. Actually, Judith rather liked being able to share some of the nursing chores. She could imagine, briefly, the advantages of polygamy. But Fern and Gordon always ended up arguing, as she was sure they had when they were married to each other. That is, Gordon argued and Fern sighed and looked pained and quoted her experts.

"My good body has betrayed me," he told Judith. "Always I've been vigorous, able to stay up all night and dance and fuck and drink, and still work the next day. It's like a great battle horse that suddenly stumbles, and you wonder if you'll have to shoot it. My body is all I think about now. It's a new kind of narcissism."

"It's not narcissism, Gordon. You're trying to recover from a dangerous illness. It takes all your time and all your energy."

Gordon was sitting in his favorite chair in the living room with Portnoy on his lap, the big gray cat who had become his constant companion. Seven years before, Natasha had found him beside Route 6, a discarded, starving kitten with a broken leg. Now Portnoy had decided to take care of Gordon, according to his lights, washing his hands, cuddling against him, keeping the other cats and dogs away. "It is narcissism, Judith. I'm obsessed with how I feel day and night. I keep a journal about my symptoms and my responses. I go through litanies of my aches and pains. I am obsessed with the chemicals, the poisons they put into me. The idea of taking platinum as a drug is fascinating. My body is becoming this expensive and useless artifact."

"With the end in sight of getting better, of being well again."

"The stupidest thing is, I felt much better before they started on me. I keep thinking—and don't yell at me, I'm not acting on it—that all that was wrong with me was a cough and a little fever and a pain in my shoulder. Now my whole body is screwed up. I can't eat, I can't drink, I can't fuck, I can't climb a flight of steps unassisted. I'm wondering if the cure isn't worse than the disease."

"Gordon, lung cancer kills."

"But Judith, it may do that anyhow. And is this living?"

Finally Dr. Ripkin pronounced the tumor shrunk enough for Dr. Barrows to operate, to remove the tumor, affected lymph nodes and, of course, a good portion of Gordon's left lung. Many new tests irritated Gordon. But he was pleased to hear he had a good heart. They always tested for cardiovascular problems before surgery. It seemed as if there was scarcely an inch of his body they did not test in some way, not a system they left alone. Judith had enough warning so that she put everything on hold, found another lawyer to cover for her and went into Boston with him. The surgery would take place at Dana Farber, where they had done the biopsies on his lungs and lymph nodes. They had friends she could have stayed with, but she preferred a hotel. She did not want to have to chat with anyone. It was easier to be alone. She spoke to Natasha twice a day, to Hannah every night and usually also to her best friend on the Cape, her frequent antagonist in court, the assistant district attorney, Barbara Ashbaum. That was as much contact and conversation as she could endure. Most of the other children called the hospital or the doctor. Ben, the oldest, called her the night of the surgery.

Gordon hated the hospital. He was depressed by patients lined up in corridors waiting for X rays, waiting for scans, waiting for doctors. He found the standard ways that nurses and orderlies addressed him demeaning. He was used to admiration, deference, used to people knowing who he was. Here he was just bald Gordon the patient to whom things were administered and done. "They speak to me as if I had lost my mind with my tumor and had the mental level of a five-year-old. It drives me up the wall. Do you know what you mainly do in the hospital? You wait. You're called a patient because you're required to be endlessly, endlessly patient."

She could not stay in Boston the next two weeks, but commuted when she was able. She could not drop her practice, or they would not survive economically. The nights she spent in the house alone were dreadful. When she was in Boston, Stumpy cared for the cats and dogs and the birds and random other animals Natasha brought home. The six cats and two dogs were some kind of comfort. They were worried. They came to her to give and take reassurance. She could not say that she slept alone, for there were up to five other mammals in her bed on any given night.

She was tremendously glad to bring Gordon back to the Cape. He was not to remain in bed, but to get up every day and walk as far as he could endure. He was to eat as much as he could, to regain lost weight. Gradually he began to regain his strength. They walked, slowly, but they walked together along the sand roads, over the hills, along the beaches on both sides of the island. They walked and sometimes they talked. He was short of breath and had to rest frequently, but he was no longer an invalid. His hair was growing back, all white and finer than it had been, like down. He had an appetite. Sometimes they were even able to make love. They tried new ways of pleasing each other, gentler ways of putting their bodies together.

She studied nutrition. Hidden in her office, she had six different tomes on cancer and cancer therapies. Now Gordon was freed from the doctors for a while. He saw Dr. Barrows once a month. Perhaps he was cured; perhaps their life would really resume. His strength seemed to be seeping back. He was at work on his long overdue manuscript. The family came in bunches, and Gordon began to hold forth, as he always had, the hub of everything. She began cautiously, secretly, to hope. To hope that she would retain this man who was the center of her life, the only man she had ever really loved.

JOHNNY

Johnny Lynch had put back a few drinks after dinner and fallen asleep on the couch when the phone woke him. Twenty past midnight, said the ship's clock in his den. Chief of police Smalley filled him in at once. "It's a tragedy," Johnny said. "Did the boy damage the dike?"

"Only himself."

"Did the parents take it hard?"

Abel said he was about to call them. He was sitting at the accident site, talking to Johnny on his car phone. His men were securing the area, and the rescue squad was taking the kid to the hospital twenty miles away.

"And you think he'll lose the arm?"

"What's left of it," Abel said.

"Jesus, Mary and Joseph." He stood, clutching the phone, and dizziness hit him. He ended the conversation sitting on the floor. "The parents will want to be off to the hospital immediately. I'll call the mother in the morning."

He struggled to his feet and climbed the stairs to his bedroom. Once he'd been able to handle a scotch before supper, a bottle of wine with his meal and a few brandies as he sat down afterwards with the newspaper. But he wasn't drinking alone back then and that made all the difference. There were selectmen's meetings and poker games, cocktails with clients and dinners with the family. He'd lost half the old crowd to illness, and the other half to politics.

The following morning he drove the length of High Street, as he did every day, slowly (he didn't care who was behind him) and took in the inn with its huge porch and columns, the churches, so white and pure in the rosy light of the rising sun, redbrick Town Hall, perfectly restored after that little fire, and the street itself, washed clean every day at dawn—he'd made sure of that, wrote it into the job description of the Department of Roads, Bridges and Waterways twenty years ago after a visit to Paris. Johnny parked in the Town Hall lot, bought his three newspapers, walked to his table in the Binnacle. Conversation dropped to a murmur. Even the rattle of plates in the kitchen stopped, the dishwasher and the cook peering through the pantry window. They all wanted to know what to make of the explosion. Was it a serious crime? A seventeen-year-old boy, no stranger to the police, attempting to make some kind of statement by blowing up public property? Or just mischief? Or was this the beginning of war, neighbor versus neighbor?

Nobody approached his table. These were tough, hardworking people; not shy about demanding their due, but respectful. They were churchgoers, some of them, but they were not moralists. There was a tradition of live and let live in Saltash. This was no small midwestern town with a distrust of what was too different, but a village whose economy had depended on the sea; that had sent its men all over the world and felt damned lucky if they made it home, no matter what their quirks and changes. What these people had always sought from him was a vision of how to proceed politically; how to survive in a state whose legislature saw their home as a playland in July and August and a hinterland from September to June. They looked to Johnny for the way around and through state laws never written for their benefit.

The waitress approached his table with a pot of coffee. "How are you today, Johnny? Two eggs, toast and griddle cakes?" He was Johnny to everyone, young and old, rich and poor, except at the office. He didn't believe in humbling people before him any more than in driving fancy cars. People resented you for it. The greatest man he'd ever known drove a Buick and had people call him Jack, until he was elected president.

"Just coffee, dear. Just coffee this morning." He made his point, saw people beyond this girl's fine broad hips stop their chewing, rethink things in light of the accident.

"You feeling all right, Johnny? There's a stomach flu going around."

"To tell the truth, it's the Compton boy, dear. I can't get him off my mind. Has he truly lost that arm? We'll have to find something for him, won't we? And we will." He lifted his eyes, addressing the other tables. "Once we make sure he gets the best damned care available."

Gary Zora twisted around from the table behind. "What in the hell did the kid think he was doing, Johnny? Dike's been through two hurricanes. And did he think he wouldn't get caught?"

Johnny shook his head sadly. "I don't think the boy himself knows. Only thing I thought about at seventeen was baseball and pretty girls." He winked at Doris Fisher at the table next to Gary's. She blushed and touched her fingertips to her tight gray curls.

"I don't know where they get their ideas," Gary said.

"What I want to know is, where did he get the explosives?"

"It was easy enough." Gary was in the fire department and had either responded to last night's call or listened on the radio. The juicy gossip attached to any rescue operation was one of the perks of a dangerous nonpaying job. "He just stuffed a copper pipe full with black powder from his father's shotgun shells and laced it all through with a candle wick."

"I don't believe it, Gary. Saltash kids don't do that kind of thing," Johnny said.

Gary lowered his voice. "You know his father. The apple don't fall very far."

Johnny said, loud enough to make himself heard, "No parent would put his child up to this. No parent would ever want to see his boy lose his arm. Not over a petty municipal disagreement. Am I right?" he asked Birdie Hogan, watching from a corner table.

"Not here, Johnny. Not since I been." Birdie wore coveralls, summer and winter, stained with motor oil, and was always coated with sawdust shavings. Going on seventy-five, he still worked his gas station and, out back, a firewood business. "Not in this town."

Johnny could feel a consensus building, a general return to normality in the clatter of plates, the rise of cigarette smoke and conversation. He had flushed the issue like a pheasant into the open. People weren't inherently mean-spirited or stupid, but the world was complicated. He left feeling better than he had in hours, knowing that he had set things right, let everyone know where he stood.

Although Abel Smalley assured him the kid had done more damage to himself than to the dike, Johnny asked Petersen, a retired engineer and chairman of the Board of Selectmen, to go down and take a look. He'd go by himself after dark when there wouldn't be too many people around, or he could hear it now: Johnny Lynch was out there checking on his dike; Lynch's dike, some called it.

He used to know all the kids in town when his own were in school, and even after, when he used to read his favorites out loud, *A Child's Christmas in Wales*, *The Legend of Sleepy Hollow*. This Compton boy was a blank. The girls in his office said there was something funny about the kid, always on his bicycle, always by himself, riding up and down High Street as if he never had a friend or a home. The girls said the kid's father was at fault. Palmer Compton was as loud as he was nasty, thought the best way from point A to point B was to run everyone down in between. He had one issue, never gave a lick about anything else in town, and he beat it like a deaf mule, so long and hard that even people prone to agree got mad sometimes and voted the opposite way.

Palmer Compton had always been against the dike. He thought the whole town was out to keep him from making a living, when everyone knew the old days of shellfishing were over. Sure there would always be a living for those who were scientific about it and had their own shellfish grant. But scratching clams from the wild? Trying to feed his family with a pail and rake? That was good for the tourists and picturesque, but the money lay in developing the land, in building. If the dike was gone tomorrow and the whole valley flooded over, there still wouldn't be enough shellfish to support more than a few families. Johnny had done everything he could to bring this town into the future, to open it up to real prosperity, to get it in the Sunday travel sections and the guidebooks. But here was this fool Palmer Compton railing about a dike drying up the shellfish, when the dike kept flood tides out of land that could profit the entire town.

Next, Johnny called Sams, the medical examiner, and asked him to find out about the kid. If God forbid the boy died, there'd be a martyr; as if a one-armed half-wit bicycling back and forth on High Street wasn't symbol enough. He'd have to come up with a job for the kid— quietly. Roads and Bridges was out, obviously. Then an idea struck him: with one arm, the kid might qualify for handicapped. There was a lot of money floating around for the handicapped; state and federal. Johnny was sure he could find a job, maybe for the county: get the kid out of Saltash.

The new secretary rapped on his office door. He liked to keep it open if he wasn't seeing a client, to make everybody feel like family. He'd been watching Crystal and he liked what he saw. The old girls cooed over her, and lately he'd heard giggling in the office, the way it used to be.

"Mr. Lynch? Selectman Petersen's on the line." She was only thirty-odd, but she'd been around the block a few times. She had a fine body, thickening around the waist, although that had never bothered him about a woman. Her skills were rusty; he doubted she had done legal work for years. He didn't hire her for her skills, and certainly not because of her father; he hardly owed any favors to Doc Sinclair. He'd kept the dentist out of jail and got the case of the woman whose tongue he had cut up settled out of court.

Then he'd urged Doc Sinclair, with his shaky hands and his drug habit and his history of trouble, to move on. The man had blown it. Sure it was paradise out here, but you had to know your limits. He'd hired Crystal for the same reason he'd sometimes go fishing instead of the office on the first hot days of June; the same reason he'd once come back from a hunting trip with a pony for his daughter. It was a willful submission to temptation, a vague infrequent admission that there was more to his life than politics and the law. He hired her because it amused and titillated him to have her around. And of course because Maria wanted her. At least she did know something about computers.

He made a point to act businesslike in her presence. He couldn't afford to embarrass himself. But the simple truth was that it had been years since he'd found himself smiling for no reason. "Put him on, please, Miss Sinclair . . . Ralph? What's it look like over there? Give it to me straight."

"Nothing to give," Ralph Petersen said.

Prying information out of Petersen took persistence, but his silence worked both ways. The man was unshakable. Never made promises he couldn't keep or shot his mouth off to the newspapers; never lashed out no matter who attacked him at a meeting. He was bald as an egg, with a straight white mustache that looked glued on. Petersen liked to make you feel as if you could answer your own question if you just thought hard enough. His only gesture was to touch the ends of his mustache, as if to make sure they were still there.

"So the explosion didn't harm anything?"

"Everything looks the way it did yesterday and the day before. There's evidence of a small fire—"

"Where?"

"On the rocks just above the dike's floodgate. There's a little carbon residue, that's all."

"The state will find something," Johnny said. The state had been trying to open the dike for years, along with Audubon and the bird-watchers, the bullies like Palmer Compton and the tree-hugging retirees. They'd commissioned scientists and studies trying to prove the dike was detrimental to the town. Any idiot could tell them that once it was removed, the water would rush right up the valley, flood the golf course and the homes and the best land in this town, destroy the natural habitat of fox and deer and coyote.

Johnny had been fighting them for years. Every time he knocked one enemy out, a new one stood up to take his place.. He needed another year, maybe two, to sell off the remaining lots and see his profits. Until then he was counting on the Board of Selectmen to keep the dike in place. If it came down to a final threat to take the case to court, the board could agree to a compromise, a small opening of the floodgate, a little each year to test the impact of change on the ecosystem. Both sides could use ecology to their advantage. He'd worked all that out with Petersen. As long as Johnny managed to keep the majority of the board loyal to him, he'd be all right. This was still his town. Nobody was going to take it away without a fight, and there wasn't anybody out there big enough or smart enough to fight him and win.

DAVID

16 Saltash wasn't a hard town, but the general consensus was that the Compton kid had it coming. In grade school he used to run people off the sidewalks with his bicycle. When he took up skateboarding, he liked to charge in front of moving cars and dare the drivers to hit him. He was a dangerous combination of a need to be noticed and a complete lack of fear. He'd finally made the local headlines last summer, when he stood up in his flimsy rowboat and harpooned a disoriented dolphin just off the town beach. A hundred sun bathers and the stunned local fishing fleet watched helplessly as the suffering creature towed the kid halfway across the harbor before it bled to death.

The kindest thing I heard was attributed to Johnny Lynch. He was going to see that the boy got the best medical care, physical therapy, and job training. Saltash took care of its own, people said—meaning Johnny Lynch did. Look at Stumpy Squeer. Look at Crazy Jane Villa, who used to pull her dress up to her chin on the town green. Johnny Lynch saw they were never sent away, that they lived in their family houses with fuel for the winter and enough to eat.

Gordon called me the evening after the accident. It had been a little over a week since I'd walked in on him and his wife. I was avoiding the two of them, determined to disentangle myself. "Here's your issue like a Christmas goose," he said. There was genuine glee in his voice.

"The dike thing? Is that what you're talking about?"

My lack of enthusiasm diminished his. "You want to see it opened, don't you?"

I didn't play golf or own land on the river or dig shellfish; I wasn't in the building trades and had nothing to gain either way. "I suppose," I said, mostly in opposition to Johnny Lynch.

"Well, you're the only candidate who feels that way and has a chance to win."

"What about Joe Pound?" Bird Man.

"Joe Pound couldn't win if he gave every voter a five-dollar bill and a ride to the polls."

"Gordon, I'm not sure I'm the guy."

"Not sure? I don't understand."

"I changed my mind. I don't want to run."

"You want to see this town built up like a fucking suburb? You want to see the shellfish industry dry up? What else have we got, goddamn it? Tourists are fickle, they like a place for a few years then flock to another. Look at Atlantic City! Look at Rockaway Beach!" He was rattling off lakes and spa towns, ski resorts I'd never heard of. He was furious.

"I said I'd *think* about running. I never said I was definite."

"Did you tell the Committee for Civic Responsibility? They've been raising money for you, David. They've been making phone calls in your behalf."

"Two hundred votes can't win an election against Johnny Lynch."

"Not if you sit on your ass. You have really screwed us, you know that? We can't find another candidate now—it's too late to file. Don't you care how people live? What do you care about? Why did you start this process, anyway?"

Because I wanted to sleep with his wife.

"Look, David Greene, it's very simple. There are four people on the ballot and only two have a chance to win that open seat. One of them is in John Lynch's pocket and the other one isn't. At least I didn't think so."

The implication was that by pulling out, I was handing the race to Lynch. "I resent that, Gordon."

"Well, fuck your resentment." I had made love to this man's wife and he hadn't said a word. Now, his voice was shaking: "You can't mobilize people behind you, then change your mind overnight. I'm asking you to get yourself straight, goddamn it. People are counting on you."

Tommy's girlfriend Michelle lived with her daughter, Kelly Ann, in the old Endicott house. Once a small hotel, later a rooming house for fishermen, and most recently apartments for young townies with little money, it sat at the top of a hill on Dock Street and seemed to brood over the bustling village the way some of its tenants sat on the front steps mulling over their lost chances in life.

Michelle's apartment was on the third floor. The residents used each landing as suburban families used garages: for storage. There were cribs and barbecue grills, box springs and bicycles. The abiding odor of the stairwell was something like mildew and boiled cabbage. As I climbed, I smelled marijuana and cat litter boxes, diapers and incense. When I reached the third floor I began to sneeze uncontrollably. Before I knocked, the door to Michelle's apartment opened. I heard clashing radios, children running; I smelled perfume and chili. What I remember best was Crystal's face, moonlike in that dingy hall, luminescent and cool. Her platinum hair seemed to absorb the available light. Her head cocked, she was obviously expecting me, inspecting me. Even before she spoke, her slightly ironic smile suggested we both knew why I was here.

"Hello, David. Welcome to the fun house." Her voice was whiskey in a tumbler with ice; hard and scratchy with a tinkle of sarcasm, it brought to mind dark cocktail lounges and cigarette smoke. Crystal wore a black cardigan with rhinestone buttons and western boots. Before I stopped sneezing, a child appeared, a thin little boy with light brown bangs. He pressed his cheek to her hip as she smoothed the hair from his eyes. "Is he sick?" the boy asked.

"Nah, he'll be all right," she said. "I think he'll be just fine."

Tommy and Michelle were sitting at the kitchen table. From the way they were dressed, I knew they were not planning to stay. Michelle had large blue eyes, meticulously lined and shadowed, and a rabbit-like overbite. Her hair was her most striking feature, a butter-yellow architecture of elaborate dips and waves as delicate as puff pastry. I'd never spoken to Michelle but I had seen her around. I judged her to be my sister's age and thought I'd ask Holly if they had gone to school together.

The apartment was jammed. Where laundry wasn't drying lay toys, boxes, piles of towels. Michelle's daughter was stretched to her extended length across Tommy's lap, poking her mother's breast with a big toe. The table was set for dinner with mismatched plates and paper napkins. Crystal served. "She was living out West," Tommy said. "That's why she makes great chili. She's a cowgirl. She even named her kid Laramie."

"It's a stupid name," Kelly Ann said.

"She drove all the way across country," Tommy said. "Her and the kid. Did it in three days like an all-night trucker."

Crystal was broad in the bust, the shoulders and hips, but seemed to diminish in size like a servant in the kitchen. She filled the children's milk glasses, got another beer for Tommy, picked up Kelly Ann's napkin when it slipped to the floor. She ate silently with her eyes focused on her son, whose appetite she coaxed with soft whispers.

"It's like fucking courageous, you know?" Tommy said. "To come all the way back here three thousand miles where you don't know nobody anymore."

Michelle set her glass down heavily. "I'm nobody now?"

"I didn't mean it that way," he said. It was not like Tommy Shalhoub to back off, not from a woman, but as Kelly Ann kept poking her mother, as each addition to the conversation only seemed to stall it further, it was apparent how deeply in trouble Tommy had gotten himself with his girlfriend's roommate and how much he needed me to get him out.

"How long have you two known each other?" I asked Michelle.

She divided her chili into four equilateral triangles so her plate looked like the Confederate flag. "We were friends in school," she said grudgingly.

Crystal began to sing: "You need no introduction to who we really are . . ." Tommy led an imaginary orchestra with his fork. Kelly Ann perked up and sang the words. "This shining star, this precious jewel, our Saltash Elementary School."

"Are you here for good?" I asked Crystal.

"Till I get on my feet."

"She just got a job," Tommy said. "At Johnny Lynch's office."

"Oh, what do you do?" I asked.

"Legal secretary," Crystal said.

"Just like a lawyer," Tommy said. " 'Cept they do all the work."

Michelle took offense. "I don't happen to think it's the same thing at all. A nurse is not the same as a doctor."

Tommy's jaw twitched. His fist clenched, then opened. "I'm trying to introduce two people who don't know each other. Isn't that what we wanted to do here, Michelle?"

"Don't kick me," Michelle exploded at her daughter, pushing away Kelly Ann's foot.

"This is good chili," Tommy said. "There's no beans. You notice that? That's the way they do it out West. You ever hear of chili with no beans?"

Michelle's chair screeched as she pushed away from the table, high heels clopping all the way to the bathroom. Kelly Ann straggled behind. Michelle closed the door. The little girl pounded on it. Tommy sighed and got their coats. When the bathroom door opened, Kelly Ann grabbed her mother's leg and started to wail. "I'll be back." Michelle knelt to hush her. "When you wake up tomorrow morning, I'll be in my bed. You come in and we'll cuddle, okay? Okay?" But Kelly Ann clung to her mother until Crystal pried her away and carried her, screaming, into the children's bedroom.

"Does this happen every night?" I whispered to Tommy.

Michelle, whose blue eyeliner was now streaked with tears, cut me an icy glare. "Not before *she* moved in," Michelle said.

When they left, I wandered into the living room and found myself alone with the little boy. Like me, he didn't seem to know where to sit, to stand, how to make himself small enough to stay out of the way. He was resting his chin on the back of an old couch, which I assumed from the suitcase next to it and the alarm clock on the coffee table was where his mother slept. Since I lived so far from my own son, I tried a little too hard with my sister's daughters. I sensed that I embarrassed them, that whatever activities they had on their busy agenda were only interrupted by my awkward attempts to make them my surrogate kids. He looked younger than Terry, and I felt for this little boy who held himself, head down, arms at his side, like a peg to be pounded into a narrow hole. When I said, "Hi," he almost jumped. "Have you started school yet?"

"Yeah." He drew his hand across the back of the couch.

"Do you like it?"

He shrugged. "They're putting me back a grade. Tomorrow. They said I have to repeat third."

"That might not be so bad," I said. "You'll be smarter than everybody because you already know the stuff."

Hope flickered across his face for a moment then went out.

"You might be the biggest kid too."

"In fourth they made fun of me. They said I have a dumb name."

"I think Laramie is a kick-ass name. Like a movie star or a rock singer. But if you don't like it, change it."

"You can't just change your name 'cause you want to. They won't let you."

"Why not? When the new teacher introduces you tomorrow, you say, 'My name is Laramie but in my old school everybody called me Larry.' You could do that."

He was thinking, hard. This was one serious little boy.

When I looked up, I noticed Crystal had inched her way inside the door frame. She'd been watching me and the boy, listening. She was a handsome woman. The confidence with which she moved, beneath the weariness and the baggy shirt, the way her smile demanded my attention and wouldn't let go, suggested she knew her way around men. We didn't exchange a word as she gathered Laramie in her arms to bring him to bed, but the heat with which she looked upon him, that same bright beam of strength and affection, included me in its widening arc. It had been decided. I was to stay.

DAVID

17

"You think you remember me, don't you?" Crystal said. Her smile was half tease, half reproach. As she settled back on the couch after putting her son to bed, her blouse was open by an extra button. She pulled her fingers through her hair and shook her head—as if to toss much longer hair in place. Although it was cut short, I imagined it touching her shoulders and trailing down her back. There was a lot I found myself imagining about Crystal because nothing connected her to the past. The crucifix on the living room wall, the sewing machine, the rock star poster belonged to her roommate. Crystal's turquoise bracelets and her platinum hair, even her little boy's name, didn't seem to issue from the woman whose hand was brushing my knee, but struck me, like her western boots, as something of a pose.

I felt a remarkable ease in her presence, however, a shared sympathy. "I probably know you from high school?" I asked.

"Right," she mocked me. "Saltash's Davey Greene, the Pitching Machine. You didn't know I was alive."

"Were you friends with my sister?"

"I wasn't in the sweater set crowd."

"Tommy said your father was a dentist."

"You didn't go to him." There was a touch of resentment in her voice, but she was right. My mother took us to a guy named Horowitz. He was the only Jewish dentist on the entire Cape at the time, and that seemed reason enough to justify the forty-five-minute drive. "Try again. I like this game."

So did I. More than a game, or even a walk through the past, it was a reality check: a contrast between the way I saw my family and the way we were seen. I remember my parents struggling to pay the mortgage, to meet the payroll. They borrowed constantly. Every unplanned expense was a crisis. But what I knew to be just one more of my father's failed businesses, Crystal saw as the factory we owned. While I overheard my father begging Johnny Lynch to ask the bank manager not to foreclose, Crystal saw only the white full Cape with pink native roses, a half acre of locust trees and lush grass.

Her family had moved to Saltash when she was three, she said. Her father had been working too hard in the city and it was killing him. He was the kind of dentist who couldn't turn people away. Rich or poor, every patient got the best he could give. In Saltash, half the time he came home with a bag of flounder or an oil painting or a promise of a truckload of garden manure instead of his fee. When he did get paid, he never kept track. He wasn't interested in money. "All he cared about was helping people."

When her parents split in Crystal's junior year of high school, her mother moved to Arizona. They lived in a town an hour south of Sedona, a little like Saltash, she said, "Poor, scenic and two blocks long." She started dreaming of water. She hated the desert and only an ocean could quench her thirst. After two years of college she headed for the nearest one.

She ended up in Seattle, met an Irishman with a red beard, a fishing boat and a voice like a lullaby. They moved into a house on a bluff with a distant view of the Sound. He cut his drinking to a six-pack a night and she worked in a law office. Then she got pregnant and he turned mean. She lived with Liam for five years, but the first time he hit her she waited exactly thirteen hours, until the bank opened the following morning, then cut out for good.

Crystal left Seattle with two suitcases and a kid with a temperature of 102. I imagined her speeding to nowhere, as I had after being cut, every exit another disappointment, a place someone else could call home. She telephoned Michelle from a service plaza. First she had to remind her they had been best friends in high school—then explain she had nowhere to go.

Crystal's story filled me with a mixture of admiration and pity, although I didn't offer either and she didn't seem to care. "I guess I was wrong," I said finally. "I don't know you at all."

"But you do. We're the same."

I was a little lost here. "Because we both moved back to Saltash?"

"Because we're both failures."

I must have been embarrassed. I laughed.

"You're not doing what you *really* do, David Greene. Admit it. You're an athlete. Nothing you'll ever do in your life will make you as happy. It's inside you all the time."

"I don't know about that," I said. But I did. I knew that I never looked at a level field without measuring out a diamond, calculating the distance from home plate to the mound. I never held an apple without my fingers closing around it in preparation to throw. When I smelled fresh-mown grass I was aware of an emptiness, the absence of a crowd.

"I believe there are people who are born for something," she said. I noticed the way her breasts pushed against the white satin cups of her bra. "I'm not talking about destiny or religion. It's just that some people are born with abilities, that's all. And if they can't do what they're made to do—" She stopped abruptly. She closed her eyes, as if the conversation had already gone too far. "They're a mess."

"And you think I'm a mess?" I said.

"I know I am."

"You didn't tell me what you were born to do."

"I said *some* people. I'm not one of them."

"I don't believe that."

"Because you're nice. Laramie said you're the nicest man he's ever met."

"I want to know. What were you born to be?"

"Just a mom," she said. "Maybe just an overwrought, overweight mom with six kids and a big barn of a house."

"I doubt that. You work in a law office. Don't you ever think of being a lawyer yourself?"

"About a hundred times a day."

"I think you'd be a good one. You're obviously smart. You're experienced. You're compassionate."

"And thirty-two. And a single mom. Much too old to go back to school. Too busy and too tired." When I challenged her, she placed her fingertips over my mouth to silence me. "I'm doing fine, okay? I don't need any help."

We were sitting in a cold room facing her unpacked boxes in a corner. The only lamp cast a sickly yellow light. Through the floorboards we heard a couple fighting. I said, "Of course you don't," and we both started to laugh.

Looking back on the night I met Crystal, I realize I might have seen her differently. I might have perceived a burden. I might have made her a project or even a friend. If all I had wanted was to distance myself from Judith, I could have simply gotten laid. But on that winter night I was kindled with a more urgent fire, a mother and a child's need for me. I thought my efforts could change everything. I thought I could enter her life like a god. What I imagined as Crystal's weakness, however, proved to be my own.

Sometimes in autumn when the storm tides recede, the soft, placid beaches resemble a killing field. Some claim to know the reason whales strand themselves, wash up to suffocate in the sand, their lungs crushed by the weight of their own bodies, their skin cracking in the sun like the walls of old tires. What faulty inner magnet could draw them to their deaths? The old fishermen say under stress and sickness, they follow a leader with the ancient memory of land in her genes, land as safety, land as home. But what if they were trying to save the leader?

Or maybe, once committed to the wrong course, they were afraid of turning back? Many times I told myself the consequences of leaving Crystal were more dangerous than remaining in her bed. Many times it seemed to me that however damaging I knew our course together to be, that she was what I deserved. On that first cold night I had no idea. Only upon looking back did I realize that to wade into Crystal's shallow life was to drown.

Her back pressed to my chest, entwining her fingers in mine as my arms wound around her waist, she seemed to project her story on the wall. I assumed that not facing me was a way to avoid the pain, but of course I didn't even know Crystal's last name at this point, or that her version of history was only a shadow play.

"Look," I said, "maybe you don't want to talk about this now. But I do think you could become something. You have two years of college? You could go back. Take one course a semester. Your life doesn't end when things don't work out the first time. You just have to start another life."

Before she kissed me, she said, "You're also the nicest man I've ever met." She opened her lips like the mouth of an infant asking to be fed. She suckled my ears, my neck, my lips with ferocious hunger. I was mother, she was child, there is no more accurate way to describe it. She put out the light before she undressed. She had heavy breasts and a soft belly, and when she saw me admiring her in the remaining light, she was ashamed. She took my cock between her breasts, guided my hand to her thighs. She told me lightly, lightly touch the rings in her nipples with my tongue. She placed me inside easily, locked her legs around my hips and rocked. But I tell you I was less a man than a source of warmth, a mass of comfort and kindness. I have never felt as purely needed by any lover nor as willing to be consumed.

JUDITH

18 By her seventh year in Saltash, when Judith was thirty-nine, she was becoming better known as a lawyer, an aggressive defense lawyer who would do a good job for anyone in trouble, a lawyer who would sue any corporation or government entity for a client. She was becoming even better known as a shark of a divorce lawyer who would get for her predominantly women clients a better deal than other lawyers even tried for. People saw her as unscrupulous, hard, even immoral, because she fought to win.

But what could she do against the enemy stealing Gordon from her? The cancer had returned, in the other lung. The cancer had touched his liver. More chemotherapy. Another operation. Sometimes Gordon could work, but not as he had; mostly his profession was his disease. He would not go into a cancer support group. "What am I supposed to do with a bunch of people whose only connection with me is that parts of our bodies are sick or missing?"

Over their years together they had dined out frequently. Now she cooked every night she could, to tempt him to eat, to get good nutrition into him. At night in bed, besides briefs she read cookbooks. She had given up low-fat cooking. Gordon kept losing weight. She was congenitally thin herself. Natasha compared her to a shrew who had to eat every ten minutes or starve. Now she cooked whatever might tempt him to eat. If it was hollandaise sauce, so be it. When she spent the night across the bridge in the loft above her new law office on the harbor, she had arranged for Jana Baer (who lived on the island) to come in to cook him a meal.

Gordon had been her rock. Since the first year of their marriage, she had relied on him as she had relied on no one since the death of her mother. They would fight, they would yell at each other, they would violently disagree about people or the exact interpretation of political events or a movie they had seen, but on the big things they agreed, on values, on their love, on how they should live. Now she would sometimes look at him, his face gaunt and visibly showing his age, and she would feel fear serrated, cold, sawing at her. He was her joy: the center of her life was collapsing.

That spring, she suggested they try to cut back on the number of summer guests, that they simply reduce their entertaining to be less of a strain on him than the usual delirium. She had wanted to cancel the big Fourth of July party too, but Gordon insisted that while he was alive, it continue. He had begun to use that phrase, which angered her.

Tonight she called him on it. "Anyone could say that. A truck could run me off the road tomorrow. I could choke on a chicken bone. I could die of food poisoning from fast food. Some ex-client could shoot me in court. Or somebody who just hates lawyers."

"Judith, you want to avoid thinking about my death. Dr. Barrows says I have two years at the very best, probably less."

"It could go into remission. You're more stubborn than he understands. It's a lottery." She would probably throw herself into the law, continuing the process that had already begun. Because of Gordon's illness, she had become a better lawyer, fiercer, more inventive, because there and only there she could still win.

"And I've never been fool enough to play the lottery. The odds, Judith, you perfectly well understand odds. I'm not sentimental and I'm not delusional. The odds are I'll be dead soon, and we have to think about that together."

"I don't want to think about it! What good does it do?"

"What good does it do to pretend I'll live forever? We have to make plans. I can't stand the pretending. I need to know you're going to be all right."

"Gordon, there's no way I'll be all right without you. But I'll go on. I have my work. I'll just work harder."

"Do you intend to go on living out here?"

"How do I know?" She threw her hands up, furious at him for insisting on talking about something she preferred to think about alone in the middle of the night when no one could see her cry.

"Your practice is here. Your reputation is growing. You have as many cases as you can handle. If you moved back to Boston, you'd have to start over."

"I hardly want to do that. I'm thirty-nine. So I imagine I'll stay."

"I've split the land and buildings between you and Natasha. Nobody else has a claim. I've left a modest bequest to all my children."

"Gordon, you gave me a copy of your will two months ago. Do we have to dwell on this?"

"Judith, you've been the best choice I ever made in my life, because you're bright and level-headed and you've always brought your full intelligence to bear on everything you do, from practicing law to choosing a broom. I love that. But you haven't been willing to bring any intelligence whatsoever to the situation we're in. When you married me, you didn't think I was twenty-seven too. You knew I was much older than you and the odds were enormous that I'd die first. Now I have lung cancer. You read all the books. You know what the survival rate is for recurrent lung cancer. About a five percent chance of being alive in five years. When you refuse to be open-minded and clear-eyed about this event so important to me, then I'm left to face it alone."

"What do you want from me? To sit down with you and plan your funeral?"

"I'm not into that yet, although given my flair for self-dramatization, I won't miss that last grand opportunity. What I have to know is how things will be with you. I have to leave you set up."

"Well, I'll have the house and my practice. That's as much set up as any person has a right to expect."

"I don't agree. I brought you out here, away from the city. It was to please me."

"Gordon, I love living here. I probably enjoy the Cape's natural resources more than you do."

"But you're here because I was an old man and I retired. Otherwise we'd both be working in the city. And this land is important to me. This compound is a crazy but vital creation. It's my monument, if you like. I hate to think of it going on the market and being dismantled by somebody who wants to replace it all with one of those millionaire's atrocities."

"Gordon, I live here. I live with you. Enough!" It was a recurrent quarrel. She did not know what he wanted from her, that she produce a projection of her life without him like an entrepreneur drafting a plan for a new business? It was gruesome.

At last Gordon finally found a project he could immerse himself in. He began writing a book with a photographer about Saltash, its history, its sociology. It was a true collaboration, and Brian Peyrera, a photographer from New York, had moved to Saltash for the duration. Gordon had begun several projects since the onset of cancer, but he had abandoned them all, losing interest. Working with someone on a project of limited scope seemed to be exactly what he needed. He began to fight less with her about the future. She was immensely relieved. The photographer, just about her age and recently divorced, was a very thin young man with a dazzling smile and lots of dark brown wavy hair.

"Brian ought to move in here," Gordon said one morning at breakfast. "It'd be much easier for us to work together. He's spending a fortune at the inn."

"Live here?" Judith squeaked. "Couldn't we just find him a rental?"

"In June we're supposed to find him a summer rental? Be real. He could live in the cabin Ben built. He wouldn't be underfoot."

She could not deny Gordon his wishes; she had never been good at that. So Brian moved into one of the cabins in the compound, and he was indeed underfoot. He was a wistful good-natured man, a little sorry for himself, talkative but not much of a physical presence. He did not dominate space the way Gordon always had, which was a plus under the circumstances. He took over making lunch and some of the shopping.

"You have the domestic virtues," Judith said as he was helping her clean up from supper. "I appreciate that."

"My wife didn't."

They had tried very hard to have a baby, but the wife miscarried time after time. Finally they had decided to adopt. They were still waiting for a baby when the marriage came apart.

In some ways having Brian around did make life easier. When she could not make it back to the island because of the tides she did not have to put in a desperate call to Jana Baer. Brian was always there, and he was good company for Gordon. The book was marvelous therapy, aside from whether it would ever be finished. Brian seemed in no hurry to be done. He was happy to live with them. Why not? Saltash sure beat Manhattan in summer. The most awkward times for Judith were the evenings, since Gordon often grew weary and went to bed early, leaving the two of them tête-à-tête for hours. Sometimes they both read. Brian was not musical, and if she put a CD on, he would talk over the Mozart until she gave up trying to listen. The trouble was, he was beginning to stare at her when he thought she would not notice, to dote visibly, to sigh and gaze and otherwise exude a gentle but disconcerting desire.

"Gordon, I think maybe having Brian living here is not a great idea."

"I thought you were getting along splendidly."

"Brian's easy to get along with, unlike myself. But Gordon . . . I think he has a crush on me."

"Of course he does. How could he live with you and not fall in love? He's a sweet young man. He's bright and vulnerable—"

"And as crazy as you are." She stomped out of the room, overwhelmed with the suspicion that Gordon was intentionally throwing them together.

Gordon followed her into her room and shut the door. "You can't live out here alone. It's too difficult."

"So I'll get a roommate."

"Judith, you're still young enough to have a family."

"Gordon, you're way off. And you're a damned control freak, you know that? What are you trying to do, plan out my life for the next twenty years?" She stalked from her own bedroom, slamming the door.

When Natasha came home from vet school, eventually Judith told her. Anger roughened her voice. She could not hold it in. "He's pushing me to have an affair with that Brian, can you believe it? As if I've ever, ever shown interest in another man! It's just sick!"

Natasha had a conversation with Gordon. After that, she saw the situation differently. "He wants to know you'll be all right. And he loves this place. I think he wants to control who lives here, who shares it after he . . . in the future."

"It makes me feel dirty."

"Why?" Natasha propped her sharp chin on her hands. Her hair was her mother's, pale apricot, but her eyes were Gordon's, fiercely blue. "Why does it scare you so much? It would give him a sense of survival, to know who you were with, to know that the family goes on. He wants to have input into the choice of your next husband, Judith. Can't you understand?"

"I can't accept it."

"Even to make him happy? Even to give him some peace about how things may go? Maybe he's right. We all want to know that we can still come here, that we can feel at home here."

"I'm not shopping for a husband. I have one. Can't you just trust me to make the family feel at home?"

"He thinks you don't know much about men. He doesn't want you to get hurt after he's gone."

Judith paced, clutching her arms. "This is unbearable!"

"He wants to have an afterlife in your life. Of course it's weird, Judith, but this family is pretty weird. You play housemother to children older than you are. Gordon tries to stay friendly with all his ex-wives, and mostly he manages, but he doesn't think much of the husbands they acquired after him. You were more like an older sister than a mother to me, but you were the main woman in my life for years and years, and you still are. Listen to me. Don't be conventional about this. You didn't marry conventionally. You didn't live your married life conventionally. Listen to Gordon. If you don't agree with him on the man he chooses, say so. Say you'll pick out your own."

* * *

She told Hannah what was going on. Hannah was silent for a while. Then she said, "You know, a minor affair isn't the end of the world. It needn't damage a central and serious relationship."

Hannah had been with the senator for nine years. Judith asked, "Have you been involved with anyone else?"

Another silence. "I don't know if I'd go so far as to say involved."

She wanted to ask Hannah how could she, why would she, but she did not, for she did not want to alienate her closest woman friend (unless she counted Natasha, whom she did think of as her daughter). She did not want to make Hannah defensive, so slowly and carefully she circled toward the questions she wanted to ask. But even as she did so, she realized it was futile. Hannah was not her; the senator was not Gordon.

Finally she spoke to Barbara. "Why a man?" Barbara made a gesture of dismissal. "It's so like a man to discount half the world. I like Gordon, but it never seems to occur to him you have other choices."

"Barbara, I respect your choice, but it isn't for me."

"You've never been involved with a woman. . . . But he's pushing the envelope so hard he could rupture it. Why do you have to torture yourself now? Why can't he let you enjoy the end of his life with him, as much as you can?"

"I wish he would. I feel coerced into a complication I don't need."

"But you don't have to do it, Judith," Barbara said calmly, putting her hands flat on her desk. "He can inflict Brian on you in the house, but he can't make you fall in love with him or even in lust. After a while he'll let it go. It will be too boring to continue."

"Barbara, you're always right, do you know that? Or at least fifty percent of the time."

"Eighty-five."

"Fifty-five."

They grinned at each other. Judith felt as if she had been an idiot. She had always taken Gordon's desires, even his whims, seriously, because she wanted so much to please him. If he saw a shirt he liked as they walked past a clothing store, she would return the next day and buy it. If he dropped a hint he was curious about a show, she would call at once for tickets. Perhaps she had had a lot to prove, being the fourth wife, being the child bride, being the youngest, being . . . the last.

Brian was acceptable as a member of the household. She could think of him as a stepson, like Larry. She could think of him as a family pet.

She could handle him: just never let him declare his feelings. She started watching television in the evenings. Renting videos. Then she began to fix up her office at home so she could escape to it. She mostly hadn't bothered working on the island since Austin retired and she moved her practice to the harbor, but it was time to refurbish her home office. It was a distance from the main house, and she would gradually begin spending evenings there. She could bring the walkie-talkie out with her, and if Gordon needed something, he had only to summon her. She would order a new computer Monday with a fast modem. All right, Gordon wanted Brian, he could have Brian as much as he wanted. But she could erect a few barriers to limit Brian's access to her and keep his yearning safely distanced. She would waste no more of their precious time together arguing with Gordon, but neither would she let herself be pushed.

DAVID

Candidates' night was a blood sport in Saltash. Every April, heron stabbed alewives, coyote fattened on nestling rabbits, and the people of this town gathered in the elementary school gymnasium with a similar hunger for flesh. Judith had invited me over to help write a speech, but I felt that as soon as she saw me, she'd know; as if that one night with Crystal could cling to my skin like the odor of sex. When Judith telephoned, I said I didn't need help. "You think I don't know why?" she said.

I felt my body square, as if to defend myself. I'd spent one night with a lonely woman while Judith herself was home with her husband. I was about to say something about our little triangle when she added: "You're determined to lose this election, aren't you?"

The election. My shoulders relaxed. "I'm just doing it my own way."

"Which amounts to the same thing. What are you scared of, David?"

Five meetings a week for three years. Small town newspapers poking into my personal life. Town crazies calling me at all hours. And that was if I was elected. At candidates' night last year, a guy running for selectman had to shout to be heard above the insults of the same block of guys now sitting with their legs outstretched in the first row. Although I was pretty sure none of them were against my stand on the issues (since even I couldn't say what my stand might be), old grudges were seldom buried in this town but polished to a shine like brass. Harlan Silvester. Jimmy Phillips. Their fathers had worked for mine. Tony Brockmann had stripped my sister to her underpants when she was ten years old and tied her to a tree. I beat him until his ears filled with blood and earned the enmity of the largest family in town. A quarter of a century had passed; he had married twice, lost his oldest son, buried his parents. Now Tony Brockmann, in unlaced work boots, legs spread wide, himself a grandfather at thirty-eight, glared at me as if to say my time was finally at hand.

The man we called Ahab smelled of beer and climbed the steps dragging his bad leg. With a permanent squint, his nose and cheeks were a crosshatch of tiny broken blood vessels and his face always seemed to be on fire. He had one issue, fishing, and spent almost all his time on the town pier. I only realized, when he raised his chin to return my hello, that I had observed him for years, hands thrust in pockets, collar upturned against the wind, but I had never heard him utter a word.

In contrast, Birdman was usually the first and last to speak at any event and had run for this office three times before. He was built from the waist up like a stack of tires, one smaller than the other as they progressed from his belly to his head—balding and fringed with wild white hair. He was well known to birders statewide for leading a campaign to save piping plovers who nested on the beach. Instead of the binoculars he always wore, he carried a large rolled-up map, which he tapped nervously against his knee.

I figured I'd make it through my five-minute speech with platitudes about hard work and growing up in this town, but I was worried about the questions and answers. I was going to lose this election. I was eager for the campaign to end, but I didn't want to embarrass myself. I had made a mistake. I had a crush on a woman. She asked me to run. Had she asked me for all the savings I had in the bank, or even to help her rob one, I'd probably have agreed. But I didn't have the mind for budgets or the wit to think on my feet. I had for one sterling period of my life mastered the ability to throw a baseball, but now I moved dirt for a living.

Sitting straight in the chair next to mine, her thin ceramic lips counting her supporters as they filled the room, was the front-runner, Blossom Endicott, whom Judith dubbed Blossom End-Rot. A teacher for many years in the Saltash Elementary School, Mrs. Endicott had so internalized her profession that she viewed the world and addressed everyone in it as if it were the fourth grade. Her hair was the cut and color of a stainless steel mixing bowl. She wore a corduroy jumper and clean white Keds. She walked to the stage with a clutch of official-looking papers, which she used like a cop used a club, to divide crowds and hint at her unleashed power.

I was attempting to look neither at Judith, pacing the aisles in her pin-striped coat dress, nor at Gordon among the *alter kockers*, nor at my mother, who was sending me little waves from the third row. I tried to ignore the stooges in the front row and to look at nothing but the double doors at the back of the gym, propped open for air, the whole time praying not to see Crystal in her fringed jacket and cowboy boots. Just as the house lights dimmed, a big late model Ford pulled up in front of the gym. I watched its headlamps die, saw its ceiling lamp flash on as the door opened. The young duty patrolman, upon spotting the vehicle in the fire lane, immediately ran outside—not to chase the illegally parked car but to escort its driver inside.

Johnny Lynch entered the gym with his hand on the young cop's shoulder. He seemed a pillar of smooth gray stone, with his strong square chin and his cropped hair gone white. He was a head taller than almost everyone around him, and his elbow shot out from his body to shake hands like the piston of a well-oiled machine. When I was a boy, Johnny Lynch used to dress up in his Uncle Sam costume to march in the Fourth of July parade. For every kid in this town, he was the living embodiment of government. I could still feel his hand, sliding along the ridge of my shoulder, locking like a vise on my nape. As he dropped a shiny new quarter in my shirt pocket with one hand, he found a nerve with the other and squeezed until I began to howl. "He likes you," my father insisted, but I had watched him torment other boys, watched his lips hitch up as they dangled in his grip like hanged men and tears moistened their eyes. If he moved more slowly now as a result of a heart operation, he seemed no less powerful. Gordon and the *alter kockers* sneered, but a small crowd sprang from their seats to wish him well. He moved up the center aisle like the father-of-the-bride. When he reached the third row—people stood to let him pass—he made his way to the chair next to my mother.

Birdman spoke first, springing to the podium and attaching his map to an easel. Before retiring to Saltash he had been a professor of Shakespeare in a small Minnesota college. His voice was stage-trained, his language precise, his research unassailable; no one doubted his facts. Even the guys in the front row, hunters and fishermen, couldn't disagree with his passion to restore the river valley, yet they watched him like a target through a rifle sight, waiting their moment to fire.

Birdman's map was a simple blowup of Tamar River, in blue, bordered on one side by the Saltash golf course, shown in green, and sixty lots on the other. Colored white and cut up in grids, they represented all the remaining land in the valley, earmarked for development. Brown arrows were superimposed over the grids, drawn in a wiggle pattern like sperm cells and aimed at the river. The speaker then pointed to the dike, explaining that a vote for him would be a vote for removing the dike and returning the yet-to-be developed land to its natural, semi-underwater state. His voice then deepened as he leaned into the microphone, "Do you know what these brown marks represent?"

"More of your shit!" came Tony Brockmann's answer.

"Well, yes. That's exactly what it is," the speaker said good-naturedly, getting in his last few words before Tony and his friends made it impossible for him to go on. The audience broke into applause. Even Johnny Lynch, the owner of the lots in question, joined in, his broad shoulders and confident smile rising above the crowd like the bust of a warrior in granite.

My mother had always been a woman who appreciated size. She liked high ceilings, big American cars, gilded picture frames heavy enough to rip nails right out of the wall. She had resented being taller than my father, having to wear flats and slouch in the company of friends. But she stood fully erect in the presence of Johnny Lynch.

Johnny had been chairman of the board of the Saltash Savings Bank when we spent two weeks in a cabin here one summer. He owned Saltash Real Properties, Inc. He presented the curtain factory to my father as a native industry lacking only good management to thrive. Later, we learned he was unloading an about-to-be foreclosed property for his bank, through his real estate firm; taking a small personal stake in the business in order to keep the town's only factory in operation. My father didn't consider problems with the building or the work force, or that the market for curtains had been replaced by vertical blinds. He was anxious to start a new life for his family, to put the shame of his last failure behind him. My father thought moving from New York City to what he called "the sticks" afforded him the upper hand. If my father took Johnny Lynch for a courtly lawyer from the boondocks who wore brown suits and wide ties, Johnny Lynch saw my father as a fool.

The consequences of that partnership were played out in my living room. Almost nightly, my father was on the phone, begging Johnny Lynch not to withdraw his profits in cash; not to support the employees' demands for higher wages; not to charge his lunches to the business or to give away merchandise as gifts to clients and friends. Johnny Lynch had promised my father that the factory would turn a profit; two years after my father's death, long after he had sold it back to Johnny, the town took the building by eminent domain for a price of $1.2 million.

Compared to Ahab, who stumbled into the podium and knocked over the water pitcher, my remarks were uneventful. Even the clowns in the front row, having tried the audience's patience heckling Birdman, did little more than make faces through my speech and walk out during the applause. Blossom End-Rot, to no one's surprise, was far and away the favorite. Having packed the hall, her reception was long and loud. Afterwards, what questions came from her camp were designed mostly to embarrass Birdman, considered to be her biggest challenge. I was asked merely to comment on the town's recreation budget. I assumed it was over. Some people were already filing out. There would be an election in five weeks. I would come in third, my brief career in politics put to bed. I did not hear her question at first, or even realize Blossom End-Rot was addressing me.

Her voice was oddly kittenish. She gave the impression, with the flutter of her eyes, of curtsying as she spoke. "I was wondering," she spoke to me through the audience, "if David could comment on the problems at the high school and what if anything he would propose to do about them?"

The question was absurd. The high school was regional, the curriculum controlled by the state. The town had little if any input. "Certainly," I said. The audience remained in their seats. "Uh, could you be more specific?"

"The high incidence of teenage pregnancies, for example. The proliferation of alcohol and drugs."

I said something about drug testing.

"Because David knows how important a good moral example is to the children. Don't you, David? Being an athlete," she said as an afterthought.

Instinctively, I searched out Judith. My gaze escaped no one's attention. "Well, we all try to set a good example," I said.

"Some try harder than others." Mrs. Endicott smiled. "Coming as I do from a family with a two-hundred-year tradition in this town, I feel I must set standards. But of course it might be different for a candidate whose family is foreign born and entered this country through Ellis Island. He really can't be expected to have the same commitment, can he, David?"

At that moment I felt only the hammer of my heart in my mouth, anger rushing through me instead of words. If anything proved me unfit for office, it was this moment, this mute and shameful inability to defend myself in public.

DAVID

Saturday, my sister found me in the greenhouse watering seedlings. The April light that morning, as it had when I was growing up, filled me with anticipation of the season to come. I could smell the yeasty mud of the oyster flats at low tide and, when the wind came up, the tree sap running. In a month we'd have more work than we could handle, the election would be over and with it the embarrassment I felt every time I saw my name in the papers. For weeks I'd heard nothing from Holly but a list of things undone. Now she grinned at me. "Were you expecting visitors, David?" She didn't take her eyes from Crystal or Laramie or let them get in a word. "Where have you been keeping these people? Why didn't you tell me you had new friends?"

My sister's marriage had produced the same effect on her as boot camp on a new recruit: she'd lopped off her hair, lost ten pounds and seemed to be on guard all the time. The lilt in her voice when she got excited and her dimpled smile had disappeared. Even her ample breasts, which had hampered her high school swimming but made her a favorite with the boys on the team, had over time been chiseled to fit the body of a lean and efficient über-mom. But as she dropped to one knee to talk to Laramie, I heard a bit of the old little flirt. "You're a handsome young man. Have we met? I don't think so, and I know all the cute guys in my daughters' school. What's your name?"

"It's Laramie but—" He glanced at his mother for encouragement. "—my friends call me Larry."

"I'd like to be your friend, so I'll call you Larry too."

The boy looked to his mother to confirm his success, but Crystal was beaming at me.

"How old are you, Larry? Let me guess." Holly made a show of sizing him up. Height, weight; she stepped forward and back, squinting, looking behind his ears. "Eight," she announced.

"We didn't mean to interrupt you at work," Crystal said. "But Larry wanted to ask your advice. Guy talk." She winked.

Holly stood, slapping her knees clean. "I didn't know you were in town."

"I just moved back," Crystal said.

"When did you meet my brother? Where did you two—"

"Tommy Shalhoub introduced us," Crystal said.

"David didn't mention it."

Until this moment, nobody but Tommy and Michelle had known anything about Crystal and me. Michelle had made pancakes for us the next morning, apparently content that once Crystal met a guy, she wouldn't be after hers. Certainly Tommy seemed relieved, if a little wistful. Crystal couldn't have been cooler. She was up before me, getting her son ready for school. When we walked out, she kissed my cheek. "That was nice," was all she said. I hadn't seen her since that night.

I felt the little boy looking up at me. "What did you want to ask me, Larry?"

"Liam says he wants to get me something for my birthday, and I want a glove."

"Liam's his dad," Crystal said.

"When's your birthday?"

"Not for a month," he said. "But Mom says I have to tell him now."

"If we wait for Liam to ask, it'll be too late. But we've never had a baseball glove, have we, Larry? We wanted to know what we should ask him for."

"Well, you look like a pretty strong kid to me. Step over here a minute. Make a muscle. Good. Squeeze my hand. Ouch!" I measured his hand by placing his palm in mine. I showed him how to throw a ball, remembering how Georgie had once shown me, guiding my arm, placing his palm in the small of my back. Attention was like food for the starved little boy. When I pronounced him a pitcher, he looked as if he'd had an audience with God.

Holly lagged behind as we all strolled to the parking lot. Crystal fell in next to me. "I've been thinking about you." She was wearing a cowhide jacket and silver earrings. Although her eyes seemed clear and confident, she sounded bashful. "We have to get something clear about the other night."

"Crystal—"

"I'm grateful for your confidence in me. For the way you said you thought I could be something."

"Well, I meant it."

"That's why I had to tell you, I've decided to go back to school. To finish up my B.A. Maybe, eventually," she said shyly, "to apply to law school. And I owe it to you. You're a very special man."

"I'm not special at all," I said, but that was a lie: in her presence I felt wise and powerful.

"I'm not the only one who thinks so." She jutted her chin toward

Laramie. "Larry thinks you're the swellest guy in the world. Look." She stopped abruptly. "You may not want to see me again. I understand that."

"I didn't say that, Crystal."

"Let me finish. Please." She was shorter than I remembered her. Standing close so that her voice wouldn't carry, her forehead only reached my cheek. Her voice seemed to quiver with fragile determination. "If you don't want to see me, that's okay. But just do me a favor, will you? Be a friend to the kid. I've seen the way you talk to him. The way he listens. If you don't think we have anything going, okay. But think about being his friend, will you, David? That's really all I ask."

Holly was waiting for me when I walked back from the parking lot. "Did you tell her?"

"Tell her what?"

"Did you tell her about Judith?"

"We have customers," I said, making my way to the register.

"My money's on Crystal."

"For what?"

"To get rid of Judith. But don't worry, David. If what the boys used to say about her is true, you're going to have a really good time."

J U D I T H

21

Stumpy came over just after breakfast to help her with the garden. She had planted the peas on St. Patrick's Day, four weeks before, but digging the entire garden was a task Gordon had always done. Now Gordon sat in a deck chair wrapped in a blanket, overseeing Stumpy's digging and her cultivating and planting. They went along in tandem until half the garden—broccoli, lettuce, beets, carrots, leeks—was put in. The sun warmed her back, even though the air was chilly. This soil was her creation, compost, grass clippings, seaweed added to the sand and decayed into a rich brown soil. She loved the feel of it in her hands, looking almost edible, fudgy. Gnats swirled in the path. A mourning cloak butterfly wandered among the pines. She had never found April cruel, but fecund, full of promises that would eventually be kept, promises of growth and productivity. She thought of David. She had not seen him alone since the morning he had arrived unannounced. Being outdoors made her wish he was with her. She had imagined putting in the garden with him instead of Stumpy.

Stumpy stayed for lunch. After he left, as Gordon was retiring for his afternoon nap, he said, "I thought you'd get your young man to help. I'm sure he has some sort of mechanical cultivator that could turn the whole thing over in half an hour."

"I'd meant to ask him, but he's been avoiding me."

"Did you have a fight?"

"I think he was upset that morning he appeared right after we made love."

"Did he think I was too old or too sick to get it up?"

Actually he usually was, but she simply smiled. "I think he knew in theory we make love, but it caught him by surprise to walk in. He'll get over it. The more serious problem, I suspect, is that after candidates' night, the reality of running for office is scaring him shitless."

"He certainly seems flightier than I expected. Do you think he'll back out?"

She shrugged. "I'll talk to him."

"Is he more afraid of winning or losing? Or is it the public process that scares him? Standing up in front of people he's known all his life and making a fool of himself. I'll really regret it if he blows his chance at the seat. He's the best shot we've ever had."

"I promise, I'll give him a pep talk. I know he can win. He has more support than he realizes. He's seen as honest, hardworking, young—"

"And unknown politically. Meaning he hasn't pissed anyone off yet." Gordon looked totally exhausted. Fatigue overtook him often with the abruptness of a blade dropping. She had to help him to bed. She sat beside him as he lay waiting for sleep. "I'm making a lamb and barley soup," she said softly. "The bakery is open and I got a nice bread. I'm always so glad when they open in the spring. The geese fly overhead, the robins come back, and the bakery opens. . . ." He was asleep, she realized, and slipped out, shutting his door soundlessly.

She decided to go over to David's after supper. She could not allow the unspoken estrangement to persist. She must work through whatever had gone wrong. His car was outside and the light on in his kitchen. He had given her a key and she used it, although once inside, she called to him. "David? David? It's me."

He leapt up from the table, apparently startled. He looked almost afraid. He must have been brooding—probably about the election.

She came to him at once and kissed him lightly. "I know you've been avoiding me."

He looked petrified now. "What do you mean?"

She suspected he was afraid that she would withdraw from him if he chose not to run. For all that she had promised Gordon she would try to get him to commit, it was even more important to her that he not feel their relationship was in any way dependent on the election. She thought it would be good for him to run and to win. It would give him confidence that he had not had since the end of his baseball career. But if he was not ready, she would not coerce him, even to please Gordon. Two relationships could be a lot more complicated than Gordon realized, balancing each of them against the other. Doing justice to both men. "I've been pushing you hard to run, and you're angry."

He scratched his head, still avoiding her gaze. "I'm not angry."

"People will be disappointed if you back out—particularly Gordon. He's sure you can win and it means a lot to him. But I want you to do what you want to do. I want you to do what's best for you, and if that involves withdrawing from the race, then do it."

"That's what you wanted to talk to me about?" Now he looked at her, finally.

He was so tense, she could feel it. She loved him even more than she liked to admit to herself or to Gordon. She was besotted with him, the light eyes in the face already tanned from outdoor work, his shock of black hair, the line of his mouth and chin, the sound of his voice, tentative, always issuing from lower in his chest than she expected. His fine blunt hands were on the table, pressing against it as if to keep the world in place. "I want things to be better between us." David was a good man, and she did not want to make things harder for him.

He sat down slowly at the table, still holding her gaze, and she sank into the chair across from him. She said, "I think it's been tying you in knots. I don't want the election to come between us. You're too important to me."

"You wouldn't hate me if I decided not to run?"

"Hate you? Never. David, you may not believe it right now, but what we have together works for both of us. We have a lot to give each other, a lot to teach each other. It may not be a conventional relationship, but that doesn't mean it can't work for us—and work well."

She could tell he was full of doubts—she could feel them churning just under the surface of his apparent calm—but when she rose and walked over to him, he stood and took her in his arms. Patience, she thought to herself, patience. It's taking him a while to get used to the situation, but he does love me.

"You're so precious to me, David. I've missed you these past two weeks."

"I've missed you too," he said, and began easing her toward his bedroom. Through her body and mentally, she relaxed with a sigh. She would have to tell Gordon she had not persuaded David to make a commitment to run, but with great relief she could feel his focus shifting from whatever had been distressing him at the moment to their bodies pressing together, the sweetness of their mouths joining. It would be all right. It would be good again, she was sure.

DAVID

Between Thanksgiving and Memorial Day there were two restaurants in Saltash open after six P.M. One served steaks and seafood and was favored by the retired crowd. The working people gathered at Penia's. Crystal asked me to meet her and the kids there for dinner on Friday night. She told me she had a surprise. Penia's was noisy and smoke-filled and dark. The beer was warm and the pizza was cold, but you could feed a family of four for under twenty dollars. It was the one place in the entire town I knew I'd never see Judith—she was suing them.

"Crystal, you didn't go and get me anything, did you?"

"As a matter of fact," her voice was all whisper and giggle, "I took something away."

Kids were kicking a soccer ball in the parking lot when I arrived and filling balloons at the men's room sink. As we stood in line for a table, Michelle's daughter, Kelly Ann, met two boys from her class, arms up to the elbows in a tank of tropical fish. No, Laramie mumbled, he did not know them. He would not lift his gaze from the tops of his shoes. After the waitress finally took our order, she slouched to the table behind ours and cleared it, chatted up her two booths and ducked into the ladies' room before entering the kitchen.

"What's the matter?" Crystal said. "You keep checking your watch."

"I'm hungry."

"You look nervous."

"Just because people stare at us when they pass."

"You're running for public office. Think that could be it?"

"I hope not."

"I know, I know. Because the last thing you want to do is win."

Laramie frowned. I didn't know much about little boys, but I had never met one so worried about his mother. He not only watched her, he absorbed her every word. His mood changed with our conversation. Every time I opened my mouth to speak, he seemed to set his jaw and wait for her response. When the waitress brought Crystal's tea, he started playing with the bag, sloshing it up and down.

"Cut it out," Crystal told him.

"It makes faster this way," he said.

I ordered two more cups when the pizza arrived, told Laramie to dip the bag in one and to leave the other alone. I gave him my wristwatch and asked him to time which got darker first. Crystal looked at me as if I was a cross between Piaget and Santa Claus.

If the kid sensed that I was tense, he wasn't far off. Sure, Penia's was cheap and a place where kids could amuse themselves. But eating here on a Friday night with a woman and her children was like an announcement to the town, WE ARE AN ITEM! People weren't looking at some guy running for selectman, they were noting who was screwing who.

"Can I ask you a question?" Her voice was apologetic and she hadn't touched her food. Laramie stopped eating and waited for my answer. Her cheeks were flushed. I imagined them warm against my fingertips. "It's a serious question."

"Ask me anything you want."

"Why don't you want to run?"

Although we could hardly hear each other above the jukebox and the rattle of plates, she seemed to be doing everything in her ability to coax me into a better mood.

"You'd be so good." She slid her hand under mine. Laramie saw the gesture and relaxed. What he did not see was the nail of her middle finger moving in circles around my palm.

"Because everybody in this town would rather hate each other than change anything," I said.

"Is that the real reason?"

"It's easier to fight about the way things used to be than to face up to what really needs fixing."

"You mean my boss?"

"Johnny Lynch got rich off this town. You look around this restaurant. There isn't one local kid here who didn't lose a piece of his family's land to Johnny. But who do they hate? Who do they make jokes about and try to run off the highway? Who do they blame for being poor? The retired people, the city people. Do they remember what school was like here when we went? You know why Tommy Shalhoub dropped out of school? Because he couldn't read. Because we had a teacher who made him read out loud and hit him on the head with a book every time he made a mistake. Guess what? She's still teaching."

Laramie and Kelly Ann fell silent. Crystal withdrew her hand. I assumed the conversation was over. Then she asked, "Is that how your friend Judith feels?"

Laramie's face turned the color of a gravestone. How would he even know her name? I don't believe a muscle moved in his entire body— or mine. Crystal nibbled on her pizza, reached across the table to put another slice on Kelly Ann's plate. "Would you like another soda, you two?" Kelly Ann sucked the air through her straw and nodded. "How about you, Larry Stone Face? Do you want to tell me about her, David?"

"Well, she's a good customer. They have a very big garden. She and her husband, Gordon, have been married for thirteen years. He's got cancer. She nurses him as best she can."

"She sounds much older than you. How many children do they have?"

"Gordon has five by other marriages. But none together."

"Mmmm." Crystal flashed a grimace of pity. "So she became a lawyer." She wiped Laramie's lips with a napkin. "I'd like to meet her."

I laughed, involuntarily. It was unthinkable.

"David, if the two of you like each other, I'm sure she and I will."

"I don't know about that."

"I won't push you. But I think it's the most natural thing in the world. Like meeting your mother or an old family friend. I hope you'll change your mind," she said.

Michelle was spending Friday night at Tommy's, a deal the two mothers had worked out, and a fact that Kelly Ann forgot until she came home. Then she refused to get undressed, to turn off the TV, to brush her teeth or stop crying or get into bed. With every story we read, Kelly Ann demanded another, until we had read four of them and Laramie had fallen asleep. When we turned out the lights, the little girl turned them on again and insisted she didn't have to go to sleep if she didn't want to, Crystal wasn't her mother and this wasn't Crystal's house. I couldn't believe how tired I was, how the effort of staying awake and dealing with Kelly Ann, while attempting to control my temper, was as much work as I did in an eight-hour day. I crawled into bed—on the nights when Michelle slept out, Crystal had a real bed—already half asleep. "Don't you want to turn the light out?"

"Then you won't see my surprise," she said.

"What is it?"

"You have to guess."

"Where is it?"

"Oh, I think you know."

"So I've seen it before?"

"Not as much of it."

"I don't understand. There's more of something?"

"Less. But I think you'll like it more." She peeled off the covers and inched her back up the headboard. Slowly and with great ceremony, as if unveiling a work of art, she drew her night gown over her knees, her thighs. I'd been watching her face, her thick, deliberate smile, when she licked her finger and dragged it down her belly to where she had shaved herself smooth. Her mons was as soft and bare and pink as a child's. "I did it for you," she whispered. "Just for you. Do you like it?"

The truth is I had never seen an adult woman shaved before. I couldn't say that I *liked* it, for it disturbed me. I felt momentarily ashamed. I only knew it excited me, that I was fascinated with the act itself, so bold and spontaneous in its eccentricity.

"But she's so cold." Crystal's voice rose and slowed like a girl child's. "Don't you want to kiss her?"

As I covered her with my mouth, she dug her nails in my shoulders. "I want to know everything you like," she said. "You can ask me for anything and I'll make it come true. Anything, do you understand me?" She lifted my head until my eyes met hers. "There are no private parts. There are no secrets. My body inside and out is yours. You can do anything with me. I'm your anything girl."

DAVID

High Street, Saltash, was two lanes wide. Local guys enjoyed a good conversation in the middle of it—windows rolled down, pickups idling, one facing east, the other west, as traffic and tempers built up in both directions. Sometimes it was a demonstration of local rights, a protest against the out-of-state license plate behind them; sometimes just business, the closest a working man came to a car phone. It was also the fastest way for news to get around, and the afternoon I took on the Department of Roads, Bridges and Waterways, they tell me cars were backed up for a quarter mile.

I'd been working the Carlson job. Bob Carlson was a friend of Marty's and one of our best customers. Like a lot of affluent couples from the city, the Carlsons paid late and changed their minds on a whim. One Monday night, they decided on a party at their country home that weekend, for which they expected their fencing erected and their landscaping complete. I hadn't scheduled the job until the middle of May. Much as I wanted to tell the Carlsons to shove it, we needed the business.

Although it was only mid-April, the air was sweet with narcissus and the acid tang of pine sap. Spring peepers trilled at sundown and clouds of gnats rippled the air like waves of heat. Even after I sent the crew home, even as the sun touched the treetops, I worked without a shirt. The Carlsons' was one of the only houses in Johnny Lynch's new development. When Bob Carlson heard that the lot across the road sold, he wanted a fence. Eight feet high, one hundred long, it had taken us three days to complete.

Just beyond the fence, I heard the growl of truck gears, heavy equipment climbing, and caught a glimpse of a front-end loader, the kind road pavers used, laboring up the hill. It was odd to be starting a job this late in the day. I couldn't see the road crew but heard them horsing around. I didn't think much about it. I was driving spikes in a tier of landscape ties, trying to finish before sundown. The stench of the diesel smoke, the noise of the big machine were unpleasant enough to ruin a mild spring evening, but when the loader's engine started straining, roaring loud enough to explode, when I noticed the big rig rolling over the property line, I ran down the drive to take a look. The driver was forcing the loader's bucket under the root ball of a twenty-foot tree, attempting to lift it. The harder he gunned the engine, the farther forward the vehicle tipped, its rear tires leaving the ground. The light was fading. A thick blue cloud of smoke billowed down the hillside, but the lettering on the equipment was unmistakable. This was no moonlighting road crew working on Johnny Lynch's road, this was the Saltash Department of Roads, Bridges and Waterways, and the idiots were three feet from my fence.

A couple of guys watched from the edge of the road—Harlan Bowman and Tony Brockmann among them—arms folded, beer bottles in their fists. When they saw me coming, they turned their backs. Tiny Sauvage ran alongside the machine, waving his arms, shouting instructions.

I called, "Hey guys." They ignored me. "This is a private road. What are you doing here?"

Harlan Bowman lifted a baseball cap stained with motor oil and ran his hand through his hair. "Clearing trees."

"It took my crew three days to put up that fence. Don't you think he's awful close?"

Harlan shrugged. "He's a new guy." The machine rocked, forward and back, spewing a shower of pebbles and sand.

I was shouting above the noise, "Well, get him out of there," when the huge yellow rig sprang backwards, hit the ground with its rear wheels spinning, shot through two sections of my new cedar fence, lurched forward and died in the middle of the road.

Tiny Sauvage screamed at the driver, "You fuck, you stupid fuck!" The guys crept up cautiously, as if the big rear tires might suddenly come alive.

"You crushed the fence," I said to Tiny. Didn't seem to bother him a bit.

Harlan took a step backward, considering the twelve-foot gap of dangling staves and splinters. "Took a hit there. Yup."

The door of the loader's cab creaked open. A hand appeared, then a boot, dangling cautiously in search of a step.

"Look!" Tiny shouted, his finger pointing at the driver's pants. "He pissed hisself! Sonofabitch pissed hisself!"

Sheepishly, the driver spread his hand over the wet splotch of his pants. "I had an accident," he said. The collective laughter was uncontrolled.

"Guys. Listen to me." I wasn't trying to pick a fight. "The fence is going to have to be replaced."

Tiny said over his shoulder, "We'll take care of it."

"When?"

"When we get to it."

"When you get to it? Guys, my best customer's coming up here to-morrow night. What am I supposed to tell him?"

Tony Brockmann spit in the dust. "Tell him you had an accident."

"It's dark now," Tiny said. "We can't do nothing in the dark."

As long as I could remember, there were two-hour lunch breaks be-hind the ice skating rink, poker games in the town golf course locker room, municipal trucks cruising the highway with their radios scream-ing heavy metal rock. This was Saltash's archaic welfare system, a sociopathic elite hired by Johnny Lynch and tenured by the town. But I wasn't some teacher from Westchester whose electric line they'd acci-dentally cut. This was my work they'd destroyed and me they were laughing at.

"I want it fixed first thing tomorrow morning," I said. "I mean that. Or I'll have to go over your head."

Tiny looked from me to his men—is this guy an asshole or what?—and left me standing alone in the road.

For all the years I'd lived in Saltash, I could count the times I'd been in Town Hall, the only brick building in town. Its long dark halls, hot in summer and clammy in winter, were bleak and dreary and seemed to discourage invaders. "We are not complainers," my father used to say. He was fond of declaring our standards. We tip well. We pay local tradesmen on time. A pitiful code of conduct to be sure, but one we ad-hered to in lieu of our religion and the customs we'd left where we came from. Throughout my life, in spite of lousy tableside service or a pipe that began leaking as soon as the plumber's truck left the driveway, I tipped twenty percent, I paid my bills the day they arrived. I did not complain.

The town manager did not know me from my glory years. He was a tall soft tired man who listened with an interest that seemed directly calibrated to the amount of trouble I was likely to cause.

"Sir, I just want you to know I'm not a complainer," I began, and out-lined the situation from the misuse of town property to the gaping hole in the fence. Without interrupting, the manager made a phone call. "Could you get right up here?" he said, and five minutes later Donkey Sparks arrived.

"David Greene!" His cheeks were pink, his collar too tight. He wore a tie beneath an old cotton sweater that announced he might be man-agement but still close enough to his rank and file not to betray them by wearing a suit. "Christ, it's been years. Do you know this guy?" he asked the town manager without waiting for a reply. Then to me: "You've been back in town how long? And did you come to see me?"

"I—"

"Best damned high school pitcher I ever saw. Damn, he was good. Went all the way to the Chicago Cubs, did you know that? Davey Greene, the Pitching Machine."

"Mr. Greene was telling me about an incident he encountered up, where?"

"This the fence thing?" Donkey waved it off. "Those assholes. Got to watch them every minute. Don't worry about it. We'll have it all taken care of. So, Davey, what are you doing now? You think you'll do some coaching for the Little League?"

"What do you mean taken care of?" I said.

Donkey was so named for a horsey staccato laugh, almost a bray, which escaped him now. "I mean we'll order some sections of fence for you and as soon as they come we'll get up there and make it good as new."

"It was new. These are important customers to me. They'll be up tomorrow night."

"Hey, Davey. Spring is here, my friend. The whole town's breathing down my neck. I told you. As soon as we can. Is that not reasonable?"

Complainers were people who didn't listen to reason; troubled people who searched out trouble. I knew the more I made of it, the less my chances of the fence ever being fixed. "Look, these are difficult customers I'm talking about. They are going to hold me up for the whole job because of that stretch of fence. I'm not going to be able to pay my crew, okay? And why? Because your guys are out there drinking and operating heavy machinery—"

"Drinking?" Donkey glanced at the town manager.

"Yes, I think they were," I said.

"You think."

"They were holding beer bottles."

"And you know what was in those bottles? You know positively that it was alcoholic beer? Because you're making serious accusations, my friend." The flush of his cheeks intensified; all the blood in his body seemed to collect in his face. His smile turned to warning: back off. "You collected those bottles and had them tested? Is that what you're saying? You have the results?"

I didn't have anything of the kind. "What were they doing up there after work, using town equipment on a private road?"

Donkey grinned. That was easy. "Making access for fire vehicles," he said to the manager. "I asked them to put in a little overtime and they were glad to do it. It's all listed in the work detail." Then, ignoring me, "Is there anything else?" Donkey waited, his short square body tensed for a fight.

When I emerged, the weather had turned. A cold fog settled over Saltash, driven by a northeast wind. I drove eighty-five miles to pick up the replacement sections of fence and worked well past dark cementing the posts.

"It's over," Crystal said, warming the meat loaf in a frying pan. "Don't be so hard on yourself."

I ate because she had cooked, but I had no appetite. With no proof—they had taken their beer bottles with them—no witnesses, there was nothing I could have done. Moreover, the fence was fixed. Did I really want to pursue this further, put five men out of work? It was over, I told myself. Over.

Since I'd started seeing Crystal, I was spending less time with Judith, but Crystal considered herself at war. To the extent that she had studied the enemy, Crystal knew that Judith was well read and interesting to talk to; that she had traveled a good deal; that she had a local reputation as a fabulous cook and hostess; that she was quoted in the newspapers regularly, often saying something witty and outrageous. Moreover, Judith was affluent, genetically thin, and to the extent that it meant anything now, my mentor in local politics. This might have been enough to overwhelm any number of women, if they respected any of Judith's virtues. Crystal did not. To Crystal, Judith was incomplete. "If you haven't had a child," she said more than once, "you're not a real woman."

Crystal had not only managed to neuter her enemy but to employ sex as her most potent weapon. She had asked more than once what Judith was like in bed (I would not talk about it), but was confident she was better. Or at least that she tried harder. For on no occasion that I spent the night with her, or as little as half an hour in a place with a door that closed (including my truck) did we fail to have sex. Crystal felt that an evening was incomplete until she had made me come.

Before we got into bed that night, I had told her honestly, sex was the last thing on my mind. Had I displayed the usual signs of disinterest, she might have believed me, but perversely, I was and remained hard as a pole. I simply could not get off. She squat-fucked me, facing front, then rear (coming twice herself in the process); she greased me with massage oil and pumped me with her fist; she sucked me until her jaw ached, all with no luck. "Where are you?" she said, rising from the bed sheets for air.

The photographs over the years show my father as a man with delicate bones, an ever thinning pompadour, and a thick blue vein that ran from his hairline to the corner of his eye. He had borrowed a small fortune from my grandmother to buy into the curtain factory. He was up at three every morning, often loading the trucks himself. When I was eight years old, he scored the biggest order the company ever had, a thousand gross of gingham curtains for a department store chain in the Midwest. His stitchers worked double time to make the deadline. The order had to be delivered on or before the first of October. But because his truck driver had been drinking and had disappeared with both sets of the keys to the truck, the shipment never made it on time. My father was furious and fired the driver. That night, Johnny Lynch stormed into my living room. As my mother paced the kitchen, he called my father a heartless New York kike.

"I'm not doing it, Johnny, no."

I was hiding in the hallway.

"Call." Johnny's voice carried the authority of law.

"The man's a drunk, Johnny."

"He has a wife and children."

"So do I, Johnny. So do I."

"*Call him!*" Johnny shouted, and the house shook. "Or the bank calls your loan tomorrow. Tell him you apologize. Tell him you had a talk with me."

I remember the ratchet of the old rotary dial, and my father's forehead in the lamplight, the blue vein throbbing, seventeen years before the stroke that killed him.

"You can't give it up, can you?" Crystal said. But neither could she. Having invested two hours in my satisfaction, she was afraid that she'd be sending me off to Judith in the morning hornier than ever. But all I felt was a weight pressing on my head from the inside, a pounding need for revenge. I had two choices: to back off or go at them, not only the idiots on the crew or Donkey Sparks above them, but Johnny at the top of the pyramid. Johnny Lynch had viewed my father as invisible, the way they all looked through me. I doubt I was the first to decide to run for political office while having sex, but something did happen just then. Something had fallen into place. Compare it to a gear, spinning for years without engaging. Compare it to catching your breath; or to orgasm itself, the explosive fusion of mind and body.

I came in what felt like a torrent of memory and emotion. Crystal swallowed, swinging her head to release the crick in her neck. "Finally," she gasped, for both of us.

JOHNNY

Johnny thought of parking in the woods and walking to the house, like the old days when the whole town knew what he was doing before he had his pants off. Around here, your car told people everything they wanted to know, what you drove and where you parked it. He'd learned that the hard way. He'd lost his first election because of that little red Triumph. It was months later before he'd understood how people here perceived him. Playboy. High roller. You could get away with a lot in this town if you knew the limits. Marry a black girl. Drink yourself pickled. Be a lesbian. But drive around in some fancy Mercedes? People wouldn't put up with it.

Ever since, he'd driven a Ford Crown Vic brown or maroon four-door sedan. The dullest car in town, everybody knew it on sight: his problem today. He didn't want the boy to see it in his mother's driveway and drive off angry. But Johnny no longer had the strength to park the car on a sand road and go on foot the way he used to: half a mile sometimes, through the woods like a tomcat.

Johnny didn't like involving Linda Greene, but what could he do? David Greene avoided him. Never set foot in the office when he picked up Crystal. Never returned Johnny's wave in the parking lot. Something had to be done.

"Hello, dear. How are you?" Johnny kissed her cheek but was careful to thrust his gift between them.

"Roses, Johnny! You didn't have to do that."

"You're putting yourself out for me and I appreciate it."

"Oh, you. Putting myself out. It's just brownies and coffee with David."

Linda Greene was a fine-looking woman still, with a high broad bosom and slender legs. Unlike the others her age, she never let herself go gray. She dressed young; a ribbed cotton sweater over black leggings. He'd watched her walking over the years, sometimes with women friends, sometimes just with her dog, but out there rain or shine on Ocean's Edge Road, keeping up a pace, working on her figure.

Johnny usually avoided being alone with Linda Greene, but thought it best to be seated at the kitchen table when the boy walked in. "You'll want to get those in some water." Linda was a little too passionate. He had his excuse now: he could blame his bad heart and her feelings wouldn't be hurt. She was a needful woman. Emotional. Not emotional like his wife, not delicate but the opposite. Before her husband passed away, she'd made her interest in Johnny plain enough. At curtain factory parties. Good Christ, in the elementary school parking lot one snowy December night after the Christmas play. She practically shoved her tongue down his throat. It wasn't for lack of desire on his part. He could have met her in Florida any number of times, where she visited her sister. But Johnny knew this town well enough to keep his hands off the widow of his ex-partner.

He anticipated her return from the sink, her cool fingertips grazing his skin above the shirt collar. "So young David said he was coming, dear? Just what did you tell him?"

"That I wanted him to see a friend."

"You didn't say who?"

"He doesn't hate you, Johnny. He just doesn't understand."

"But you didn't—"

"No, I just told him somebody he hadn't spoken to in a long time wanted to talk to him about running for selectman."

"That's good. That's very good." He let her fingers drift up to his cheek before he removed himself to the window. He supposed he was no better than any man; he enjoyed being wanted. But the truth was, he'd always liked Linda Greene. Far more than the husband who'd never learned to play the game, she was a practical woman. Sure her feelings were hurt when he ignored her interest in him, but she got more out of him as a friend than she ever would in bed. The son was like the father, looking at the dark side of everything. Sure enough when he rolled into the driveway and saw the Crown Vic, he stormed from his truck like a company of marines, throwing open the kitchen door.

"What's he doing here?" David Greene said, without so much as the courtesy to address Johnny by name. He was small like his father but an outdoor man, well-muscled, a scrapper. For a moment Johnny feared for his safety. He studied the boy's eyes, light gray like storm clouds.

The boy had always been a cold one. He'd never sat at Johnny's knee with the other children for stories but hovered back. Even when Johnny had picked the boy to ride with him in the big parade—two hours in the backseat of a convertible, creeping along Main Street in the scorching July sun—David Greene never spoke a word. "Hello, son. Your mother and I were having coffee and cake. Will you join us?"

"Why didn't you tell me this is the friend you wanted me to see?"

"David—"

"Because I asked her not to," Johnny said. "You wouldn't have come."

"You've got that right."

Linda Greene placed herself between them.

"And why is that?" Johnny asked.

David folded his arms. "Where do you want me to start?"

"By sitting down. Stop embarrassing me," Linda said. "The past is the past. You don't know everything."

"I know he bled my father's business dry."

Linda looked away, as if from a photograph she didn't want to see.

"When I first showed him the factory, I told him there was a good life to be had in this town. The idea was to give people jobs, draw a modest salary, enjoy his life. Your uncle George understood that. I told your father again and again to wait, the factory would pay off eventually."

"David, you were so young." Linda Greene was close to tears. "Your father was a very impatient man. There was only one way, his way."

"Enough of this," Johnny said. "I didn't come to rehash the past. I came to wish you luck in your run for public office and to ask you, man-to-man, if you're planning to turn this election into a referendum against me."

"Is there another issue?"

Johnny caught Linda's wrist. "We need a little time alone, dear, the boy and I. Is that all right with you? If David and I take a ride together?"

"I'm not going anywhere with you."

"Then we'll sit right here and have it out in front of your mother, won't we? Is that what you'd rather?"

"Any closer to that car door, son, you'll be on the sidewalk."

David didn't answer. He sat as far from Johnny as was possible in the front seat. His face was a mask of stone. Only the police scanner broke the silence, spitting out the urgent business of the Saltash P.D. *"Roger. Who has the jug of windshield wiper fluid? Over. I think Duffy had it last. Over."*

Johnny caught the boy smiling. "You've got to love this town," he said.

David, obviously uncomfortable, shifted in his seat, staring frontways, sideways, anywhere but at Johnny. He looked at the backseat covered with election posters for Blossom Endicott.

"First thing Monday, she'll have these up at every traffic light on the highway, every window in the center of town."

"Why would you tell me that? Why rat out Blossom?"

"Because you might win."

"Where are we going?" David sighed, sounding almost resigned.

Johnny continued through Saltash center and out Dock Street along the harbor, up the state highway ten miles, then into the neighboring town of Sandy Bars. Only when he signaled a left turn toward the bay did he answer, "To what they call their town pier."

"What the hell for? There's nothing there."

Johnny pulled into a cracked asphalt parking lot, a peninsula surrounded on three sides by muddy tidal marsh. A row of dories and small motorboats lay one against the other along the back fence. A couple of old-timers in hip boots hung out on the steps of the Sandy Bars harbormaster's shack. This was a high-tide harbor; boats sat in the mud until the tide came up. Until then, there was no channel, no access to the sea. Johnny nosed the car up to a guardrail and shut the engine. "What do you see here?"

"What am I supposed to see? Nothing."

"How does it compare to Saltash harbor?"

"It doesn't," David said.

Saltash had thirty draggers, ten lobster boats, fifteen sport fishing charters. Johnny knew the numbers by heart. In season there were slips for 215 sailboats, 180 powerboats and a waiting list triple that. There were tackle stores and restaurants; two thriving boatyards, a summer theater, picnic tables, parking for four hundred, a bandstand, public showers and a fish market. Johnny stretched his arm across David's seat, sending him sideways to the door. "Now why the fuck do you think that is?"

The boy hedged. "We have a better natural harbor."

"Study your geography, son. Saltash harbor is a shallow embayment with a tidal amplitude of ten feet, about the same as what you're staring at. Sandy Bars could have had a fine harbor too, but nobody had the brains or the balls to make it happen. Thirty-five years ago I looked at Saltash and saw a town crying for an industry. That's why you're looking at this mud puddle in front of you while ten miles down the coast we have a beautiful working harbor."

"On which you bought up and sold—how many waterfront acres was it? Land you made valuable with public money."

So it was a pissing contest he wanted? "All right, David. Let's say I made a little money in my time. Let's say also that I managed to do something for my people along the way. What have *you* done? What did Gordon and his wealthy retired friends do? They don't give a fuck about who works or who doesn't because they don't have to work. As far as they're concerned, the local women can clean their toilets and the men mow their lawns. Take your best shot, son, go ahead. What else do your fancy backers accuse me of? Keeping the state from turning half of Saltash into a fucking bird sanctuary? Am I supposed to apologize? The land we kept out of the state's hands is what we call the tax base, son.

That's what pays for the police and the rescue squad and the best school system within a hundred miles."

"Isn't the principal of the school your sister, Johnny? Maybe we ought to rename the place Coincidence, Massachusetts. Because we sure have our share." The little prick kept pushing. "And didn't the selectmen happen to buy *your* land to build the school on? And didn't you handpick the contractor so the roof always leaks and the foundation is cracking?"

"The people of Saltash always made out," Johnny said, a little louder than he meant to.

"Is that all you wanted to tell me?"

Johnny sighed. He was tired, as if he could sleep for the rest of the afternoon. "What do you say we have a drink together?"

"Thanks. I don't have the time."

Johnny laughed to himself. "Neither did your father, do you know that? In all the years we did business together, he never once had the time for a drink."

As he drove back, Johnny tried to figure it out, how this cocky little high school pitcher had come back to haunt him. Johnny had heard he was screwing Judith Silver, Gordon's child bride. For all the cheap gossip Johnny himself had generated, this town had never seen anything like Gordon Stone and his drugs and naked orgies and string of women. But the kid had been hanging around his new secretary too. He'd have to find out what was going on.

David Greene was a lightweight; youth and resentment, that's all he had going. So what was so upsetting? Why did Johnny feel like he could pull the covers over his head and sleep the day through until morning? In front of Linda Greene's house, Johnny offered his hand. "Well, son, goodbye and good luck. Tell your mother thanks for putting herself out."

The kid nodded and slammed the car door, never acknowledging Johnny as a man or an adversary with whom he'd have to contend in the future.

And that was it, Johnny understood. That's what was bringing him down. Under this boy's contempt, Johnny was disappearing, shedding his importance. All his talent to move people, gone; his influence and the fear he instilled in men, gone; his eyesight and his stamina; his dear wife and what once seemed a small fortune. He was losing his life in pieces.

History and experience, all his accomplishments meant nothing. They kept coming at him: ambitious young pit bulls, smelling weakness, hungry for a fight. If it was a dogfight David Greene wanted, then a dogfight he'd get. The old schoolteacher wouldn't have been Johnny's first choice, but he'd backed worse and he'd won. Her family had been in the town two hundred years, and if people weren't crazy about her, they remembered her dad or her brother fondly. The Endicott clan alone were worth forty votes. It would be a dirty campaign, but Blossom could lick David Greene, and that was all he needed to get this depression off his back. To win, again. To win.

JUDITH

25 Judith's secretary Mattie told her that David had been seen with a woman who just moved back to town. When her partner Austin retired, Judith had kept Mattie on. Mattie was fourteen years older than Judith and doubted she could have found another job as good. Therefore she offered Judith a fierce loyalty that Judith cherished. Mattie had white hair braided around her head in an old-fashioned style, hair that would come well past her shoulders if loosened. She wore thick glasses and was stooped, but bright and fast. She had made herself comfortable with computers. She kept up, with an edge of desperation, for her divorce had left her with little but her house and debts. Her two sons who lived on the Cape were more a drain than a resource.

Mattie knew who Crystal was: the daughter of a dentist who had left town under a shadow. "His hands used to shake. The story was, he was addicted to painkillers and wrote himself script all the time. He got into trouble in two other states, people said, but his license was still good in Massachusetts. Finally he hurt a woman bad, our kindergarten teacher. A sweet lady. Johnny Lynch hushed it up but made him go."

"So how old was Crystal when her family left town?"

"Most of the way through high school, I'd say. A pretty girl, but her reputation wasn't. The parents split up. The mother went out West, I heard, and the father moved to Troy, New York. He and my ex-husband used to go fishing together and, every year, he sends my husband a Christmas card with a fish or a duck on it. I sent him a postcard years ago that Mick had left, but he just ignores it and sends him a card at my house every Christmas."

Mattie paused for a moment, her mouth dipping down. "I don't know if I should say this. I never cared for Crystal. My boy Cal went out with her in high school, and it made me nervous. She had him twisted around her little finger. I kept finding condoms in his drawer, although he'd deny there was any of that going on. I was terrified she was going to get pregnant and he'd have to marry her. I was so relieved when they left town, I can't tell you. She's a sly one. She used to try to butter me up." Mattie shook her head. "It makes me nervous, just having her back. Even though Cal's married. I'm not even going to mention that she's in town again."

Mattie reported two days later that Crystal was living with another woman, her own boy and a little girl at 114 Dock Street. That meant she had no money. Mattie also reported she was working for Johnny Lynch. Was David consorting with the enemy? To what degree? What was Crystal to him? Probably he knew her from school.

Crystal Sinclair. Now she had a name. Judith sat in her office, a little ashamed of herself for her curiosity. But David had withdrawn from her. Even when she was with him at his place she had the sense of something working against her, besides his squeamishness about the unconventionality of their arrangement. Someone perhaps; perhaps Crystal Sinclair. She had felt a kind of shadow between them that had not been there.

Gordon asked what was troubling her, and she told him, briefly, trying to downplay her anxieties. She disliked keeping anything from him, but she did not want to burden him with her worries. He frowned. "Is she pretty?"

"I have no idea. She's younger than me, of course."

"It seemed to me, the way he looked at you, the way he acted, that he was deeply involved." Gordon muttered something she did not catch. Then he said, "You'll have to fight back."

"Perhaps. How many battles can we fight at one time?" Dr. Barrows had told her there would be no more operations. He could see no point to removing more of Gordon's lungs. "We should make him as comfortable as we can," he said. It sounded like a death sentence. She was sleeping badly again. Gordon was weaker. He was on painkillers, a system that released what he needed when he felt he needed help.

"But couldn't he become addicted?" she asked Dr. Barrows.

"That isn't really a problem at this point."

She sometimes felt as if Gordon were headed out to sea in a kayak, alone, paddling into the distance. He had drawn into himself more than at any time since they had been together. All his attachments seemed at a remove from his passionate concern with his body and his illness. If only David had been willing to run, that would have helped, for the only thing that had seemed to absorb Gordon was the possibility of defeating Johnny Lynch and finally ousting him from power, from control of the town. That snagged his attention, that roused his passion and his remaining energy. Sometimes she had thought that hope was keeping him alive. Johnny Lynch and Gordon had squared off against each other years ago. Gordon was convinced Johnny had been behind the great pot raid on his compound, that he had used his influence to cause trouble. He was also convinced Johnny had pushed through building codes specifically to prevent him from playing with his building projects. Johnny,

Gordon said, had always been sick with jealousy of him, what he imagined as his scads of women, the pleasure and the celebrity he enjoyed. With Judith, it was a purely political animosity; but Johnny had brought the authorities down on Gordon's head, costing him thousands in legal expenses.

She was fighting a child custody case for a lesbian jewelry shop owner. It was being pushed hard by the father and his Boston lawyer. By this time he honestly hated his divorced wife and her new lover. There would be no compromise. Barbara had sent the woman to her.

She found herself sitting in her office brooding about David, lying awake at night thinking of him. She missed him. It was unfortunate that she had fallen in love with him. Had she fooled herself about his feelings? Or was the problem the woman he kept being seen with? Was he in love with Crystal? Perhaps she should simply forget him. Or had he withdrawn from her because he was ashamed of backing out of the election? If only he would open up and talk.

Barbara and she often had lunch together when they were both in court, even when they were on opposite sides of a case. They discussed forming a partnership in a few years when Barbara was ready to leave the district attorney's office. The major pull keeping her there was the hope that her boss would be appointed a judge in the next year or two and she would then run for his office. Barbara would like to be the district attorney.

Judith told Barbara about what was happening with David, or not happening. She repeated what she had learned of the woman who had come to Saltash when she was a little girl, who had lived in Arizona and in Seattle. And Nevada. Mattie knew Marie, who worked for Johnny Lynch; Marie told her that Crystal had gone to college in Las Vegas. A wandering woman looking for a better life? A better man?

Gordon was eating less and less. Occasionally he still had a good day. He rallied when old friends visited or when his children came home, particularly Natasha. "I'll be interning on Sanibel Island, where there's a facility that treats wild birds and animals. I'm excited about it. I was lucky to be accepted." Natasha arrived with an injured crow. He was moved into the shed that was an aviary, with a screened enclosure on the side.

"Can you be here for the summer?"

"I'll stay for June. Then I have to report to Sanibel. It's near Fort Myers. I can fly back, if it's necessary."

Neither of them said aloud why it would be necessary. Judith began to feel an invisible guest at every meal, the Angel of Death.

"Natasha, do you think I made a mistake getting involved with David Greene? Did I see more in him than there is?"

Natasha shrugged. "You know him better than I do. I was surprised by your choosing him. I supposed you'd find an intellectual."

"No one I found could ever compete with your father. But I thought he was a good, solid, kind man. I sensed that he wanted to learn things, to grow. And he's a Jew. I feel more comfortable being involved with a Jewish man. It's one less problem. Besides, he has great physical presence. I guess I like that. And he loves the Cape."

"Good physical presence." Natasha grinned slyly. "In other words, he's a hunk."

"Not that, exactly. He's comfortable in his body. He doesn't sit in a little cab up on the top of the machine." She did not tell Natasha that after several years of nursing Gordon, health itself was a treasure to her, strength and health moved her in and of themselves. "I thought he was as serious about me as I am about him. Now I have doubts."

"Maybe he figures he can have a girl on the side, since you're married to Gordon."

"That may be. But I'd feel much better if I didn't sense him withdrawing. And I'd feel much better if he was talking to me about it. He's never mentioned her. Not once."

"Maybe he's scared to. You know, Daddy had affairs when I was growing up. It wasn't a secret."

"But I never have, until David. Now I feel vulnerable."

"Gordon loves you. I love you. If David doesn't, he's an idiot."

Barbara summoned her for a special breakfast together. "I have information on your friend's friend. You're not going to like this."

When Judith returned to her office at ten, she started a file labeled GLASS and encoded it for herself only. Crystal Sinclair had left no record in Arizona except for her driver's license. After six years in the Seattle area, she had gotten in trouble for bad checks but had made restitution and the case was dropped. She next turned up in Vegas. She appeared in police records because a friend, a prostitute, had reported that Crystal had trashed her apartment and threatened her with a scissors. Apparently Crystal accused the woman of interfering between her and her boyfriend. According to the police report, they had been drinking together when the fight broke out, and Crystal, the other woman alleged, had gone crazy. The case dragged on for a year with many delays. Finally the woman disappeared, Crystal pleaded no contest and began to attend alcohol rehab meetings. Apparently the next year she left Las Vegas.

So that was Crystal Sinclair, David's new friend. Judith did not think David naive enough to have become seriously involved with her. Probably he knew her from school and felt sorry for her. She had had a hard life, obviously, and it could not have been easy for her son. Johnny Lynch had protected her father, the addicted dentist, so perhaps he viewed the daughter as owing him, or as under his protection also. She did not intend to tell David what she had learned. It would be unethical, as well as exposing Barbara. Moreover, if he had slept with the woman, she would come off as jealous. But the woman was trouble. She would keep that history in mind.

DAVID

I'd heard a couple of stories about fistfights, shouting, the time Slow Boat Richardson pissed on a candidate's literature. I'd put it off every day this week, but this much I knew: you could call them, write them, post signs in their faces, get your name in the papers and promise the world, but if you didn't have the nerve to greet people face-to-face in the Saltash post office parking lot and ask them for their vote, you were not going to get it.

Saturday, I got there earlier than the postmaster and sat in my front seat with a stack of six-by-eight cards, my picture on one side, on the other every endorsement for my good character I could come up with. The first to pull up was the Corn Man. White hair in a ponytail, red suspenders. Every August the land surrounding his small gray house, front and side yards, every arable inch down to the road, was crowded with stalks of butter and sugar corn.

When he stepped out of his car, I waved. He looked away. I took a step toward him. He jogged to his left. I stopped in front of him with my hand out. He gave up and waited.

"Good morning." I pushed my literature against his tightly closed fist. "My name is David Greene. I'm running for selectman."

He looked from the picture on the card to me and back to the picture. I was indeed the asshole I said I was. Now what?

"If you have any questions you'd like to ask?"

"No, no." He gazed longingly over my shoulder at the post office door.

"Well, sir, I hope I can count on your vote."

"Yes, yes," he said, brushing past my shoulder and deftly pitching my card in the trash.

As the sun rose and the wet surface of the parking lot shrank to a small dark puddle, I pressed myself on the Passionate Plumber who wore the zipper of his coveralls open to his navel and doused himself in Old Spice; to my ex–sixth-grade teacher, who proofread my literature; an electrician Holly dated in high school; the chief of police; a couple who tried to sell me a water filtration system; and a man who warned me away with open palms, his wrists and arms slathered pink. "Poison ivy! Poison ivy!" he said, slipping past me like a leper into a dark Calcutta alley.

As afraid as I had been, each person was more afraid of me. What did I want from them? Time? Money? What if they snubbed me and I actually went on to win? "Hi, I'm David Greene. I'm running for selectman. Could I ask you for your vote?"

He was bald and stout and wore brown rubber waders up to his chest, which made me think of something half dipped in chocolate. "You want my vote?" He folded his arms. "Where do you stand on the dike?"

"Out of the wind, so I don't fall in."

"So you don't fall in?" His face brightened like a newly polished coin. "I like that." He slapped my shoulder. "So you don't fall in."

"Hi, I'm David Greene. I'm running for selectman."

She was maybe twenty-five, long black hair, sweater tight across her breasts, with a four-year-old trailing behind. She took my card and asked, squinting into the sun, "You the guy who told Donkey Sparks about those guys getting drunk on the job?"

I said proudly, "That was me, yeah."

"You son of a bitch." She ripped my card in pieces and threw it at me. "My boyfriend could have lost his job."

When Blossom End-Rot drove up to get her mail, her face turned the color of boiled meat. "Well. David Greene." She choked on a smile. "I didn't realize you were mounting such a campaign?"

"You never know what to expect from us pushy immigrant types." I left her to approach another voter. "My name's David Greene . . ."

She wanted desperately to see my literature but couldn't bring herself to ask. As soon as she thought I was distracted, she ripped a card from the hand of someone she knew and studied it front and back. She lifted her eyes to the hip boot man, walking to the car with his mail. "Ask him where he stands on the dike!" he said, waving me a victory sign. "God knows we need somebody with a sense of humor in there."

Could I win? I doubted it but it sure felt good to ruin Blossom's day. Of all the cars that pulled up, however, the one I was waiting for did not: Judith's black Jeep Cherokee. I didn't want to *tell* her I was running. I'd already done that and backed out. I wanted her to see me in action. When I left the post office just after noon, I drove by her office. Closed. I headed for Mary's Tea Room. Judith sat at a rear table reading, her back to the door.

"Hi, my name is David Greene. I'm running for selectman." I handed her a card.

"Where have you been?" I didn't know what I was seeing in her expression. Skepticism? Annoyance? Maybe just my own guilt.

"Incredibly busy. It's the big season for landscapers." I sat down. "How's Gordon?"

She shrugged, not wanting to get into a discussion about cancer. "Do you think he'd still be willing to help?"

"You'll have to ask him."

"Would you still be willing to help?"

"Do you really want this?" Her eyes grew darker, somehow more serious, and I wondered if we were talking about the same thing.

She was wearing a blue silk blouse with long French cuffs and a wide collar, through which I imagined the delicate lacework of her underclothes. "Yes, I do very much," I said.

"I'm talking about *this*." She fanned my card in front of my eyes.

"Do I actually want to be a selectman? I won't know until I win. Do I want to make trouble for Johnny Lynch? Big time, I do. Don't you think that'd be fun?"

The meeting took place the next afternoon at Judith and Gordon's. Along with the *alter kockers* for lynching Johnny, they had rounded up twenty people. There was a table of sandwiches and drinks, and street lists with voters' names. This was serious politics, Saltash style.

Gordon set the tone. "No offense to the candidate," although he looked at me as if I was a sorry excuse for one, "but I want to make it clear we're here for one reason. To put the last nail in Johnny Lynch's coffin."

The drinking started just after dark. The tide was low, the beer was cold, and no one seemed in a rush to get home. I milled around the room attempting to ingratiate myself, until Judith motioned me into the kitchen.

She said quietly, "Say goodbye to everyone personally." This struck me as a sensible idea. "Then leave through the side door."

"Now?"

"Now." Her hand grazed mine. "And meet me in my studio around back."

She joined me half an hour later with a satisfied smile. She drew the curtains and stoked the stove, and just when I thought I knew what she was thinking, took a seat in a rocking chair facing me.

From the house we heard singing. "I missed you," she said. "I've been busy. So have you."

"I'm here now."

"Yes, you are. Yes, you are." She took my face in her hands and outlined my lips with her tongue. She was tentative. Do you still want me? her fingers seemed to ask. Temples and earlobes, biceps and belly. My body was a new land she was mapping. When we began, it was cool in the cottage, the little stove working against the evening chill. We dove beneath the covers and clung together, shivering until our bodies warmed to the boiling point and we came up to cool off and breathe.

Judith took a deep breath. Outside, it began to rain and droplets fell from the eaves, drub, drub, drub, to the wooden porch. An offshore buoy clanged in the early spring wind. She lay in my arms playing with my nipple. She sighed, "I missed you so much."

When the phone rang, Judith sprang from the bed. Upon answering, she looked at the receiver incredulously. "It's for you. It's a child."

The phone sat on her desk, plugged into a jack along with the modem, among law books and journals and briefs in towering piles. I crossed the room, naked, to answer it while Judith took my place under the covers. It was Laramie. "My mom said it was okay to call you."

"It is, Laramie. Sure. What can I do for you?"

Judith mouthed, "Who is Laramie?"

"Um. She wondered if you could pick me up from school on Thursday because she has an—" From somewhere behind him I heard Crystal say, "an interview." "—an interview about college."

"Thursday I can't, Laramie. I'm sorry."

"David?" Judith said, but I looked away from her when I heard the boy say, "Oh," like a small puncture in a lifeboat, and I felt him going under.

"But listen, man, we'll get together soon."

He sighed and I heard traces of a whispered discussion. "Uh, my mom says you should call her, okay?"

"Sure. That'll be fine."

"Thanks. 'Bye," he said, and hung up.

Judith watched me return to bed. "Who's Laramie?"

"He's a little boy I know. My sister's crazy about him."

"He sounds very sad."

"He doesn't have any friends. A new kid in town. You know how it is."

The bed was warm and the sheets smelled of perfume and sweat. I wanted the conversation over and done, but Judith was still curious. "You never mentioned him," she said.

"I just met him pretty recently."

"Pretty fast friendship. His parents approve?"

"Approve of what?"

"Don't be naive. It's not easy for adults to be friends with kids these days. You have to be careful. A lot of charges are thrown, a lot of things imagined. I think twice before I befriend a kid. Parents can be suspicious."

"His parents are split up. His mother's all for it. Okay?"

"That's all I wanted to hear," Judith said. She pushed her hair back and frowned at the far wall, looking past me. "Do you know her well?"

"What is this? Do you want to say what the hell it is you're thinking?"

"All of a sudden there's a child who calls you at my house, a little boy whose name you never mentioned. Naturally I'm surprised."

"That's because you don't have children in your life, Judith. You're not used to them."

"Tell me I'm off here, David. But that sounds like an accusation."

"It's not an accusation. There are just things you can't understand."

"David, I don't want to be mean, but I spent far more time raising Natasha than you did your own son. This sounds like you're trying to create a surrogate son for yourself, all of a sudden."

I had to remind myself where I was. In Judith's shack, with a little fire in the stove casting shadows on the walls. In bed, naked, with a woman I was about to make love to. I could still taste the coffee on Judith's mouth. How had this happened?

"Judith, let's start over again. One. He's a kid I feel sorry for. Two. His mother is cool about the whole thing. Three. I did not mean to imply that because you don't have children you don't know anything about . . . about how weird this world is around kids. I'm sorry. Please accept my apology."

As I drew her against me, she turned. I loved the tight and delicate curve of her back, her small sickle-shaped breasts in the crook of my forearms, my sex thrust between her buttocks. But I could feel a taut coil of resistance inside her. I wasn't surprised when she said to the wall, "Who is his mother, David?"

"Somebody I met."

"Obviously." Judith disentangled herself. When her back was flush against the wall behind the bed, when she had covered herself, she dropped her hands in her lap and stared at them. "She has a name."

"Her name is Crystal."

"And you sleep with Crystal."

"Yes. Like you sleep with Gordon." Even as it left my lips, the comparison felt crude. Gordon was a shell of a lover and had been before I met Judith.

"I understand your justification, David." I had heard her use this tone with workmen who failed to live up to their contracts.

"I don't have to justify myself. It doesn't mean anything. It's casual."

"She called my house," Judith said rising. "She knew you were here. Did you give her the number? It's not listed."

"Holly must have given her the number."

"She's a friend of your sister's." Judith nodded as if chipping away at the truth. Everything I said seemed to make it worse. "A single woman with a child. Of all the stupid people to pick."

"What's better, then? A married woman? A young student? A widow? Who? Do you want to set me parameters, Judith? Give me a list?"

Her face seemed to melt. Her lips trembled and when she finally spoke she sounded helpless. "Why did you do it?"

"Because I've never been involved in anything like what we're doing."

"We're just loving each other, David."

"Fifty yards away from where we're sitting, your husband is entertaining friends. And you're in bed with me. Is that any better or worse than a few lonely nights with some secretary who just moved to town? I love you as much as I ever did. I admit I made a mistake. We'll come back from it."

"I hope so, David. But if she thought the relationship was so casual, she wouldn't have tracked you down and called here."

"She didn't call, her kid did."

As she got out of bed, Judith said mockingly, "Right. As if we both believe that."

"Aren't we going to make love?"

"Do you have a condom?"

"What for? We haven't used a condom since the first time."

"Then get used to it, David. You're screwing two women now. That changes things."

DAVID

27 Some afternoons, between the time school let out and Crystal got off work, Laramie took the school bus to the nursery. It was Holly's idea. She always had a job for him, watering seedlings, bagging wild bird food mix. He could work methodically for hours, seeming to absorb silence the way plants thrived in humidity. Watching him bag one-pound packages of thistle seed—not one-point-one pounds or point-ninety-nine—was like observing a chemist measure acid into a test tube. Holly paid him two dollars an hour. After work he and I drove around town putting up my election signs. Laramie held the wooden stakes in place as I pounded them into the ground.

I knew early on I hadn't the experience or the organization or the base of support; that all I could really hope to do was to raise some questions, kick up a little dirt. But I was a trained competitor. Although speeches and land use policies were a far cry from lobbing baseballs, I couldn't help playing to win. I'd ordered a hundred signs and put up eighty. Like a rancher in his pickup cruising his spread, I was up every morning before sunrise to check on my signs. Once, I'd dreamed of headlining the sports pages, but it was oddly satisfying to see the solitary squares proclaiming my name in block letters, black and white against the wet grass like Holstein cattle. One morning on my patrol, however, three of my signs were missing. Ten of Blossom End-Rot's had sprung up overnight. I replaced the three. That afternoon, with Laramie's help, I pounded in ten more. The following morning twenty more of hers appeared. Four of mine were down. Blossom had six nephews, but I was obsessed. At work that morning I called in an order for fifty more signs.

"What do you think you're doing?" Holly said.

"I can't let them get away with this."

"People already know you're running, David. They're not more likely to vote for you because you fill the roadsides with cardboard."

"Is there a problem, Holly? Let's have it."

"No, there's no problem. You know I want you to win this thing."

"Do you?"

"If that's what you want, but . . ." Here it was. The reason she was not at candidates' night, and why I saw her scowling while I was cutting scrap wood for sign posts. "It can't be good for this business, David.

We've worked so hard to build it up. You know how crazy people in this town are about politics." Our own father, after seeing a Nixon's the One sign on the lawn of a local farm stand, never bought apples there again. "People hold grudges. If you win, they're going to hate you for some stupid decision you'll have to make. Even if you lose, you ran against someone's candidate."

"But you're not talking about people in this town, are you? You're talking about Johnny Lynch."

"He's an old friend of the family, David."

"You think Dad thought so?"

"I think Dad would have been happy to know his wife was taken care of."

"For fuck sake, Holly, that's how half the town thinks. He gives everyone a little piece of something and keeps the rest for himself. Everyone's so damned afraid of losing their little piece."

"Johnny owns the house Mother lives in."

"Our old house?"

"You were away, David. You were having your own problems in Florida. Daddy couldn't pay the mortgage. Johnny bought it, the way he likes to pick up property. He's let mother live there for years for a nominal rent." Holly looked at me with something like pity.

"She never told me."

"Did you ever ask?"

Late one afternoon I met Judith in her office for a quick update on the campaign that turned into drinks as the sun went down and an invitation to the island for dinner. The kitchen smelled of chicken and garlic. Gordon was sitting near the fireplace with a red wool blanket wrapped around him and a glass of scotch in his big hand. "She'll have it all together in half an hour. Now tell me how the campaign is going."

"Well, as I was putting gas in my truck today, who should pull up?"

Judith ran in from the kitchen. "Blossom End-Rot?"

"Go on," Gordon said.

"Did you see the picture in her ad?" Judith perched on the arm of Gordon's couch. "The meanest teacher you ever had."

"Judith, let him tell the story." Gordon settled back.

"She didn't say hello," I said. "She could barely return my smile. She stuck a newspaper article in my face about some proposed antiprofanity bylaw."

"I never heard of it." Gordon asked Judith, "Have you?"

"Neither had I," the chair screeched as I leapt to my feet. "But once

I knew she was for it, I felt the need to oppose it, to draw crowds, to orate, to reorient people's hearts and minds so that we will always and forever have the right to call each other assholes in public."

"He's got the fever," Gordon said. "Blossom's your only real competitor. The professional widow."

"He was a war hero, right?" Blossom invoked his name regularly, and right in the middle of town, on High Street by the Town Hall, was Lieutenant Phillip Endicott Square. Every Memorial Day a wreath was laid against the street sign.

"He was a local boy who went off to Korea. He came home on furlough looking for a good time, and he got hitched to Blossom instead." Gordon shook his head. "In Korea, he lasted two months."

"It's always been my opinion," Judith said, "that she's far happier as a widow than she ever would have been married to Phil Endicott, who liked his bottle and his feet up, or so Mattie tells me. It was a mismatch. She's the matriarch of her clan in spite of not having children. She gives money, advice, whatever, to her eleven nephews and nieces, and she plays them off against each other. The heroic status of her dead husband—and remember, they were only together for two weeks—has grown with every passing year."

"Her signs are everywhere," I said. "They're green and red to my plain little black and white ones. They're wider than mine. I measured. And longer by six inches. I'm developing a case of sign envy."

Gordon liked my joke. But his laughter caused him to cough hard. Throughout dinner he seemed distracted by pain. He would suddenly drop his hands to the table, eyes alert but otherwise motionless, as if listening to something inside himself. Three or four times Judith suggested he lie down, but despite his obvious fatigue, he refused.

I told them what I'd learned from Holly.

Gordon sat back in his chair, his eyes half closed. "He plays fast and loose and he plays hard. If he can't get what he wants one way, he tries another. Remember the Town Hall fire?"

"Sort of. I was in high school. Wasn't it some kind of accident?"

"That's what the fire chief said. But you always have to ask yourself, who won, who lost, who benefited most? All the records were burned. All the titles, all the deeds. All the town correspondence."

"Are you saying he did it?"

"Funny thing. Johnny was under investigation at the time. All the records the state probers wanted were lost."

"What was he being investigated for?"

"Conflict of interest. Obtaining state grants for the town to build roads through land he owned, to dredge the harbor for a fancy new marina built by his friends. The very site selected belonged to his wife. Sweet woman. Spent the better part of every year in a mental hospital." Gordon seemed to drift off into the past. He was silent for several minutes. "Saltash might have had thousands more acres of protected land if it wasn't for old Johnny. Powerful man. His connections ran high up. You didn't fuck with him. He could be very good to you or come down hard. Two sides of the same coin . . ." His voice trailed off.

"How is he?" I asked Judith when Gordon finally went to bed.

"I'm worried," she said.

"For a while he seemed so lively."

"He's getting a lot of pleasure out of your campaign. He's having fun."

"Isn't that odd? Why does this backward little place mean anything to a man as successful as Gordon?"

"Gordon knows that small places are just as real as large ones. Since he's 'succeeded,' as you call it, on a grand scale, he knows what's at stake here: the well-being of the land, the local economy. He has high hopes for you, David. He thinks you're bright. He told me you have a sharp instinctive intelligence."

"That's a very kind thing to say."

She smiled. "Kind? It's something that his graduate students would have killed to hear."

We finished the dishes together quietly. Before things had changed, I would have taken my sweater off, made myself comfortable. Now I felt like a guest. "I forgot to ask about the tide," I said when we finished.

Judith cocked her head, as if to consider an interesting ploy. "Are you asking if you have to stay or if you can?"

"I'd like to."

"Good." She kissed my nose. "What's wrong?"

"Why do you put up with me and her?" I asked.

"You and Crystal? Is she very much on your mind?"

"No," I said quickly. Unless I was in bed with her, no. Even when sex was over, when she'd offered me something I'd never dared ask a woman to do, we lay side by side without a thing to connect us except what we'd just done. So we did it again.

"How well do you really know her, David?"

"Why? Do you think she's hiding something?"

"Most people are, David. Some more than others."

One afternoon, when business was slow and the back lot was alive with insects and wildflowers, I asked Laramie if he wanted to play catch. He was sweeping up the stock room in his quiet, meticulous way, seeming content, but I felt like a sweatshop foreman keeping children from the light. "I thought you liked baseball?"

As if annoyed with the interruption, he continued sweeping. "I don't have a baseball glove."

"Use mine."

"Too big," he said.

"Well, you're going to get one soon, right? For your birthday. Your dad's sending it."

"No, he's not. He never sends me anything."

"He sent you a tape deck last year. I saw it."

"My mom got it."

"That's not what she told me."

"Yeah, she did. Her handwriting was on the box."

"Maybe he sent it to her and she rewrapped it."

Laramie swept the dirt into a perfect conical pile. "She says my dad sends presents, but she does it. 'Cause she wants me to think he loves me."

Most nights, after Crystal left work, she had both kids to care for. She did the shopping and all her other errands, the laundry, gave the kids supper, cleaned up afterwards, supervised their homework and put them to bed. Two nights a week she came straight from work to my house with clothes for the next day. She loved those nights, she told me. She loved having supper on the table in my house with its shabby furniture and cold drafts, because, she said, "I feel like somebody wants us."

That night, as she usually did, she threw the door back and spread her arms wide. "Where's my guys?" I had brought Laramie home with me from the nursery.

She gathered Laramie up in the folds of her coat and kissed his sallow face until he squirmed and turned pink. Me she dragged behind the closet door and shot her tongue into my mouth murmuring, "Thank you, thank you, thank you, for saving my life." Then the kid and I settled down with her at the kitchen table.

"This is great," she said. "What is it?"

"Obviously not too good if you can't tell."

"Beef stew! We made it," Laramie said.

"You two made this? No sir. I don't believe it. It's takeout from a fancy restaurant."

Laramie's laughter was as pure as water splashing on a ledge of slate.

"I really do not believe you made this," she said to me with a wink. "Is there something you want?" Then, sotto voce, "Because I think you're going to get it."

Laramie studied his mother, not quite understanding the sudden huskiness in her voice, the tip of tongue brushing her upper lip, but trying to.

"So what'd you do in school today?" she asked him.

"I don't know. Nothin'."

"And you, Daddy? Nothin'? You guys." She shook her head. "Well, I have good news."

Because she said it quickly, because it blew across the table and was gone, we continued our conversation. Although I played at being Daddy two nights a week; although I was often mistaken for Laramie's father by shopkeepers and placed in that role by school officials beside themselves in the presence of a man of appropriate age, a working man, taking an interest in a child, I was not Laramie's father. In his presence I watched the years I'd lost with my own boy and imagined taking Laramie down to Florida with me the next time I went to see Terry. I cared a lot for Laramie. In my way, I loved him. But every time Crystal cast me as Daddy—and I believe she did it when I wasn't around—she created expectations that could only break his heart.

"There's a party after work on Friday. For Mr. Lynch's birthday. I know. I know." Crystal deepened her voice. "He's the evil Darth Vader. But he asked you especially to come."

"Well, send my regrets."

"Can't you put politics aside? He's been very nice to me, David. He may give me a recommendation to law school."

"Johnny Lynch can be very nice when he wants something."

"Maybe you'll meet some new people. Isn't that what politicians are supposed to do? Show up and mingle?"

"I doubt anyone in his own office would vote against his candidate."

Her voice became liquid sugar. "That's not what the girls say. They've seen you in the parking lot, David. They think you're adorable."

"I'm sorry. I can't make it on Friday."

"No, of course not, that's not my day, is it? It's Judith's."

I looked at the clock, the wall, anything but the little family I could only seem to disappoint. Crystal took a second helping of stew and wiped the gravy up with stale bread. Laramie's eyes moved from one of us to the other. He barely seemed to breathe.

I was in bed pretending sleep when Crystal crept under the covers and kissed my nose. "I want you to know you're the sweetest, most wonderful boyfriend I've ever had."

"Except that I see another woman."

"That does hurt me. But I know you care about me. We have plans together. For me to go to law school. That's what you, and only you, convinced me I could do. And I believed you. I believe in myself because of you." Crystal turned on the beside lamp. She was wearing a black nylon nightgown. Crystal complained about putting on weight since she'd moved East, but if she had, it only made her breasts bigger and more attractive to me. I had no particular reaction to the small roll of flesh that swelled over her skirt waistband. Her face was round and luscious. "Look, David, you don't know where I came from. My ex didn't want Laramie. When I told him I was pregnant, he—" She stopped abruptly.

"He what?"

"He got very angry. I thought I would lose the baby."

"You never told me."

"It's behind me now, and you're the best thing that ever happened to me."

"You can't mean that."

"At least I have you three nights a week. I know where I can call you if I need you. Liam used to go off for weeks at a time. If the baby got sick, I was on my own. Sometimes he'd have wads of money, stacks of bills. But not for me."

"From what?" Dealing drugs? Gambling? Where did a guy get stacks of bills?

"I didn't ask questions. But then it would be gone as fast as it came." She yawned heavily. "You're great, David, for me and for Laramie."

"Compared to Liam."

"Compared to anyone." She yawned again. "We better do it before I fall asleep."

"We don't have to *do it*. Not if you're tired."

"But you want to, don't you?"

"You were up at five this morning. You got two kids off to school, worked a full day and then did the laundry. We can skip a night."

"You really are the best man in the world." She set the alarm and kissed me. "I'll make it up to you."

"You don't have to."

"Yes, I do." She curled into the crook of my arm and fell asleep within seconds.

The alarm rang in what seemed the middle of the night. Crystal ran off to the bathroom. I was still fumbling with the clock when she returned. "We don't have to get up for another hour."

"But you're seeing her today," Crystal said.

"So what?" The room was cold. A sharp light knifed into the room from the hallway we kept lit for Laramie. I smelled perfume and tooth-paste as she crept beneath the sheets. "You want to make love? Now?"

"I want to fuck you dry."

I struggled to get to the toilet but she pushed my shoulders back. "You have to piss, don't you?" She squeezed my balls. "You feel like you're going to burst." She knew men's bodies, the pressure of necessity and desire.

"Just stay here," she said, and began licking me, feathering my cock, lips and tongue, drawing the edge of her teeth across the shaft, giving me pleasure to the point of pain. "I'm going to come," I said, at which she tugged my balls and swallowed me down the tunnel of her throat. She threw her leg over my head and buried my face in her crotch. Smelling of piss and sex, night sweat and traces of perfume, she ground herself to the beat of a primal tune. Feeling me shudder, she scuttled off and presented her ass. "Shove it in deep," she said. I fell into her, quivering. I melted. I ran my palms up her thighs, the plane of her back, her nipples, her throat. Her mouth. She bit my fingers and we collapsed, liquid and skin, into the twisted sheets. "Do you want to do it again?" she said.

"Are you crazy?" I was gasping. Breath and strength had left my body. "Do you?"

Her face half in darkness, half light, her voice cool in spite of the sweat that glistened on her breasts and upper lip, she said: "I can't send you to her with anything left."

JOHNNY

28 Through his office window Johnny watched Crystal running out to her car in the rain—a bit of thigh showing as the wind lifted her skirt—settling herself in the driver's seat, fixing her hair in the rearview mirror. He found himself smiling. Women were all the same. As if she wouldn't have to leave the car in the same pouring rain and get mussed up before anyone saw her. He heard her try the engine, try it again and again until the starter motor screeched and she banged the steering wheel with her fist. As she struggled to open the hood, he ran out with his umbrella, blown inside out by the northeast wind. "Come inside! Come inside now!" he shouted.

Crystal hadn't heard him and jumped, startled, when he appeared behind her. "It won't start!"

"Go back inside and we'll call the garage."

"They won't come in a storm like this."

"They will if I call them. Now get under this umbrella." She resisted his grip but gave up and followed him inside. "That's all I need," he said, "you getting sick and nobody knowing how to work the damned computers."

"I have to pick up my son." She shook out her hair.

Johnny was on the phone with the garage. Whatever idiot they'd left in the office had no idea to whom he was speaking. Johnny gave him the address and hoped for the best. "Now sit down next to the radiator and dry off. The office is closed for the day. Relax."

Crystal seemed uneasy, but no more than he was, he supposed. He hadn't spent ten minutes alone with her since the day of the interview. He didn't want to be caught staring, an old man at a pretty girl. But he could enjoy a glimpse of her profile, the little turned-up nose, the lovely shadow of her earrings against her cheek. As her clothing dried, he smelled roses, probably her perfume. "Let's get you something warming to drink. Would you like that? Would you like a scotch?"

"Oh, no," she said, as if frightened. "I can't drink!"

"Tea then. I suppose I can still boil water." As Johnny lumbered around the staff kitchenette, he saw her watching the window. "We'll give the tow truck the time it takes to drink a cup of tea. If they don't show up, I'll give you a ride."

"You're very nice," she said. "Thank you. Every time it rains, my damned old car gives me trouble."

"It's hard, isn't it? My mother worked all her life," Johnny said. "But people had their families around in those days, cousins, grandmothers."

"I get help sometimes," she said. "I have a roommate."

A roommate. She was raising a child, for Christ's sake, and she lived like a stewardess. "And the boy's father?" He set down the cups and searched for the sugar, asking absently, "He doesn't live in the area?"

"Wouldn't much matter if he did," Crystal said, more amused than angry. "Liam might have been a good father, if he had ever grown up himself."

"I see that all too often, I have to say."

"But you would have liked him," she said. "He was born in Ireland."

"Where? Do you know?"

"Dublin. He had an Irish music band. They were really good. We traveled all up and down the coast in a Volkswagen bus. Going to a different coffeehouse every night and just getting by, making friends everywhere we stopped." He heard a wistful, almost songlike quality in her voice, like his own when he was reading to children. "Once in Lake Tahoe we got arrested for camping, and Liam took out his fiddle and got us off."

"Sounds like a charmer."

"Oh, you don't know the half. He sure got everything he wanted from me."

"But not a baby."

"How'd you guess? Once Laramie was born, Liam had to choose between his music and his family."

"But your boyfriend, dear, if you can bear the questions of a nosy old romantic, is there no chance of wedding bells? I see how David looks at you."

She responded with a self-mocking scowl. "Except I'm not the only one he's looking at."

Johnny expected her to turn away again, to bolt, having offered too much of herself. But she sat quietly, staring into her cup. Johnny sighed. "Two paths in a yellow wood. If he's a good man, he'll know which one to take."

"But he is," she insisted. "She just puts ideas in his head." Everyone in this office knew who *she* was.

"Dear, I've fought Judith Silver for a decade." He felt Crystal's attention. "She's the worst kind of adversary. She fights on moral grounds, tries to persuade you you're acting out of selfish motives, when she and her husband are the most corrupt couple this town has ever seen. The drug parties, the sexual display . . . Gordon Stone has an FBI file as thick as a volume of the encyclopedia. It's not hard to imagine a good man getting mixed up with her. We men are all weak. A woman like that comes along and tells us what we want to hear."

"I think it's the election," Crystal said. "He didn't know her before she asked him to run."

"Didn't he?" This was interesting. Johnny hadn't realized they'd actually recruited the boy. He'd thought David one of the pretty young people they were said to share, to pass between them in bed. But this made perfect sense. David Greene. Local hero. Angry young man. Out of town for almost fifteen years. No political history. A clean slate. He had underestimated Gordon. However slow on the uptake and soft-spoken, David was an excellent choice, far better than his own old witch. He was sorry he hadn't gotten to him first. "You see, they simply have no values, these people. David is a man who was trying to do the right thing by a woman and a child, and they lure him away from his family. I bet you don't see enough of him, do you?"

"Two nights a week. David says after the election he'll have more time."

Johnny saw the tow truck circling the parking lot. He had to work fast. "Not if he wins, believe me. Meetings every night, calls about everything from where a yellow line gets painted down Main Street to who gets to be fire chief. You see, people like Gordon and Judith could never get elected themselves . . ."

The tow truck sounded its horn. But Crystal didn't move. "Look at that," he said. "One beaten up Olds with its hood unlatched, one brand-new Ford, and the idiot can't tell which needs help. Hold on, dear." He ran outside to instruct the driver and at the same time take care of the bill.

Back inside, he continued, "Gordon Stone and his people have been waiting for a puppet for years. Once they attach their strings, they own him. Believe me, as much as he might want to, he won't have time for a family. God bless my dear wife, she would tell you I didn't."

"But David doesn't think he has a chance to win."

"That's not what I hear. People like him. The fishermen go for their man, the environmentalists for theirs. It splits the vote. I think he stands a hell of a chance. Come. Get your coat. Looks like our genius out there has your car started. What's the matter, dear?"

"Nothing. I just . . . I was hoping . . . If David heard me say this he'd kill me. I was hoping he'd lose and the thing with her would be over."

Johnny led her to the door, his hand on her shoulder. "If hope is all we've got, we haven't got much, have we?" He opened the umbrella to the rain and urged her close. She leaned into him; she didn't resist. "But if we had something that might help people see things differently, that might change the voter's mind, then . . ."

Crystal stopped in the middle of the parking lot. "Like what?"

"I have no idea, dear. You're the one who knows David. Just something that might tarnish that fresh-faced image for his own damned good. That might save him from falling permanently into the clutches of that woman. If he loses the election, he'll be of little further interest to that pair."

The following morning Crystal wrote him out a check, paying for the tow service. If anything, she seemed more reserved with him. Polite, always; efficient and helpful, but perhaps a little ashamed of what she had revealed. He couldn't blame her, and in truth he was probably lucky. He had crossed the barrier between boss and employee. He was a silly old man. He wouldn't make a fool of himself again.

At Friday noon, just after the other girls went to lunch, Crystal stepped into his office and closed the door firmly behind her. Approaching his desk, she said softly, "Mr. Lynch. I think I found something you can use." She reached into her purse.

JUDITH

Judith studied the flyer Blossom had put out, simple, vulgar and effective. The headline asked WHO BEST REPRESENTS THE PEOPLE OF SALTASH? One photo showed Birdman in a safari jacket peering through binoculars out to sea, gesturing to some unseen audience like a priggish private school science teacher. Ahab clung to the deck of a boat run aground on a sand bar, waving his arms wildly, red-nosed and demented. Judith remembered that little accident. Could happen to anybody, given the way the harbor bottom changed from season to season, but Blossom had come up with a photo. Next, Blossom with her sleeves rolled up collecting trash on Beach Improvement Day. Finally there was David—David and Gordon and herself. They were lying on a bed together, Gordon in his pajamas, his arms around David and her. A bottle of champagne stood on a bed tray as they all toasted Gordon's last birthday for the camera.

"Well, at least we look as if we're having a good time," Judith said mildly, handing the flyer back to David.

"How did they ever get hold of that picture? Natasha took it, right?"

"Of course. But she's at Cornell, and why would she give a copy to anyone? I suppose it could have been someone in the pharmacy, where the film was left. Or someone in Hyannis, where they send it to be developed. But why are you so agitated?"

Gordon was lying on the couch, eating from the coffee table, perhaps one bite to every ten of theirs. "It can't hurt you unless you act guilty."

"I don't know . . . It makes me out to be some kind of playboy."

"David, everybody sees how hard you work at landscaping and nursery." But in the car afterward with the two of them on their way to a small Shabbat service in the Universalist meeting house, Judith felt she could speak more bluntly. "What upsets you? Are you ashamed to be seen with me—in a photo or in person?"

"Of course not. I'm proud to be with you."

"We never go out together."

"Judith, where do I ever go?"

"I assume, wherever young couples with children go. To Little League games. To the movies. Out for pizza at Penia's."

"We were talking about the election."

"Yes, and you told Gordon you see the photo as an attack."

"I was talking about how Blossom got hold of it. I had a copy in my drawer—"

"Where Crystal won't see it?"

"It's not Crystal. I checked this morning, and it's still there. . . . But it makes me look like a drunken bum."

"We both know what the picture is supposed to say, or Gordon and I wouldn't be in it. So what? If there were two people in town who didn't know about us, they just learned. It seems you have two choices. Either you cut off the relationship—"

"I wouldn't do that!" His voice sounded almost panicked.

"Or you start acting proud. This town is too small to hide in. People know if you go skulking around. Believe it or not, I'm a respected person in this town, and so is Gordon."

"You're married."

"And you're my friend. Married ladies are allowed to have friends. I think you're the one who feels married, David. You act as if Crystal is real and I'm not. Because she has a child and you two play mommy and daddy go to market, mommy and daddy take their son to school. Unless you feel like an adulterer, why be ashamed?"

"I'm not ashamed of you. I never have been."

"Then act it. Gordon and I have a lot of friends. I think we can win this election—but not if you hold us back. I'm asking you to say, 'This is my life, take it or leave it.' You have to be willing to fight and you have to be willing to take the consequences."

Judith listened to herself as she lectured David. It was time to cool down. This was not the way to approach Shabbat. But she decided it was past time she took her own advice. Fight and take the consequences. Go public. Act proud.

When David addressed the Taxpayers Association in mid-week, Judith stood against a back wall with her arms folded, keeping her eyes on him, nodding when he made a good point. She had been practicing his delivery with him; his public speaking was improving. He was going door-to-door every evening, talking with a few families. His literature was being churned out, courtesy of the Greene Team, Judith Silver, Chair. She had written most of it.

Sunday at six she had a get-together for all the volunteers she had been able to line up, everyone from friends of Natasha to old clients, the "reform element," women who simply liked her. She laid out a spread in her office, chicken, vegetarian lasagna, snacks, beer and soda, food for thirty-two who had come out for David and for her. She got commitments from people to put bumper stickers on their cars and to stand on the highway Saturday mornings holding signs. She found a finance chair and two people who offered to drive older people to the polls. Judith was at David's elbow: she was the heart of his campaign now that both her crusades, to elect him and to keep him as her lover, were public. She had been told that Crystal clung to him when they went out, hung on his arm, called him Laramie's daddy. That would never be Judith's style. She simply claimed him publicly. She intended to prove herself essential. The Greene Team banner was draped on the outer wall of her office. If Johnny Lynch considered her the opposition, she would be right in his face. She wanted him to know that win or lose this election, she was not going to vanish. She wanted him thinking about her whenever he pulled something under cover of darkness; and she wanted to have the identical effect on Crystal.

DAVID

"Crystal, stop crying."

"Don't tell me what to do! I'm sick of being ordered around."

"I am not ordering you. I'm asking you to calm down so I can hear you." I assumed there'd be a price to pay for Judith's party. When Holly ran into the yard to tell me Crystal was on the telephone, so upset she could barely speak, I knew this was it. "Calm down, please. You're at work. You can't cry like this, you'll get in trouble with your boss."

"I'm in Mr. Lynch's office. He told me to use his phone. I'm in trouble. I'm being kicked out in the street with my kid. I'm going to be homeless."

"Stop right there. What's going on? Start from the beginning."

"It happened last night. I tried to call you. You weren't home."

Because of course I was with Judith and thirty-two of her loyal friends. Holly was watching me from the register, dying to lift the extension.

"When I got up this morning I found the telephone and electric bills on the kitchen table and a note from Michelle that said she wanted the money by tonight or we're out, me and Laramie. Where can we go?" Crystal was about to start crying again.

"So it's just finding the money?"

"No, she's crazy. You don't understand. The money is an excuse. She wants me out. Everything I do is wrong. She likes it well enough when I take care of her kid. And I take care of her kid a hell of a lot better than she does. I never told anyone this, but she hits Kelly Ann. When Michelle gets angry, her hands fly. That's why that little girl is so messed up."

"Please, let me get this straight. Is it or isn't it a matter of money?"

"I won't be treated this way. I won't be accused of something I didn't do."

"Accused of what?"

She sighed deeply. "She says I was playing around with her boyfriend."

"Tommy? Why would she say that?"

"I don't know. She hates me. She's crazy. Don't tell me you don't trust me either."

"I just asked. I'm trying to understand. How could she say something so ridiculous?"

"She came in late last night and he was here, okay? We were watching TV. Is that such a big deal? He was only waiting for her."

"And that's it? Just because he was waiting for her?"

"She says because the lights were off and we were sitting on the couch. Like there's a lot of furniture in her living room, right?"

"So it's all a misunderstanding? Maybe we can talk to her."

"That's what you care about, appeasing her."

"What I care about is that you and Laramie have a place to live."

"What kind of place to live is it with an ax over our heads that could fall any minute? Any time she wants she can march in and say *get out*. I don't have the money for two months' deposit on a new apartment, *if* I could find one, and a month's rent and heat and utilities and a telephone."

"I can lend it to you."

"I won't take money from you. I never take money from guys. I'd rather be on the street. That's just what she wants, the bitch." I could hear her labored breathing, her voice beginning to crack.

"Stop. You won't be on the street."

Holly was listening openly now, standing at my elbow.

"We will. Laramie and me."

"No, you won't. If Michelle throws you out, you can come to my house."

"Oh, that'll be cute. You and me and Judith."

"Judith has her own house. When I see her, I go over there."

"Always?"

"We can work it out. The two of you can move in temporarily. Until you find your own place."

"Temporarily. Of course. Judith would be upset otherwise." Although there was a bitter cast to her voice, she was noticeably calmer. The crying had stopped. A peace settled over the telephone lines like a baby suddenly falling asleep. When she spoke at last, her voice was matter-of-fact. "All right, I'll go back to work now. But you're all wrong about Mr. Lynch. He had Maria make tea, and he gave me a Valium, or I'd be too hysterical to talk. He's like a father to me, David, just like my own father was. I really do feel less scared for Laramie, now that I've settled what to do. You always make things better."

JUDITH

31 Judith felt cold through and through, although the first Wednesday in May was balmy, the air moist from the Gulf Stream, the buds on the silver maples breaking their seals. She felt cold with desperation. She had called Lynch's law office at ten yesterday and asked for Crystal, suggesting they have lunch today. She selected Mary's Tea Room because the booths offered a little privacy. She often brought clients there, and she had asked Mary to save her the booth at the end.

With Crystal moving in on David, Judith had to put a face on her and try to reach an understanding. Would it be possible? She had to make it possible. If she could reach some sort of rapport with Crystal, they would stop tugging on David like children fighting over a doll. If the situation had an end in sight, she could simply endure it. If it did not, then Crystal and she must work things out. She did not want the subterranean war they had been waging. It made her feel rotten.

She must not make Crystal think she was trying to bribe her, but at the same time she wanted Crystal to understand that she could help. Crystal was a single mother, as Yirina had been. Judith had to make the younger woman see that she was willing to be a friend. Helping raise another woman's child was a familiar role to Judith. If that's what it takes, she thought. It frightened Judith that Crystal had moved in, that David had allowed it, even though he was apologetic, even though he insisted it was an emergency measure. Judith doubted that Crystal would be in any hurry to move out. She was in residence; she was in possession. When Judith told Hannah, Hannah said, "Well, that was fun while it lasted. Wake up and smell the exhaust. He's gone now." But Judith did not want to believe that Crystal had simply taken him over.

She dressed normally, a silk shirt dress, because while she was not in court today, she had a string of clients all morning and all afternoon. Two divorces in progress, a child custody defense, a suit involving an improperly laid roof that never stopped leaking, a defense of a doctor accused by his patient's family of aiding her desire to die. The last was the most interesting case. She took it on with full fervor, because she was terribly aware of the pain of cancer and how ineffective the means to relieve that pain were. Dying took a long time. Not everyone had

Gordon's patience with the process. He claimed to find it interesting. So far, endurable.

As she walked from her office the six blocks to Mary's, she still felt cold, on a sunny day when dogs were trotting in happy packs and in the marina six different boats were waiting to be launched from winter storage. Gordon and she had talked about buying a boat after Natasha was done with her schooling. Now it would never happen.

She walked briskly, afraid she would be late, but she arrived well before Crystal. She had time to order a cup of coffee and drink it before Crystal arrived. When she saw Crystal enter, she stood and waved. She thought Crystal probably recognized her, but after all, they had never officially met. Crystal was got up in a fashion not exactly appropriate for a law office, or for that matter, lunch in this town. She was wearing western boots, a fringed leather skirt cut a little too tight with a turquoise satin blouse. Her dangling earrings were turquoise also—cheap silver, chip-glued turquoise. She wore a black leather belt with silver conchos and much perfume, one of those horrors they sprayed on hapless passersby in department stores. Judith was not sure exactly what this costume was supposed to signify, but it did serve to remind her that Crystal had spent years in Las Vegas.

They shook hands. Crystal's hands were as warm as hers were cold. Different reactions to stress? But she saw no stress in Crystal's face, only a glitter of hostility barely masked by a sweetish smile and a gush of words. "So nice to meet you finally . . . David talks so much about you. It's been really kind of you to take an interest in his campaign. I know you're so much more experienced than he is in politics and everything else. It's been a real boon to him—that you're willing to help a man not only so much younger, but I'm sure David seems very naive to someone like you."

"Someone like me? David's smart, educated. And a ball player sees quite a lot of people on their best and worst behavior."

"I mean someone older, more sophisticated. Married to a famous man. A lawyer everybody's heard of. People just keep telling me stories about what a great time you and your husband had, parties and all those . . . high times."

From the phrase and expression, she assumed the young woman had heard the story of Gordon's great marijuana bust—long before she met him. "Actually we both mostly work. My husband hasn't produced twenty books by dancing all night. I'm afraid you'll find me simply hardworking and involved in my job."

"David has told me how kind you've been to him. How grateful he is. How . . . obligated he feels to you."

She realized Crystal had gone immediately on the attack. But Mary was standing over them now. "We should order."

Crystal ordered the chef's salad. If Crystal had been a friend, Judith would have warned her that the chef's salad was a few cubes of ham and processed cheese in iceburg lettuce with a couple of canned olives. She ordered a hamburger with french fries (which would probably give her heartburn; she never ate french fries). If there had been anything palatable that was even fattier, she would have ordered that also. This was a silly war, but it was obviously war. Time to go on the offensive.

"So you come to us from Las Vegas?" She let her eyes drift over Crystal's outfit. She decided it was supposed to say S-E-X.

"I went there to be a blackjack dealer. I needed to make good money to support my son. I was running away from his father."

"I've been in Las Vegas," Judith thought it only fair to say, in reference to the dealer fairy tale. Larry, Gordon's youngest son, had gotten in trouble there and they had flown out to pay his debts and take him home. "Why were you fleeing Laramie's father?" She dropped the boy's name intentionally. If Crystal wanted to imply that David talked about her, which she doubted, two could play. Crystal waited while Mary set down the pale salad and Judith's sizzling burger. Mary made good meat and seafood dishes. She just had no interest in vegetables. "Do have some of my french fries. Mary gave me a mountain of them."

"I couldn't!"

"Watching your weight? So often it's a matter of watching it steadily rise." Judith ate her fries one at a time, smiling. "You were going to tell me about Laramie's father."

Crystal shuddered and put her hand up to her face as if feeling a bruise. "He started slapping me around when he was drinking. But after Laramie was born, it got worse. One night he beat me unconscious. The next morning I took Laramie and I left, with what I could throw in a suitcase. I left him everything we owned. I drew half the money out of our account and bought a bus ticket to Las Vegas."

Judith had had perhaps fifty battered women as clients. Why didn't she believe Crystal? She was not sure if she was being intuitive or whether she simply wanted to withhold sympathy. Her doubts made her feel guilty. "It's difficult to leave the father of your child, even if he's violent."

"It was hard. But I couldn't wait any longer. He had been hitting Laramie too. . . ." Crystal closed her eyes and sighed heavily.

"But if you had the money in the bank to leave, I don't understand why you got in trouble for bad checks?" High hard line drive to right field. It's going, going, gone.

Crystal stared, her face going blank and tight. "I don't know what you're talking about. Who told you that?"

"I have friends in Seattle," Judith invented. She could hardly say that the assistant district attorney had told her.

"Well, whatever those *friends* told you is a pack of lies. The problem was Liam kept drawing money out of the bank. He had some bad habits. I was trying to pay bills, and he never told me he'd taken money from our account. But the important thing is that I got away from him and I got Laramie away. . . . He's the treasure of my life!" Crystal's voice took on a breathless quality. She reached out and touched Judith's hand. "Is there anything like the bond of giving birth? It's the richest experience we can ever know, isn't it?"

"I've never had a child." As if you didn't bloody well know that.

"Oh! I'm so sorry." Crystal drew her hand back as if burnt. "Are you still trying? It must be a little late."

"I've never tried. I never felt the need."

Crystal's eyes were wide and pitying. "Having Laramie was the best thing in my life. Until I met David." Crystal beamed.

Judith made herself smile. She motioned to Mary. "I'll have a slice of your wonderful blueberry pie. A la mode." She'd probably fall asleep in her office from eating such a pig-out lunch, unless heartburn kept her awake, but it was a small revenge. Crystal had observed every bite of her hamburger and every french fry. "And coffee," she called after Mary. She had to stay awake this afternoon. She'd have Mattie brew her a big pot.

"I'd never be satisfied with one child," Crystal was saying in the same breathless voice. "I couldn't feel fulfilled. And I think only children are at a disadvantage."

"If you're going to law school, believe me, you don't want another baby. Not until you're established in a practice."

"I'm sure you know all about being a lawyer, but I'd never give up bringing life into the world for anything so . . . dry and dull. I see all day what a successful lawyer does. The opposite of motherhood. The opposite of being nurturing and loving."

"David thinks you're planning to go to law school."

"David is my angel, you know that? He saved me from despair. He restored my faith in men. He wants to be the father of my child."

"Does he?" Judith was coldly furious. Either David was lying all of the time to her, or Crystal was lying. Either way, it was ugly. If David had a child with this woman, she would never, never forgive him. Had she made that serious an error about David? Was he as much a liar as she suspected Crystal to be? Had she made David up, or was he trapped, manipulated? If so, how?

"More than anything else, I want to bear his child. That's how much I love him . . . David and I grew up here. I think we're fated for each other. We probably seem like a dull ordinary couple to you, but I think we'll have a good family life together. Because we really love. Don't you think that's the most important thing?"

When Mary brought the check, Judith did not volunteer to pay. She told Crystal she'd pay two thirds, since she'd eaten more, and handed Crystal the check. It took Crystal three tries to figure out her share, and then she was off by a dollar thirty-two. Judith simply made up the difference.

As she walked back, she shook her head. She knew a little about gambling because she had defended a few gamblers. Dealers in casinos were in the direct line of fire. Besides dealing, they sold chips, paid off winners, and collected from losers. Every move they made was watched by the floorwalker, the pit boss, the casino manager. They had to be fast and cool as ice. They had to do sums in their head. Crystal would never have made it onto the floor of the smallest and cheesiest establishment. It was a story, a romance. Crystal the battered woman, Crystal the dealer. Judith had no idea what it all meant. Was Crystal covering up something? Or nothing? Did Crystal herself know the difference? Perhaps she simply wanted to make herself interesting to whoever was before her. Perhaps she needed to make a more compelling story of her life.

Whatever Crystal was or wasn't, there was one truth evident: she was an enemy. She was trouble.

DAVID

32 Getting out of my truck to help Crystal load her things, I'd expected an icy reception from her roommate, but Crystal and Michelle were laughing together. Michelle couldn't seem to help her enough. "Anytime you want me to take Laramie," she said.

Crystal gathered Michelle's little girl into her arms: "Now you *know* I'm not leaving you. I'm just moving in with David not two miles from here."

In fact things proceeded as they had before: except that whenever I came home, Crystal was in my living room, my kitchen, my bathtub, my bed. Crystal found curtains for the second bedroom and the kitchen windows. She covered the old couch with an Indian madras spread. The women in her office gave us a cast-iron frying pan and a set of plates, a bedside lamp, and a coffee table. Although I didn't want her to start paying rent, she insisted. She found an old student's desk in the garage, stripped it and painted it yellow. The more she invested in the house, the more it became hers. I had not asked how long she might be here. I could never ask "the question" in front of Laramie, although he seemed to be waiting for it. Whenever things got quiet between his mother and me, he inched closer or took a seat in a corner, drawing his knees to his chest. Nor did Crystal offer an answer when we were alone. The night she moved in, while I ran out to Penia's for pizza, she started scrubbing the kitchen floor with steel wool. The next night after work, she began on the bathroom, and the next night shampooed the carpet. "David, is there something you wanted to ask me?" she said when she noticed me watching her.

Caught off guard, I muttered, "No. I mean, yes. You don't have to do all this." Or something like that. Anything else just felt plain cruel.

Soon after they moved in, Crystal and Laramie started arguing. Sometimes it was about getting up in the morning or finishing his toast or cleaning up his stuff, it didn't matter. The kind of terrible rows that used to go on between Crystal and Kelly Ann became a commonplace occurrence in our house. I started spending more time with the boy, making him breakfast, getting him off to school, reading his books together.

One day I heard Crystal shriek from the bathroom. Laramie started crying soon after. Crystal's frustration was humiliating and sharp. "What is this? You're going to be eight years old. You can't do this!"

I arrived to find Laramie in tears, his pants and underwear swaddling his shoes. "Look at this!" Crystal stood over a small puddle of urine in front of the toilet bowl.

"It just happens," Laramie said. "I can't help it."

"Well, you better help it, young man. Or we're going to be asked to leave this house, and you know what I mean."

A ripple of guilt tore through my gut. Did I have that kind of power? "Crystal, please," I said. "Leave us alone for a minute."

"You don't have to do this, David. He's old enough to know better."

"Please," I said, and ushered her out. Laramie stood before me with his eyes down, arms folded. I had not seen my own boy naked since he was three years old. I had never taught him anything about his body. And who was going to teach this kid if not for me? "Laramie, what's going on?"

"Sometimes when I sit down on the toilet, it just happens." Fear and shame clotted his voice. "The pee goes all over the floor."

"You know what you have to do? This happened to me when I was a kid."

"It did?"

"Happens to all little boys. You have to hold your penis down so the pee goes into the water, instead of between the bowl and the seat." I didn't touch him; he wasn't mine, after all, but I illustrated what I meant with my hand and he understood. Nothing that I'd ever done before had made me feel as much like a father.

Most nights after work, I attended a meeting, spoke to some group or stood outside the post office during its last hour before closing to shake hands. Half the people I spoke to sought me out with an ax to grind. Some said they admired my drive. "I don't know you from Adam," an old man told me. "But I'm voting for you because you believe in yourself. You must, you're out here every damned night." He didn't realize he was casting his ballot for a guy who was putting off going home.

Thursday nights I had a standing date with Judith, but the week before, the week Crystal moved in, Judith had to take Gordon into the Dana Farber clinic. I was nervous about the following Thursday date that Wednesday night when I took the "family" out to the movies and then to the supermarket. "You okay?" Crystal kept asking me, stroking my thigh in the dark theater, placing her hand on top of mine as I pushed the grocery cart. We talked about getting shelves and painting the living room. Crystal didn't mention my seeing Judith. As we drove back, Laramie asked if he could get a dog, mother and son waiting in reverent silence for me to decide the fate of their lives. It was half past nine when we got home. Another hour passed before we got the food put away and Laramie to sleep. Still, we made love that night. Crystal made love to me every night that week, but Thursday morning she set the alarm a half hour earlier than usual. When she came back to bed, she took me in her mouth. "Shove him all the way in. All the way down my throat."

As Crystal showered, I realized that one difference between Crystal and Judith, between Crystal and any woman I had ever known, was that sex for her had little to do with her own pleasure. She was glad to have an orgasm and sometimes seemed surprised; but her satisfaction derived not from the intensity of her pleasure but mine. I felt no small amount of shame sometimes. I knew, despite her cries of delight, her grunting in my ear, "You stud! Your cock is God!" that the excitement was an act, a sideshow, and that I was the audience. Yet I could not stop myself. Use me, she said, use me, and I did.

When she stepped out of the shower and was toweling her hair dry, she said, "I forgot to tell you, Tommy's coming over with some stuff I forgot at Michelle's."

"When?"

"Tonight. When you're at Judith's."

"Why?"

"I told you. I forgot something. The exercise bike I bought at the flea market."

"I could have picked it up."

"I didn't want to ask you. You've done so much."

"But why tonight?"

"That's when he said he could do it. You won't be here. I'll be all by myself. You said I should make some friends. I thought it would take some pressure off you if I didn't always depend on you. What's the matter? You're going to be doing what you want to. You're going to be with another friend."

A friend? I made love to Judith. What did that say about Crystal and Tommy? What *had* Michelle walked in on that night? Why had they been on the couch in the dark together? There were lights in that room. There were two other chairs. Did she think that because I slept with Judith that she had the right to sleep with Tommy? Did Tommy think he could walk into my house when I wasn't here and make love to the woman I was living with? I left for work that morning with raw intestines and my head on fire. I couldn't accuse her, not when she knew exactly where I would be and what I would be doing. It was a silent threat: be with Judith and I'll be with someone too.

The following night was Friday and Crystal was waiting for me at the door. She ushered me into the kitchen. "Do you like it?" So much seemed to depend on my answer.

"Of course!"

"It's all here, right?" The table was covered with an old lace cloth instead of the usual vinyl. "I did the whole thing like the book said. I got it all, I think."

"I helped with the bread."

"Oh, I know you did, Laramie," I said. "It's beautiful." He was wearing a dress shirt and a Bruins cap. My sister had lent Crystal *The Complete Book of Jewish Observance*. Crystal, doing her best to create a Shabbat meal, had fashioned candle holders from upturned egg cups and baked a braided bread. "They didn't have poppy seeds. Is sesame all right?"

"It's beautiful," I said. "Thank you."

She had located—probably from the back of my sister's liquor cabinet—a bottle of cherry wine labeled Kosher for Passover. She and Laramie stood at something like attention as I recited the blessings. She wore a silk kerchief and a white Greek fisherman's shirt with balloon sleeves. She had roasted a chicken, and instead of the potato kugel in the "Suggested Menus" chapter, served macaroni and cheese. They began to eat only after I did (Laramie watching for the nod from his mother), and sat in dead formal silence, waiting for something to happen. I had never been one to initiate dinner table conversation. Moreover, my father had led the few ritual dinners we had, and after his death, Marty did it. When I shared Shabbat with Judith, she was the source of prayer and song, shadowy memories for me. The truth is, I didn't know much about being a Jew or how to teach anyone else.

Crystal poured me another glass of cherry wine, half cabernet sauvignon, half Robitussen. "Eat slowly," Crystal reminded Laramie. "I know it's not as good as *she* makes it but—"

"It's wonderful," I said automatically. "It's very good. Don't put yourself down."

"—but it's my first time. I wasn't putting myself down. Did you have a good night last night?"

"What do you mean?"

"I haven't seen you since yesterday morning. I just asked if you had a good night."

In fact it had not been good. The question I could not bring up to Crystal was the first thing Judith asked. How long is she going to be there, David? I said I didn't know. Why? she asked. Why can't you set a date, tell Crystal she has two weeks to find a place? That's a little stiff, I said. All right, two months, David, but make a deadline. How long am I supposed to go on like this? You live with her now. So what? I said, you live with your husband. So you see her five nights a week and I see you two, Judith said. So I'm involved with a man whose house is off limits to me. So you're not even with me when you are here.

Because all I could think about was Crystal and Tommy. I had driven past my house on the way to Judith's at seven. Tommy's truck was not there. Which meant he could have come and gone—or that he wasn't coming until after dark.

"Judith and I mostly dealt with the election," I said. "It was business."

She swept crumbs from the table into her palm. "What kind?"

I didn't want Crystal to be jealous of Judith and me, but the fact that she did not show the slightest concern seemed to prove she had gotten even. "Strategy stuff," I said grudgingly. "We decided to send out a last campaign letter to arrive in the voters' mailboxes the morning of the election."

That night I wanted her with a fierceness fueled by pure anxiety. Everything I'd felt a hundred times seemed new: the tickle of her hair as it lay on my inner thigh; her nipples dangling above my lips. Her breath in my ear made me shiver. I came the first time just kissing and again inside her.

We lay together afterwards in a cold sweat, barely able to move. Sex had left us more wounded than satisfied, more exhausted than content. I listened to her breathing as she certainly listened to mine. Neither of us could sleep. "You want me out of here, don't you?" Crystal said in the dark.

"It's just that I'm used to living by myself."

"Tell me the truth. You think I can't feel it? Nothing I do can make you want us. If I wash the floor, you just think I'm doing it so I can stay here. If I try to make the kind of ritual you like, it doesn't compare to the way she does it."

"I never said that."

"I can feel it. You're mad at me all the time." I reached for her and she pulled away. "Do you think I want to impose on you? It's just so hard for me, David. You don't know how much it costs to have a kid."

"I told you I'd help you. I mean it."

"I don't want your money. If you want us out, okay, just say it. If it wasn't for Laramie I wouldn't even be here. His father doesn't help. He never sends anything. Do you know how hard that is? Laramie thinks nobody loves him. I don't want him to grow up like that."

"You're a good mother, Crystal. There's none better."

"I've made such a lousy life for him."

"No, you haven't. He's a good, beautiful kid."

"He really loves you, David."

"And I love him."

She was suddenly still. "You do? You mean that? I don't care how you feel about me. But if you could care for him. He can't take being kicked again and again."

"Nobody's going to hurt him or you."

"We'll move as soon as I get the money together. I promise. I want to pay off my debts. And then I'll work on saving enough to rent a house. I won't be a burden to you."

"You're not a burden." What else could I say? I had the sense if I ever said flat out, *I do wish you would move, I feel crowded out of my own house,* she would utterly collapse. I had to go gently around her. "I know how hard you work to please me. I know I'm not easy. Don't cry, Crystal. You can stay as long as you need to. Why are you crying?"

"I wanted to hear you say that."

DAVID

33 The only campaign weapon we had left was our letter, secretly typed, copied, stamped and, by arrangement with the postmaster, delivered in time for voters to find it in their boxes the morning of the election. Gordon suspected that people had tuned out the signs and forgotten the issues. They were tired of the election and might not bother to vote. We needed to goose them, he said, at exactly the right time and above all with a light hand. Gordon had three photos of me taken, each one recalling those in Blossom's letter of attack. Under a photograph of me in a pea coat, looking something like Ahab, was the caption: "a sobering choice." Underscoring me in a Birdmanlike safari shirt, a pair of binoculars around my neck, were the words, "Looking to the future of Saltash." Under a picture of me on the beach holding a garbage bag, just as Blossom had posed, were the block letters: "He doesn't have to talk trash." In place of the photo of me and Gordon and Judith, there was a picture of Blossom and Johnny Lynch, above the caption: "David Greene is his own boss."

But upon delivery at exactly five P.M. the night before the election, we were told by the postmaster that Blossom had sent out a second letter at the same time as ours, unheard of in Saltash politics. Gordon's face was all furrows; lips, cheeks, and brow pinched together in a ruminative grin. "Looks like we have ourselves a mole."

"The voters will get two letters and throw away both," I said. "We're finished."

"Maybe. We'll know tomorrow morning."

"The polls don't close until seven."

"We'll do exit polls."

"In Saltash?"

"You'll see."

Meeting that night with our committee, Gordon looked sharp despite his pallor and weakness, like a general on the eve of battle. His gaze, sometimes prone to wander off, was fixed on the registered voters street listing, a pencil steady in his hand. We would have poll watchers keeping track of who had yet to vote, telephone volunteers to remind them and a driver for those who couldn't drive themselves. More than once Judith urged Gordon to rest. He refused more rudely each time.

Gordon's exit poll worked this way: on election morning, the earlier the better, each candidate staked out a corner where the voters had to pass on their way out of the polls. My job was to wave furiously at each and every car. According to Gordon, their vote was apparent on their faces. Those who would not look at you had not voted for you. They were embarrassed. Those who gave you an enthusiastic wave had certainly been in your corner; and a thumb up and a toot of the horn meant they liked you enough to tell their friends. A middle finger in your face didn't matter. The crude ones didn't bother to vote. A middle finger slyly directed at your opposition, however, was good, because it meant they not only liked you and had probably enlisted their friends to the cause, but had some dirt on the other candidate they were spreading.

At six-forty A.M., I claimed the northeast corner in front of Town Hall, beating the opening of the polls by fifteen minutes and the other candidates by an hour. Blossom was next, her mouth twisted into a plastic smile. For the first two hours we were even in the thumbs-and-toot department but I had gotten more enthusiastic waves. At around ten I caught a middle finger and three no-looks in a row and tried to shrug it off. By noon, when Judith stopped to wish me luck, I was waving my sign and enjoying myself. What the hell. It was lunchtime; seven hours till the polls closed. But right behind Judith's Jeep, Crystal pulled up in her Olds. She approached me with a brown bag lunch, just as Judith had. Standing there between them I couldn't think of a single word to say.

"We're going to kick ass!" Crystal said.

"It's looking good," Judith said, nose-to-nose with Crystal.

"People in my office are all coming out!"

Judith smirked. "To vote for Blossom?"

My face was sunburned and desiccated. My lips were parched from calling out to cars. "You've been out since dawn, poor baby," Crystal said. "As soon as you get home, I'm going to give you a hot meal and a bath."

"He can eat at the victory party," Judith said.

"Victory?" I said through a smile as tight as clenched teeth. "Don't jinx me."

"What party?" Crystal stared from Judith to me and back at Judith.

"At my office," Judith said. "There'll be a lovely buffet. We're having David's supporters over to wait for the results."

"You didn't tell me." Crystal turned to me, her eyes enormous.

"I didn't know about child care. I thought it would be a late night for Laramie."

"Too late to see his father win an election? Are you coming home first?" Crystal said.

"I, uh, don't know if I have time."

"Do you want to come to the party, Crystal?" I knew Crystal was the last person Judith wanted to invite, but she was too polite not to ask her. "I'm sure there'll be people you know."

"Sure," Crystal said, backing away, the glint of broken glass in her eyes. "Maybe I'll do that."

They count the votes one by one in Saltash, reading the names from a paper ballot and shouting them out in an open hall. I swung by Town Hall at nine, when the poll counters were breaking for dinner. The town clerk said there had been a near-record turnout and they wouldn't be finished for hours.

I knew I should go home to change and shower, to touch base with Laramie, but if my time belonged to anyone tonight, it was Judith and Gordon. In spite of my tangled sex life, my disappearances and indecision, they wished me well. In ways that surprised me, I was becoming like them. Small things surfaced, like a taste for meat cooked rare instead of overdone, a liking for vegetables as long as they weren't boiled, a belief that olive oil and garlic were part of a good meal. I'd begun to read, for the first time in my life enjoying books—a memoir about Tip O'Neill that Judith had given me. I was thinking differently too, looking at situations in a way Gordon had taught me, not dwelling on how they affected me so much as asking who stood to lose and who to gain. Judith and Gordon had become a part of me and felt, more than friends, like family. What I was with them was better than what I had been or could be without them. With them, I grew.

Mary, from Mary's Tea Room, and her daughter Jo in white shirts and cummerbunds were setting up platters of cold cuts and tubs of shrimp salad in Judith's office. One of the oystermen was shucking oysters and clams on a folding table. The bar was set up by the windows overlooking the harbor. When I walked in, about twenty people were watching the last bright pink light squeezed between clouds and the horizon. Judith's secretary Mattie put a drink in my hand. She was off to take care of somebody else before I could thank her. People pressed close. How did I feel? Did I think we had taken it? I hadn't hugged or shaken hands with so many people since the day I left town for the Cubs.

Judith made her entrance in a red crepe dress, devastating but simple, slit along the side with a U-neck just low enough to show the slightest hint of décolleté. Between her breasts she wore a heavy silver necklace; her earrings were discs of hammered silver. She had changed for the party but also for me. Our eyes met and did not let go. "I called the town clerk. I couldn't wait," she said between gritted teeth. "They're only three-quarters counted." Later, over the dancing, she shouted, "David! I just got word. They'll be finished by eleven."

The music was a mix of sixties rock and big band swing. Mattie was doing a lindy with the passionate plumber, placing her palm over her bosom to cover it whenever she did a dip backwards. The Birdman, with no party of his own, was chewing Gordon's ear off. If Gordon hadn't looked tired during the last week of the campaign, he did now. Judith got him into a comfortable chair. Stumpy Squeer cleared himself a corner of the buffet table; a fork in one hand, a beer in the other, he looked alternately at each as if unable to choose which to place in his mouth. Twice Natasha called from school, and twice Judith told her that they were still counting ballots. Tommy had come in (without Michelle) and was hunched over the bar. Judith looked worried about the election results, about me, about her guests' wine sloshing over the Xerox machine.

At five to eleven I was summoned to the telephone. "Hello, David," a woman said somberly. "It is my sworn duty as clerk of the Town of Saltash to call each of the candidates in descending order of the number of votes they received. . . ." As I waited, I realized the music had stopped. A crowd of perspiring bodies had formed a horseshoe around me. For all that I'd convinced myself I didn't want to run, blood beat against my temples like a rubber mallet. "And I'm calling you first."

"That means I won?"

The cheer was so loud I didn't hear her response. My knees threatened to give. Had Gordon not been the first to shake my hand, had a hundred people not lined up to wish me well, I might have run to Judith's arms. I might have rushed her upstairs to the loft and knelt in front of her to press my cheek to her belly. I wanted to undress her slowly and thank her in the dark. She had given me much more than help; she had given me a new vision of myself, proven to me I could win again. "Thank you so much, thank you," I said, to anyone and everyone, fighting my way to Judith, drawing her into a corner.

"I knew you could do it! I knew you could!" She pressed her lips to my cheek, demurely, for Gordon was here and she would never embarrass him. "My friends!" Suddenly she was addressing everyone in the room. "I know all of you are as proud as I am. Not only of David," she linked her arm tightly in mine, for all to see, "but of yourselves. For what we've accomplished. David Greene is the rallying point for a new kind of politics, an era of open, accessible, democratic government in the life of this town." Over the applause she said only to me, "You came through. You stuck with it." I could barely hear her. "I'm so proud of you."

"Judith, I want you."

Through a smile, just beneath the noise of the crowd, she said, "Can you stay with me tonight? Can you come back to the house?"

"Yes, yes," I said. "Why not?" But followed the doubt in her eyes to the crowd in front of me, parting for a woman in a fringed western skirt and satin blouse, with tears running into her smile and a little boy in pajamas in her arms.

Crystal spoke as if there was a period at the end of every word. "We. Are. So. Proud. Of you. Tell him, Laramie."

"I love you, Daddy!" Laramie jumped into my arms. There was nothing I could do but catch him as the crowd stepped back and sighed. A flashbulb popped. Judith was gone.

The music began again. A new line formed at the buffet table. Cars streamed into the parking lot. Word had gotten out. Even Holly came, leading my mother in her royal-blue suit. The forces of good had won. A new day was dawning in Saltash. I swung around, searching for Judith. Laramie spotted the desserts and asked for a piece of chocolate cake. I lowered him into Crystal's arms.

Judith was not looking for me. She was standing behind Gordon, massaging his shoulders as he held forth in a circle of friends.

"I lost you," I said. "In the crowd."

She smiled coldly. She could hardly say what was on her mind. She could hardly ask, Why, David? Why did you do this to yourself? Why did you sink so deeply, so unnecessarily? Why couldn't you trust me and Gordon? Why couldn't you give us a chance? "Yes, it's gotten very crowded in here."

"Could I see you tomorrow?"

"Tomorrow." For a moment I was sure she'd say no. She seemed taller, harder. There was no trace of emotion on her face. "Yes. That would be a good idea. Call my office. We have a great deal to talk about."

People touched my shoulder. They grabbed my hand. One man said, "You must be exhausted, son. You look ready to keel over."

Crystal had come to stand beside me again, pressed into me as she held Laramie upright. He was falling asleep on his feet.

My mother studied my face. "I thought you'd be happy now that you've won? Aren't you happy?"

"Sure, Mom. Just a little tired, that's all."

"You look as if you're ready to kill somebody, doesn't he, Holly?" She had no idea who. Or why.

JUDITH

The morning after the election, Gordon slept until ten. Judith worked at the kitchen table, hoping to have breakfast with him before she took off. He came out grinning with pride after a very personal victory over Johnny Lynch. But he knew what was on her mind. He said, "Look, you don't understand because you aren't susceptible in the same way. You're divinely pragmatic, sane and sensible. But I wasn't. I was as stupid as David with some women I got involved with."

Judith was forcing herself not to pace. It was not fair to Gordon to dump her grief on him. "Never that stupid. She's one of the most blatant manipulators I've ever encountered. I've met murderers I trusted more."

"Judith, isn't it possible she's just desperate? A woman with a family that's apparently of no use to her, a kid to raise alone. Little training or education. The boy's father doesn't help her. She's in that old situation of women, where she needs a man to support her. It's unfortunate for us she picked David."

He was right, of course, about Crystal's desperation, but that didn't excuse David. "But he picked her too! He could have refused to allow her to move in. He never had to get involved in the first place!"

"Remember the second Mrs. Stone? Beverly, now Caldwell. Beverly eats gold. Her proper environment is pure money. She can't breathe without it. Yet it took me ten years and two children to figure out I could never satisfy her. And to bruise my ego further, while I was used to being now and then unfaithful, I was not accustomed to having it done to me. She had an affair with her therapist. She had an affair with Larry's orthodontist. Believe me, I feel for David. I understand. That bimbo had me eaten up with jealousy."

"You call Beverly a bimbo, but you invite her here every summer."

"She was my wife, Judith. She's the mother of two of my children. I have an obligation to get on with her. Besides, I can enjoy her now that I don't have to support her. You have to admit, she can be funny. She knows how to enjoy herself. Dying puts a lot of things into perspective, including exes."

"She drinks like a fish."

"I used to, my Judith. I used to do the same." Gordon sighed, collaps-ing on the couch. Half an hour later he returned to bed. Every day he had managed to get up, but now that David's campaign was over, he seemed empty. He was supposed to be revising one of his most fa-mous books: *The Sociology of Fantasy: Americans Who Want to Be Some-body Else*. Over the past months, he had made scant progress. She wished she could provide him with an assistant who would keep him interested.

Thursday, Judith was glad her office was air-conditioned. The tem-perature had risen twenty-five degrees since yesterday. As suddenly as if the heat had hatched them, tourists were everywhere, driving too fast or too slow on every road, standing in clumps staring at buildings as if the town were a museum. She had a court date tomorrow, and the tides were not cooperative, so she was staying in her office. She expected David, but she was feeling anxiety instead of pleasant anticipation. She ran over her memos, her notes and her brief while she waited. The leak-ing roof case was finally coming up.

Mattie had left for the day. Judith rubbed her temples. A year ago the thought that she could love a man besides Gordon had appeared ab-surd. She simply did not look at other men as sexual or romantic ob-jects. Gordon had primed her for experiencing a possible attraction, but until David, none had occurred. Then it had happened quickly, without her willing it or even becoming aware until it was there, full grown, in the middle of her consciousness. She had not quite realized until one night in her office when they were sitting before her gas fire discussing his running for selectman, that she was going to become involved with him. She had not considered the possibility. She was used to men look-ing at her as David had, with evident attraction, but in fourteen years she had not responded.

She wondered sometimes if she had not plunged into this out of her habit of pleasing Gordon. She knew he was worried about his ultimate creation, his menagerie of buildings, as Natasha worried about the ani-mals she had brought home and who now lived with them, cared for by Judith. They were both terrified she would move away.

Now she considered herself a fool. She had fallen hard, seriously, passionately, for a man who seemed to prefer a coarse and manipulative woman—younger, yes, a liar. Who had grown up here. Who had a child for whom David seemed to care a great deal. All those points Judith had gone over with Hannah, with Barbara, with Natasha, and, in a more re-strained way, with Gordon. She had found herself distracted in court last week when she should have been paying close attention to a hostile witness's testimony. She had not been so sloppy and absorbed in something irrelevant to a case since Gordon had been diagnosed with cancer. Her intense focus was her best weapon and she had almost lost it. She owed her clients a housecleaning.

David stood in the parking lot, looking weary and uncertain. He could not guess she was observing him. He grimaced, almost a wince, and then came slowly toward the building. Did he dread seeing her? Did he guess how estranged she felt? More likely the latter. He was observant and smart about people; mostly, that is. He had no smarts about Crystal.

She offered him coffee. They sat facing each other. She needed the distance. They spoke for a few minutes about the election. However important that had felt twenty-four hours before, it did not seem to be foremost on either of their minds. "David, don't you find it a little embarrassing to have Laramie, as sweet as he seems to be, call you Daddy? He has a real father, doesn't he?"

"He was abusive. Violent. Maybe dealing drugs . . . I've never told Laramie to call me Daddy. Crystal tells him to. I can't hurt him by telling him not to. I can't, Judith."

"Do you intend to be his father?"

David shrugged, running his hands roughly through his dark coarse hair. He was darkly tanned. His eyes seemed lighter than ever, chips of something luminous and rare. "I don't know what to do."

"Are you going to marry her?"

He gripped the sides of his chair. "No, but what am I supposed to do? I feel trapped. She had no place to go. Laramie has to have a home."

"David, she has a job. She ought to be getting child support from the boy's father. Do you want me to check if Massachusetts has a reciprocal agreement with Washington? I would pursue this for her if you want me to."

"I should try calling him," David said dispiritedly.

She wanted to shake him. He seemed flaccid, without will. "I ask you again, do you want to marry her? You seem bound on that road."

"I can't hurt the boy, Judith."

"Do you think you'd feel this guilty about a boy you met twelve weeks ago if you saw your son on a more regular basis? If you felt truly involved with Terry?"

"I can't deal with that many 'ifs.' Terry's my son, and the more I'm around Laramie, the bigger hole I feel in my life, hardly seeing him. . . ." He shook his head as if he had no hope.

"How long do you intend for her to live with you?"

"Just until she finds a decent place."

"Is she looking?"

"Is this your best courtroom manner?" He tried a grin. It didn't come off.

"I use the tools I have at hand to come at the truth, David." She forced herself to lean back in her chair. "I assume your lack of answer means she is not looking. So you plan to live with her until death do you part?"

"I read the real estate ads to her every week."

"David, we can barely see each other. When we do, I never know when she is going to have the boy call or charge in herself. We can't be together in your place. You're always nervous with me now. If you want to go on seeing me, give her a real honest deadline."

"I'll try to talk to her again. I'll do something. I promise."

"Are you using condoms with her?"

"This is not something I want to talk about. Besides, she's on the pill."

"She told me she intends to have another baby with you. And that you want to have one with her. Those are her plans. Not law school."

He looked as if she had slapped him hard. With a sharp intake of breath, he sat in silence for several moments. "You misunderstood her."

"Not possible. She said she wanted to have your baby. And you wanted to father a child with her. I am quoting."

"I never said that. She never asked me. No, I don't want her to have a child with me. That's all I need!"

"It is one hell of a lot more than I need, David." She folded her arms tight across her chest. "I've told you before, and I meant it, that I would help you with getting a better situation with your son. You need an arrangement where Terry spends part of every year with you here, maybe a month in the summer, or you'll never have a genuine relationship with him. If you really want a child, I would never rule out that possibility. More and more women my age have babies. But not while Gordon's alive. If you want our relationship to continue as more than political allies and somewhat distant friends, then you will change your life. You will get her out of your house or at least begin serious preparations for that happening. And you will straighten things out with her about whether or not the two of you are going to make a baby. Am I getting through?"

"Loud and clear."

"Good, because, David, I mean it all. I really mean it."

DAVID

35 I found Liam's telephone number in Crystal's address book. I copied it while she was sleeping. I did not want to call him but I had no choice. I was not Laramie's father. I loved him but I did not want to live with his mother. I hated feeling that the choice was her becoming homeless or becoming my wife. Everything had moved too fast. It was Judith who said, "Do you realize you're living with a woman and child you only met twelve weeks ago?"

I was going to ask Liam to take some responsibility for his son, to cough up some child support. Fifty dollars a week could go a long way out here, could mean Crystal finding a decent place of her own. If Laramie knew his dad was thinking about him, even enough to write a check once a month, it might give him a little confidence. In Crystal's photograph album, Liam was a slender black-haired Irishman with a clenched smile and an icy stare. He was wearing black slacks, a white shirt, with his feet propped up, drinking a beer. I carried Liam's picture in my mind as I carried his telephone number in my wallet. I enacted threats. Attempts to reason. Warm stories about his son. I don't know how many times I sat behind the wheel of my truck rehearsing. I decided finally that calling him would do no good. Then, one day at work, I picked up the phone and dialed simply because I was afraid to. It was Saturday, one in the afternoon here, ten on the West Coast.

Crystal talked about Liam the way some 'Nam vets remembered the war. With a trembling bitterness, her eyes glazed over in anger and pain. He hit her when she was pregnant and wouldn't look at his child. Finally, I didn't see any point to a soft approach. I wasn't the law, but neither was Laramie just some unpaid debt.

"Hello?" It was not a man's voice. It sounded like a little girl.

"Who's this?" I asked, wondering if his number had changed.

"I'm Molly! It's me . . . Is this Uncle Mike?"

"Is Liam there?"

"Daddy!" she yelled. "Daddy and Sean are washing the car."

"Could you get him please? I'm calling long distance."

"Okay . . ." She let the phone fall with a clatter and I could hear running steps. I could hear some kind of Irish music playing and some appliance running—a mixer? a blender? It stopped. A woman's voice called something. I waited and waited. I was ready to hang up when a man picked up the receiver. "Uncle Mike? Is that yourself, back home safe and sound?"

"No, this is David Greene calling from Massachusetts. I'm a friend of Crystal Sinclair." She had once mentioned that he had not lost his accent. What she hadn't said was that there was music in it, a kind of whimsical, almost poetic rhythm. But as soon as I announced my connection to Crystal, the music turned to sarcasm. "A friend, you say? That kind of woman doesn't have men friends. So you're screwing the little lady, am I right? She's your problem now."

"That may be. But the boy is yours."

"Christ, man, that's a laugh. How do I know he's mine? I wasn't her only one. You should know that by now."

"I think he's yours, Liam. I think you couldn't pass a blood test to prove he wasn't and you know it."

I was bluffing. I didn't know a thing about blood testing, less how you went about forcing him to take one. Nor had Crystal mentioned other boyfriends. I heard a shuffling on the other end of the line and half expected the receiver to slam down on my ear, when Liam let out a long mournful breath. "I told her I'd pay for her not to have it. I begged her not to. I got down on my knees and pleaded. But she was always pushing. First she moved in with some cock and bull excuse. Then she got herself pregnant."

"I don't think she *got herself* pregnant."

"Think what you goddamn want. I kept telling her I didn't want a child with her. I liked to be with her, sure, but not after she did that. Not after she tricked me, told me she was safe and to mind me business then went and got knocked up."

"Look, there's a child. Laramie's yours and he's a good boy."

"Then you raise him. Because if you think I'm sending a dime so you two can live off me, you're wrong. Let me tell you, if I were you I wouldn't be spending me time hounding some poor bloody waiter, I'd be thinking hard about saving me own ass."

"How can you pretend you don't owe anything to your own son?"

"I got two other sons that I know are mine. And my little daughter. My wife works in a hospital. I kill myself lunches and dinners six days a week and we just squeak by. I'm a family man, Greene or whoever you are. I never asked her to have a baby. I begged her not to. If I was a rich man, I'd send her a whopping big check and tell her to go fuck herself— not that she'll ever have to. But I don't have an extra buck to buy a lottery ticket—you get the picture?"

"You know, we could take this to court."

"If I hear you doing that, I'll take hold of me family and move back to

Dublin. I have over two dozen relatives there. Listen, I screwed her maybe twenty times. I moved out and left her me damned apartment. What else could I do? But I won't talk with her and I won't let her near me wife and me kids. She's poison. Now she's your poison. Sure, and she's not a bit of mine, thank the saints and angels on me knees. And yes, me good wife does know about her, so don't be trying to blackmail me about that sad old mess." And then he did hang up.

DAVID

The wheels of government don't stop long enough for a new official to learn. Elected on Tuesday, you vote on Thursday—on an issue as routine as a business license or important as a man's career. I spent the first day just hanging around Town Hall, trying to read more than I could digest in a year and convince the secretaries I wasn't some clock-watching reformer out to make their lives miserable. The last time I was in this building, I'd stood nervously beside the town manager's desk. Now he ushered me into his office and offered me a padded leather chair. Through the window onto Main Street, I watched the regulars going in and out of the Binnacle, and the Compton kid on his bicycle, a one-armed teenage moron dodging delivery trucks to impress his friends. The town manager was talking policy. "I'm sure you're concerned about our efforts to keep the tax rate steady."

I nodded, lips tight, the way Georgie had taught me twenty years ago: Don't let anyone know what you don't understand. Keep your mouth shut.

"But of course, next year we face a property tax reval."

Whatever the fuck that meant.

He glanced at the clock over my shoulder. "Is there anything in particular you were curious about, Selectman Greene?" Meaning: What kind of an ax is this guy out to grind?

I shrugged. "Not really. Just trying to get the lay of the land."

"Well, then." He needn't waste his time.

"Maybe, if it's not an inconvenience . . . I was wondering if I could take a look at your performance evaluations for each department."

"That could take a while."

"I took off work today."

"What is this for, exactly?"

"My information. Exactly. According to the charter of this town you serve at the pleasure of the Board of Selectmen. I was just elected one."

"Yes, of course. I didn't mean to imply you weren't entitled."

"Glad to hear it."

"I just want you to understand that everything we do is subject to state law. You can't get elected one day and expect me to let good people go the next."

"I'm not talking about good people." I wondered if I was going to have trouble with this guy. He was already having trouble with me.

"Good or bad, Selectman, there's a chain of command that must be followed in this town."

"And we all know who's on top, don't we?"

"Yes, and it can't change overnight."

"I've got three years," I said. "How long do you expect to stay around?"

"Please wait here." The town manager left me alone in his office while he talked with his secretary outside. He came back with an armload of files, explaining, "This isn't all of what you want. But we're looking. I don't want to get off on the wrong foot here. I just want you to understand that the town can get into a great deal of legal trouble unless every case is handled carefully. Regardless of performance, each employee has legal rights."

"I was wondering. Is it true Abel Smalley and Donkey Sparks are up for reappointment?"

"Chief Smalley has done a good job for many years. He may not be up on his computer technology and grant writing, but his people skills are a real asset in a town like this."

"And Donkey Sparks?"

The town manager knew all about my problems with Donkey Sparks. But he didn't leap to defend him. Instead, I felt him taking my measure, studying me, wondering just who he'd have to sacrifice to save his own job. Anyway, that's what I imagined. He may have been planning his next move. He may even have known I was bluffing. Still, I appreciated the key to Town Hall he pressed into my hand; and the little card with his home and his car phone numbers and the stack of files the secretary came in with, especially the ones stamped CONFIDENTIAL.

On the way out I remembered something that Gordon had said the night of the victory party, calling me over with his eyes. I had knelt to hear his whisper. He was right. This was going to be fun.

JOHNNY

37

"It's true!" Crystal was laughing. Her laughter was ticklish, making him smile. "Don't you know guys like that, Mr. Lynch? Ugly guys who walk around like movie stars and really dumb ones who think they're Einstein."

"Too many," Johnny said, watching a slice of roast beef slide out of his sandwich onto the wrapper he balanced on his lap.

"Then there are these really good-looking guys whose self-image sucks. No matter how much somebody loves them, they just don't believe they're good enough. And do you know the reason for that? Mr. Lynch? Are you laughing at me?"

"Well, there is a daub of yogurt right there on your nose."

"Oh, you!" She licked it off with the tip of her tongue.

If any of the boys, Donkey or Abel, saw him eating lunch with a pretty girl in the front seat of his car, they'd never believe it was business. He'd only planned to familiarize Crystal with the river valley and the dike. She'd suggested the picnic. But the wind was up today, blowing sand in their eyes and forcing them back into the car.

"And the reason is the person's mother," she said, oblivious to the grandest view Saltash had to offer, the vast harbor bluer than heaven itself, then narrowing upriver of the dike into a placid stream. Aspen leaves shimmered like silver dollars. Seabirds wheeled overhead while Crystal, God bless her, rattled on about motherhood. "Between the ages of birth and five years old, that's the window. That's where you have your shot. If you really dedicate yourself to making that one little person feel special, then you're giving the gift of lifelong confidence, and that's as important as any college education."

Johnny had hoped she would grasp the beauty of the place. But he might have known, since she'd never hunted or hiked and fished here as he did, that she was simply one of those people for whom the natural world was just scenery. No matter. A little naiveté could work in his favor.

"Mr. Lynch, are you listening to me?"

"Actually, I was applying what you said to my own boys. My wife did just that. Dedicated herself. With Jackie at least. By the time William came along, well, things had changed."

"Parents aren't perfect." Crystal was lecturing him now like a little schoolteacher. Maria said since David's election, she was holding forth on everything from school budgets to dogs on the beaches. "Parents are people first. But no parent ever intentionally does anything to harm their child. Mrs. Lynch was sick. They didn't understand things like depression back then."

Johnny was uncomfortable now. "You don't know what you're talking about." He crumbled the bag on his lap. He'd told Crystal a great deal about himself, but he'd never mentioned Emily Ann. That was Maria's doing. They chattered like hens. "Now for the reason we're here, then." He heard the coldness in his voice. Crystal jerked upright like a child reprimanded. "Do you see how the trees grow right up to the bank of the river? Those are gray birches."

"They're pretty trees," she said. "This valley is beautiful."

"Beautiful to us, dear. Home to countless of God's creatures."

Since the election, Johnny had a new plan to keep the dike in place. He'd give his adversaries a dose of their own medicine, raise a grand and public stink about the environment. There had been a causeway any storm surge could overrun and a rickety wooden bridge constructed forty years before he'd even heard the name of this town. Behind the bridge there had been a salt marsh and a tidal river useful only to a few shellfish scratchers. He had replaced the bridge with a proper dike, able to withstand hurricanes and ice pileup, protecting the new land behind it. There, the old marsh had been drained, filled and had grown up into meadows and woods. Since then an entire new habitat had been formed. He didn't know all the technical details; Crystal had agreed to work overtime to come up with the proper language, interview a few biologists to get it straight. But he knew this much, and this was his line: if the dike was torn down and the saltwater of the harbor allowed to fill the valley, thousands of animals would be flooded out of their homes. Little red foxes. Innocent baby deer. Weasels, voles, opossum. Coyote would lose their food supply and begin gobbling kittens, mauling the family dog. The issue was environmentally arguable, and sentimental as a children's tale. The timing couldn't be better. It was the summer people who had influence with the legislature, over twenty thousand of them, from districts all over the state. If his luck held out, if time was on his side, he would take the issue of the dike right out of the selectmen's hands and turn it over to the media and the State House.

After eating, they returned to the office in silence. He knew the girl's feelings were hurt, but he didn't know how to smooth things over. She had set herself up a desk in a back corner of the office by the copy machine, an area formerly used to store dead files. Only when the file cabinets were moved did he realize they'd been blocking a window. Now there were plants in it. She had three pictures of her son on her desk, and one of David being sworn in by the town clerk. There was a teddy bear and a dish of hard candy, a coffee mug with red hearts. He made a few forays to the copy machine in hopes of thinking of something light to say, but the other girls were always around. As he was heading back to his office the last time, Crystal said, "Mr. Lynch, I finished those letters you asked me to write."

She handed him three, each handwritten in her loopy feminine curlicues, each addressed to the editor of a different local paper and signed in her own name. They were each two paragraphs long, as he'd advised her, and quite good. "David won't mind?"

"I have a right to protest the killing of innocent animals no matter what he thinks. He never asked *me* what to say in the election."

Johnny hoped people would assume her opinions were David's. But her relationship to the new selectman was too valuable to jeopardize. "I don't want to cause any family problems."

"Family . . ." Crystal repeated. She looked pleased at his choice of words. Then she looked down in embarrassment. "Mr. Lynch?"

"Oh, now." He was afraid she was going to cry. Because he'd used the word "family" to describe her arrangement with David Greene?

"I didn't mean to be sticking my nose into your private affairs. I mean about Mrs. Lynch and your children."

"You mean William?" He rarely mentioned his second son to anyone in this town except, on occasion, Abel Smalley, who could obtain information about the California prison system. But Johnny had a hunch. "You're about his age, aren't you?"

"He was a nice boy," Crystal said.

"I doubt if there are many around here who remember him that way, but thank you, dear."

"He was nice to me. He took me to the junior prom, even though I was a sophomore."

William had many girlfriends before he got involved with drugs. Had Crystal been one? He tried to figure out what she would have looked like at age fifteen. William had gone out with many pretty girls, but in Johnny's memory, they blurred.

"Anyway, I'm very sorry."

Those eyes, like an infant's, that was the only way to describe them, so sad and vulnerable. Johnny looked away. "Crystal, you didn't get yourself arrested for armed robbery. My William did."

"I'm sure he just got in with a bad bunch. It happens, especially when you're away from home and off on your own. I understand that, Mr. Lynch."

"We were talking about children. Which you know a great deal about. I only pray to God your boy doesn't end up the way mine did, and that I have the strength to help William when he finally comes home."

"You will," she said, her hand hovering above his but not touching, not yet, he thought. She said "You're the best boss in the world, Mr. Lynch. I see all the time how many people in town you help. People nobody else seems to care about. You don't turn anybody down. You have the biggest, kindest heart in Saltash, Mr. Lynch."

JUDITH

Every social worker in the county and every health worker knew Judith would take on those unpleasant cases of abuse, not only unsavory, but sometimes dangerous for the lawyer as well as the client. When a woman left an abusive man—or began to get ready to leave—she was in acute danger. Sometimes her lawyer too could come into the line of fire. But occasionally domestic troubles were plain bizarre.

She had two new cases. One was a bigamist. Betty Clausen and/or Sirucci had married Sirucci without getting divorced from Clausen. "But Sergio was ready to marry me. Dick wasn't paying child support. He never paid his child support after the first two months. What could I do?" Betty was a slender nervous woman with dark brown hair cut very short, who hailed originally from northern Maine. Her children were being entertained in the outer office by Mattie, who was great with kids. She kept a supply of toys and games in a box.

"Divorce would have been a really good idea, Betty."

"But that takes time. And Sergio was ready to marry me right then. How do I know he'd marry me in a year? I have two kids and he was willing to be their father. They never really had a father, not a loving one. Not a good man like Sergio. And I didn't even have a current address for Dick."

To Betty it all seemed logical. Her kids needed a father; here was a father. Ergo she had to marry him immediately. "But you'd told him you were married?"

"He's such a sweetheart. Of course I told him I'd been married. How else did I get two kids? But I said their father was dead. In Sergio's family, there's no divorce. At least I could say I wasn't a divorced woman, because I wasn't. But if a man picks on you all the time and hits you and hits your kids and doesn't pay a penny for them, how can that be marriage? So if you aren't really married—"

"The law doesn't distinguish between a good marriage and a lousy marriage, in that both are equally valid marriages and require a valid divorce to end them. Betty, there are places like the Dominican Republic where you can get a divorce overnight."

"First, I don't have the money to fly to the Caribbean. Second, how would I explain it to Sergio?"

"How are you explaining the situation now?"

"He's very upset with me." She began to cry. "I couldn't take the chance on him not marrying us. We needed him. We were having trouble making it. This is a real marriage, not like my last one."

Betty hoped if she could only explain to the judge how badly she wanted and needed Sergio, the judge would understand she had been obliged to marry him right away, and everything would be all right.

Judith had ten minutes before her next new client to make notes on the interview. Perhaps she should plea bargain and represent Betty as a devoted mother only trying to care for her children. That might go over. Sooner than put herself and her children on welfare, your honor, this mother of two . . .

The other new case was a reasonably straightforward divorce. The only question was why the woman had stayed so long with a man she described as abusive, unfaithful and often drunk. She was four years older than Betty and looked ten years older. "But where would I go?" she asked, as if she had never heard of a rental unit in her life. She had married out of high school, worked as a waitress, a salesperson in a tee-shirt shop, a chambermaid. She had always worked and never made a living.

After that interview, Judith sat in her office feeling overcome with despair. The lives of women were often so grim and desolate and patched together. No wonder a woman like Crystal grabbed at a hardworking and affectionate man. She despised Crystal because Crystal had destroyed her best hope of a good relationship with David; Crystal must hate her for the same reason. They were in each other's way. Pontificating about how good a woman Crystal was or wasn't, was irrelevant.

She was having supper with David on the island, but meeting him here. Natasha was home for the interval between vet school and her summer internship, and tonight she was cooking. Natasha was a good cook, taught by Judith. At seven-thirty oyster stew and corn bread would await them. She needed the time alone with David before the family scene.

"Any progress?" she greeted him.

"I called Laramie's father." He told her the conversation. "I don't know what to believe."

She could not come down unreservedly on the side of Liam, as she would have liked. "You have to understand that his wife no doubt was listening to every word. The truth in these matters usually lies somewhere in the middle. It is likely they did actually live together for some period of time. It is likely that Crystal was more interested than he was, and didn't believe in his attachment to his family. Most probably when he learned she was pregnant and meant to have his child over his protests, he moved out. He may have hit her or just yelled enough to frighten her. We have no witnesses. Certainly he did not exhibit good-will toward her once she announced her pregnancy."

"You sound like a lawyer again."

"I am a lawyer, David. I deal with desperate women every day, women who think they're helpless and some who actually are. I look for remedies. I send them to counselors and social workers, I send them for medical assistance, I send them to safe houses. I go to court for them. But their desperation sometimes causes them to do foolish and self-destructive things. . . . What worries me most is Crystal's penchant for getting pregnant as glue in a relationship. Have you straightened out the matter of a second child?"

"I'm dealing with that," he said, his face and tone warning her, no further trespassing.

"I hope so, David. I hope so."

Although they made love that evening and he spent the night with her, she had to recognize that it was not as it had been. She was more reserved. She could not help it. She needed a sense of commitment to let herself go sexually. She did not feel that commitment from David. She was reluctant to end the sex, for she and Gordon no longer made love. He simply did not have a sex drive, and any brisk physical activity could cause a dangerous coughing fit. But she had to recognize that the intense almost overwhelming pleasure she had felt with David had di-minished into something merely pleasant. She had felt for a while that she had two mates. That had been an illusion, for David had not felt mated to her. If Betty was a desperate bigamist, one could say she her-self had tried to be a sane and pragmatic bigamist. She had failed as thoroughly as Betty.

Perhaps Crystal's need was greater, and she should simply get out of the way. If David would only fight for his relationship with her, she would persist. But if it did not mean that much to him, then she could not allow it to mean a great deal to her. He seemed to be choosing Crystal, or at the least allowing Crystal to choose him. She did not sleep that night. As she lay beside David, she found herself reluctantly but inevitably beginning to let go.

In the morning after he had left for work, she lingered at the table with Natasha. Her first appointment had canceled; that couple had rec-onciled. Her next appointment at ten was with the insurance company representatives. She finally had a good deal for Enid from the fall through the planking outside the pizza parlor. "I'm on the verge of giv-ing up on David."

"But why?" Natasha put her sharp chin into the cup of her hand. "Don't you think you're better for him? Don't you think he loves you? I see the way he looks at you."

"Crystal will do anything to keep David. She's a mother alone with her son and little ability to support him. I keep thinking about Yirina. My mother wasn't the world's most honest and truthful woman, but she did really love me, and she did her best. Men were a means."

"But you know you're better for David."

"I don't know if David understands that, and I'm beginning to think what's best for everybody is for me to give up and get out. I can't go on fighting her. It's demeaning. And I can't help knowing how hard it is for her. Like my mother. Like so many of my clients."

"But if you love David, you have to stay in there and fight for him."

"I thought I loved him, but I'm not sure any longer if I ever knew him well enough to love him. I can't go on combating Crystal. She's the wife now. Let her take what she needs. I can survive without David. I don't think she can."

Natasha said, "Or she thinks she can't."

"It amounts to the same thing, in the end." Crystal needed him; he seemed to want Crystal. What room was left for her? Only the way out.

DAVID

I saw a small red car race up the dirt road, stopping just behind my truck. Alan McCullough shouted over the lawn mower, "It's your sister!" and the two of us watched her run up the hill. "David, Mom's had an accident." Holly was gasping. "They've taken her to the hospital. Come on."

My mother volunteered two mornings a week in a day care center in the Universalist Church. Crossing High Street at noon, she was struck by a kid on a bicycle. "Did she break something?" I asked. "Did she hit her head?"

"I don't know." Her nose almost touching the wheel, elbows pinned to her sides, Holly's whole body seemed to be aimed at the hospital, as if steering a bullet through summer traffic.

"Did they catch the kid?"

"How do I know? Crystal was calling from the ambulance."

"Crystal? How the hell—"

"I don't know, David! I just don't know anything."

I left Holly to find a space in the lot and ran to the E.R. entrance. I was halfway to Reception when Crystal called out to me. "We're okay," she said breathlessly. "It's a minor concussion. That's the good news. But she's in X ray now. They think the ankle is fractured. Her kneecap may be cracked. Over here!" Crystal waved to my sister. She draped her arm around Holly and repeated what she'd told me. "I saw a crowd outside my office window. I ran out when I heard the sirens. When I saw who it was, I couldn't believe it. She was so strong, she kept trying to get to her feet. She wanted to kill the kid. He was laughing. I swear they had to hold her down. She kept yelling, 'You little one-armed worm.' "

"It was Jimmy Compton?"

"He thought the whole thing was a joke. The rescue squad was hovering around him as if he was the one who was hurt. But he just got on his bike and rode away. I think we should press charges. I'm going to ask Mr. Lynch. I think we have a case."

My mother's accident was like a reunion for the Greene family, the first time (I'm ashamed to say) since my father's funeral that we spent more than a seder or Thanksgiving meal together under one roof. My mother left the hospital in a cast, making cooking for herself, even showering, difficult. Ten months of the year finding help would not have been an issue. However, in Saltash everyone had a summer job or two or three. In her way, she managed to put a cheerful spin on a bad situation and see herself, after years of living alone, as the matriarch of a small but dutiful clan.

Marty grilled chicken on her first night back, which we ate surrounding her on the screened-in porch. Laramie relished the extended family. He chased my sister's girls through the grove of locust trees, in and out of the barn and Georgie's old apartment upstairs. Although Laramie was between the girls in age, he was more a mascot than a friend. For hours he searched for them in a game of hide and seek. They dressed him in silly costumes. They played fish and giggled constantly, their voices rising in shrieks and then falling in hushed exchanges.

"I'm so lucky." My mother beamed that night. The following morning Holly volunteered for the breakfast shift and I arrived to prepare lunch. Still no luck in finding a caretaker. That evening I made a lasagna and the happy family dined under the mottled shade of the tall black locusts. I volunteered for the morning shift the following day, but my mother looked uneasy. "I'd rather Holly came. I have to wash my hair or I'll look like a scarecrow."

"Sorry I won't be around for dinner," Marty said. "I'll be in Toronto."

"Of course, Marty." The demands of my brother-in-law's schedule were never questioned.

The girls were looking pensive and whispered in Holly's ear. She sighed, "Mom? Do you think David could do the morning? The girls have an ice skating lesson at eight and it's almost an hour away."

"In the summer?"

"We're trying to keep their training consistent."

"I'm learning a double axel," Kara said. "My instructor says I have a good line."

"How wonderful!" my mother said.

"But I'll be here at seven," I said.

"That's not necessary, David."

"But Mom, I want to make you breakfast."

"I said it's not necessary. I need help getting dressed and . . . things a daughter should do. Not you, David. You go to work. It isn't right for a son to be playing nurse. It isn't right."

The happy family sat in stunned silence. Holly was once again in the wrong. I was uncomfortable, but how could I force myself on my mother? I tried to think of some reliable teenager to hire.

"I can come," Crystal said.

My mother protested.

"But I can. I don't have to be at my desk until nine. If I'm a little late, Mr. Lynch will understand. He's the best."

"Are you really all right with this?" Holly was still frowning.

"We'll have fun. Won't we, Laramie?"

Tonight the girls had dressed him up in lipstick and rouge, an old white shirt of my father's and a velvet curtain sash. No, he didn't mind. For Laramie, clearly any attention was better than none. He liked it, he told Holly when she offered to wash him off. He liked having sisters and a grandma.

Johnny Lynch had no problem with Crystal coming in late every other morning after caring for my mother. One day he showed up for lunch. With my mother sitting in a kitchen chair and supervising, her ankle propped on a cushion, Crystal made sandwiches and served iced tea. She'd begun wearing a blouse I remembered as my mother's, blue linen with embroidery. Another day, Holly touched Crystal's rose ceramic earrings. "Mom, I gave you these."

"They were too heavy for me." My mother never seemed to enjoy Holly's presents.

Holly liked Crystal but had always mentioned her to me with a kind of mischief in her voice, as if to suggest sex. Now the two of them conferred about my mother daily. They went over their schedules at the kitchen table, sharing shifts, giving each other a little extra time at work.

In early August a Mrs. Falco, the librarian's mother, called to say she had lost a client and had time to care for my mom. She had a good reputation. I thought we should grab her. Holly agreed. Only Crystal insisted there was no reason to waste the money. She said my mother shouldn't have to depend on strangers.

The evening before Mrs. Falco was to start, I was watching a Red Sox game with Laramie when Crystal came in with a large box. "What's that?" Laramie was intrigued.

"Mom gave it to me," she said. Since the accident, Crystal had begun speaking about my mother as if she'd known her all her life. Like dolls at a tea party, we'd been assigned roles. I was Daddy. My mother was Mom. Laramie and my nieces were the Kids. Nobody questioned it; nobody blinked. Crystal had simply redefined our family with herself in the middle.

Laramie began pulling at the wrapping tape. "Please can I see?"

"No," Crystal said, with a harshness that drew my attention. She wasn't looking at Laramie but straight ahead, almost blindly. Her fingers grazed the edges of the box as if feeling her way through some dark inner landscape. "It's time to go to bed."

But his curiosity only grew. "Please?"

"They're glasses. Blue cobalt glasses. But we can't unpack them now."

"What's cobalt?"

They were dark blue goblets, dessert cups, water glasses. Because my parents rarely entertained, they were arranged for show on a shelf in our dining room. They'd been relegated to the attic when my mother had new wallpaper put up. I hadn't laid eyes on them since.

"Why can't I see one?"

"Because we don't want to open them here. Because we'll just have to pack them again when we move."

Laramie's face turned the color of newspaper, white-gray. I imagined I could feel the blood leaving his lips, but of course it was my own pulse I felt, behind my eyes, in my wrists as I rubbed my hands against my sides.

"Mom said she was saving these for when we were married. But since David found us another place to live, I might as well take them anyway."

"Crystal . . ." I had not found them another place. I had merely asked a friend of my mother's who managed a cottage colony if there wasn't a year-round unit available. The conversation had lasted thirty seconds. I was opening my mail in the post office. The woman was tossing her duplicate catalogues. Although the situation sounded ideal, the woman had not yet gotten back to me. "Laramie, maybe you should go to bed," I said. "Put your pajamas on. I'll bring in the radio and you can listen to the game until you fall asleep."

It was as if I had not spoken. "Are we moving, Ma?"

"You know Aunt Holly always wanted these, Mom said." Her fingers were peeling the stiff brown tape as her face, her eyes, all but her lips remained absolutely still. "Aunt Holly doesn't need them because she has a house and a business and Uncle Marty to take care of her and buy her things. But we don't have any of that, so we get these. Aren't they pretty?" She lifted a blue water goblet to the light. "Aren't we lucky, Laramie? To have such pretty glasses?"

The boy was looking at me, pleading with me to stop something he had obviously witnessed before, when she raised the glass high and brought it down on the table's edge. The glass was thick and did not shatter with the first blow. She brought it down again. Then she grasped one of the jagged blue edges of the goblet and drew it along her arm.

She was not aiming to cut a vein. This was more the work of an artist, a carver to be precise, for as Crystal backed away from me, as she drew the glass across her flesh she seemed to admire the long white striations that swelled to pink and burst into rivulets of blood that flowed one into another.

"Crystal, I never asked you to leave—"

"But you want us to." Her voice sounded distant, controlled. She drew the glass across her arm again.

"I don't want you to go anywhere. I told you you could stay here as long as you need to, as long as you want to. . . ." As I neared his mother, the boy was at my side, watching her face and the pressure of the glass on her arm. Yes, he seemed to tell me, not with words but the subtlest distortion of his features, his teeth on his bottom lip, the movement of his gaze from his mother and back to me. Keep talking to her, he seemed to be saying. Keep telling her what she needs to hear. "Crystal, remember the morning Michelle asked you to leave? Remember you said that you'd be interested in a place that didn't charge two months security deposit?"

Good, Laramie seemed to be saying. This is the way.

"Remember? You said you didn't want to borrow money from me?"

Her grip on the glass seemed to loosen.

"Well, that's when I asked the lady from the cottage colony. Because she was looking for a family to move in as caretakers. For no deposit. That's when I spoke to her."

"That was two months ago," Crystal said.

"That's right. And I haven't spoken to her since."

Go on, the boy seemed to say.

"Because it's just fine for you and Laramie to be here. Because you can stay here as long as you want."

"You mean that?"

"Of course I mean it. This house is your house too."

"Mine and Laramie's."

"I don't know what my mother was talking about. She gets confused. That's why I think it's best that she has a real nurse. That's why we're getting Mrs. Falco to come in. Because Mom needs real care. She's getting older. . . ."

"She is. She forgets things," Crystal said. "Just last week she forgot Laramie's name and ran through all the kid's names before she got to his. It was really funny. She said Kara, Allison, David . . . before she got to Laramie. Remember?"

The little boy nodded.

Crystal looked at the gash on her arm as if it was nothing, an insect sting, a rash. She placed the broken goblet in my outstretched hand. "You really do want us to stay here, don't you?"

"This is your house now. I mean that sincerely," I said. And I did. It was all hers. If she wouldn't move, I would come up with another plan. I looked at Laramie, wondering at his calm. He seemed ashamed for his mother, but not surprised. I could not risk another scene like the one I had just been through. Neither could I stay in this house.

DAVID

The Board of Selectmen was divided. Two men, Ralph Petersen and Fred Fischel, were said to be in Johnny Lynch's pocket, while Sandra Powell and Lyle Upham had been elected with Judith's help. I knew why I couldn't call Judith—I had nothing yet to say. I hadn't moved out yet. I had plans to gradually detach, cut back. But I thought of Judith. I wanted every meeting night for her to show up, hoping to explain afterwards. It was like being in a storm and remembering a quiet clear place. I missed her voice, her intelligence, her body that seemed an extension of her personality and her mind, instead of a sexual morass into which I had sunk almost over my head. But I understood Judith would not be with me while I was living full-time with Crystal. The way things were now, I rarely saw Judith, and never alone.

The hearing before us was a simple conversion of a license, from wine and beer to a full liquor license. Powell and Upham were opposed and presented arguments against drunk driving, teenage alcohol abuse, and high school kids crossing the line from Wiggins Neck, the next town over. Lyle stood up to address the crowd and asked if one more place to buy hard liquor would improve life in this small town. "I don't think there's anyone here tonight who can forget about last year's rape in the parking lot." This was greeted with a loud rumbling in the audience, gaveled down by Chairman Petersen, who recognized Fred Fischel, a retired accountant with delicate, almost paper-white hands that he nervously rubbed together throughout the meeting. "You can't legislate morality," he said. "These people run a good clean business and follow all the rules. An incident like that can happen outside anyone's store, or anyone's home." Petersen voted with Fischel, for the full liquor license; Powell with Upham, against.

"How do you vote, Mr. Greene?"

Gordon told me Upham had contributed to my campaign. I knew he was pro-environment. That he'd voted for a new school. Sandra ran the local day care center. She was a perky five-foot-two who wore enormous red-framed glasses and her hair in bangs. Her youngest daughter, a budding star on the high school track team, had been hit by a truck a few years back and walked with a permanent limp.

"Mr. Greene?"

Didn't Sandra have the kids' interest at heart? Didn't Petersen and Fischel always toe the Johnny Lynch line? "I vote no," I said.

Promising to take us to court, the owners stormed out. Petersen demanded silence. The next order of business was called. I was warmed from the inside with a feeling of having stood up with the forces of good. I acknowledged a demure smile from Sandra Powell.

On the way out that night, Johnny Lynch grabbed my arm. "Tell me something. Did you know Sandra Powell's nephew just married the owner of the liquor store across the highway?"

I continued past him. "Don't know anything about it."

"Got married three weeks ago Sunday." He would not let go of my sleeve. "You gave them some wedding present there, Davey Greene. Took away their only competition. Nice work."

It was Johnny Lynch who made sure I do everything in my power never to be ignorant again; Johnny Lynch, eyeing me from the back row, waiting for me to fail, who unknowingly encouraged me to study the state ethics laws and the statutes concerning conflict of interest, to dedicate my weekends to research at Town Hall. I would not be used again. I would question and dig and ferret out every small connection and innuendo until I had it right. I would not be caught unprepared. I studied policies and labor contracts, reading sentences twice over, repeating them aloud until they made sense, studying half the night through sometimes, hoping Crystal would fall asleep before I got to bed.

We had stopped using condoms three months ago. When I put one on again, Crystal laughed. "What is that for?"

"Just extra protection."

"Against what? I take the pill, David. You know that. Or do you think I'm sleeping with someone else? Is that it?"

"I never said that."

"Did you pick up something from Judith? Some kind of infection?" Crystal said. Then hopefully: "Is she fucking someone else?"

"It's not about Judith. It's me. I don't think we're ready to have a child right now." Liam's voice had never quite left my mind. Beneath the anger, I'd heard a desperate terror. She tricked me, I could still hear him say. She's poison. "I want to use a condom, okay? There's nothing wrong with being safe."

"Fine. Use a condom," she said. "But you won't feel anything." Crystal lay on her back, legs spread, eyes on the ceiling, as still as a frightened bride, determined not to feel anything either. In turn, I moved on top of her with grim determination. "Enjoying yourself?" she asked.

*   *   *

The boat captain wore a sleeveless black tee-shirt and orange rubber boots that squeaked as he entered the hearing room. One infant son in the crook of his arm, his lean cocoa-skinned wife holding the other two boys—Saltash's only triplets—Dominic approached the selectmen like a jungle cat protecting his young. Those of us who weren't moved to sympathy understood his threats. "I got me a lawyer now and I ain't gonna be shoved around no more." He kicked the chair in front of him. "I already been punished for what I done. Fined by a judge. If you people take away my license, that's double jeopardy. It ain't right and it ain't legal."

Dominic Riggs was nineteen. His father had fished in Saltash, and his grandfather before that. Tall and wiry, with a patchy red-blond beard and a long red ponytail trailing from the back of his baseball cap, he had the kind of drive you encounter in young corporate executives who'll do anything to get to the top. But as a dragger captain, the top wasn't high enough to buy a home and support a family. Dominic was often on the wrong side of the shellfish warden: caught scalloping before the official start of the season, caught in areas closed to fishing. The warden warned the kid repeatedly and often looked the other way, but this time he was pissed off. He not only took Dominic to district court, where he'd been fined for possession of twelve bushels of oysters when the legal limit was ten, he was asking the selectmen to suspend Dominic's license.

"That fine was five hundred dollars. And another seven fifty for the lawyer." Dominic stood shoulder-to-shoulder with his wife, Jamaican born and herself the daughter of a fisherman. "You people are killing the working man."

According to the warden, the oyster harvest had been dwindling for the past two years. If some guys took more than the legal limit, there was less chance for the others to survive. Shellfish would go the way of the halibut and the cod; the resource would disappear.

Nonetheless, Sandra Powell said the boy had been punished enough. Who would feed his family if his license was suspended? Weren't we in the business of helping young people? She moved we deny the warden's request.

"Second." Lyle Upham repeated the dangers of opening the town to a law suit. Fred Fischel, facing reelection, was counting votes in the audience, packed with shellfishermen who preferred to curse the selectmen in the lobby, rather than speak their minds in public. Dominic smiled; opinion was moving in his favor.

"Mr. Chairman," I said.

Petersen responded tiredly, "Mr. Greene," as if this was not the first time I'd raised my hand to speak this evening but the fiftieth. Obviously, once was too much.

"Mr. Chairman, I move that we take the shellfish regulations of the Town of Saltash and flush them down the nearest toilet."

"Order." Petersen banged the gavel. "I said order!" He quieted the crowd. "There's a motion on the floor, Mr Greene. I assume that was meant to be a facetious remark."

"No, sir. I'm waiting for a second to my motion," I said. "Everybody in this town knows everybody else. Everybody is somebody's neighbor or daughter or cousin or friend. We try to look the other way when one of us breaks the rules. Okay. But that means we have no rules. Why pretend we do? Let's just flush them away. Now I know Dominic, and I know he works hard to feed his kids, but so do a lot of other guys. If we start ignoring the rules for every one of them, there'll be no harvest at all. Now if that's what we want, fine. But then let's not pretend we have regulations. Let's just flush them down the damned toilet and call it like it is."

Fred Fischel raised his hand. "Mr. Chairman, I move to order the previous question."

"What does that mean?" I asked.

The chairman didn't even look at me. "It means debate is closed, Mr. Greene. Do I hear a second?"

Within minutes the vote was taken. Dominic won.

"You're in the newspaper!" Crystal said, spreading the *Saltash Eagle* on the kitchen table. Laramie propped his chin on his fists to watch. She read: " 'At last Monday night's meeting, Selectman David Greene likened unenforced regulations to that which is commonly flushed down the commode . . .' "

"I didn't say anything like that."

"You know what Mr. Lynch said? He said you had real balls to take on the Riggs family." Crystal dropped her hand in my lap. "And don't I know it."

I was embarrassed in front of Laramie, who just smiled dreamily at his mother and me. Crystal thought that his stock had risen since my election, that kids who'd never been interested before were pursuing him. I thought the few new friends he'd made came from his association with my sister's girls. If anyone's social life had taken a turn for the better, it was Crystal's. Like my mom, whose status had soared when I pitched for the high school team, Crystal imagined herself the First Lady of Saltash. Sometimes people would call the house with questions— When is my road going to be repaved? Is it true they're planning to build a bike path through the woods?—which Crystal would officiously try to answer. Sometimes she came home with advice from Johnny. "He says never tell reporters anything unless you want it published. Don't mistake them for your friends." One night I heard her tell Laramie, "You have to set an example. People are watching us."

Crystal's wound was shallow but wide. It formed a scab quickly but needed to be protected or it opened and bled again. This happened once when we were in bed. Several times I saw Laramie bandaging it for her. She could have done so herself, but it seemed a ritual for them. Seriously and awkwardly he would put far more gauze around the wound than necessary. The oversized bandage served as a warning to all of us.

After the liquor license hearing, I spent almost all my time at home reading, an activity Crystal elevated to the legal ruminations of a Supreme Court justice. As soon as I opened my briefcase, she would deny Laramie access to the TV. She would make me a pot of coffee and clear the kitchen table and tell anyone who telephoned, "David is studying policy," in the same protective voice my uncle Georgie had used to clear kids away from my practice sessions behind the school.

But what Crystal took for diligence was also a way to hide. Friends had warned me during the election, "You'll never have enough time for the nursery or a personal life." That was exactly the point. I belonged to the town now. Not since I played baseball was so much expected of me; or so little. I worked for everyone now, too busy to be touched.

JOHNNY

Johnny found it odd that Crystal should sometimes remind him of his dear departed Emily Ann. Crystal was a woman who had been around the block a few times. He suspected it was more her vulnerability that had got her into trouble than wantonness—although there was a kind of perfume of that about her at times. He put it down to her sorry upbringing. Her father had preferred drugs to his family. Her mother was a petulant woman, far more involved with her own disappointments than with her two daughters.

It was Crystal's desire to please that reminded him of his wife. Emily Ann had wanted to make everything better for him, for her sons, for everyone around her. She must feed every hungry bird. She took in any stray that came by. She had raised an orphan girl, Mary Rose, now living in California with her salesman husband. Turned out better than his own son William, although it hurt him to admit it. Crystal was a good mother, as Emily Ann had been, until she could no longer manage.

Watching Crystal with the other girls, he observed her basking in her role as the more-or-less wife of a selectman. But there was the rub. Living with was not marriage, and Crystal knew it. That was where her vulnerability had got her in trouble again. If you could milk the cow free, why own it? There was a slightly broken quality to her, a resonating fragility like a good porcelain set being used for every day, that made him connect her in his mind to Emily Ann.

His wife would have labeled Crystal a bad woman. Emily Ann had a proper upbringing, her uncle a priest, her parents watching over her, and her aunt and her grandparents all protecting her not only from danger in the world, but from knowledge of danger. Her innocence, her purity had touched him from the first time he met her, at a victory dance held in the ward where she lived in Boston. He had been working for the reelection of a city councillor, his apprenticeship in politics. That very purity had broken her over the hard years. He could read faint cracks in Crystal's composure too. But once she was safely married, she would heal. She was not as pure or fine a creature as his Emily Ann, and marriage would not weaken her but make her stronger.

He was used to looking out for his own, and she had proved to be his, loyal to him, openly admiring, trusting him. She was his hidden weapon in this long struggle to hold on to this sleepy village he had made known to the rest of the world. He would reward her.

That afternoon, he called Crystal into his office. "I want you to take another look at those lots along the river. Come on."

He drove her out there again, taking the road across the dike. She perched forward on the car seat chattering about her son, his good teachers and his bad teachers. He nodded and made encouraging noises, planning his approach.

He talked about what the land here meant to him, although he was sure she was only half listening. Then he got to the clincher. He parked the car in a cul-de-sac and went around to her side to open the door for her, with a courtly little nod. "This is a prize piece of land, Crystal. Can you imagine a house here?" It was hot, but a brisk breeze was blowing off the bay. That was lucky, because his pitch wouldn't go so well if they were both slapping mosquitoes. This near the river, some days they hung in the air like a living fog bank.

Obediently she stared around her. "Right at the end of a road so that you wouldn't worry about your kid being run over. And a nice view of the river." She was trying to sound interested, and he appreciated the effort.

"Near the river. It's too shallow here to worry about your son. Wouldn't this be a lovely spot for him to grow up?"

"My son?" She turned to him as if she didn't understand. "I don't even dream about something like this."

"Crystal, you're working so hard to save this land. I want to show my appreciation. I could sell you this lot so cheap that you and David could afford to build on it. I could arrange a mortgage. I could make sure that you can raise your son in a proper house on your own land."

She stared at him, her mouth slightly open. "Would you really do that?"

"Don't you deserve it? Doesn't your boy?"

Tears formed in her eyes and rolled down her cheeks. She hurtled forward and hugged him, raising her face as if to kiss him, then caught herself. She stepped back, embarrassed. "I didn't mean—"

"You were showing your gratitude, child. You make me feel young again. But of course this can only work if we win the battle. If those maniacs open the dike, this land will be waterlogged. It will be wetlands again and nobody can build on it. And I won't be able to sell it to you, because I'll have less than half my lots buildable. . . . But don't fret. We're going to win. For you and your family. For all the young families that deserve a home." On his shirt and linen jacket he could smell the flowery perfume she wore, still clinging. He could feel her soft big body against him. His member rose in his pants. He smiled in surprise. There was a bit of fight in him still, and a bit of life too. It had been four years since the last time he had used his old friend, a quickie with Maria at the cottage.

There were women whose touch could raise the dead. Crystal was one of them. He would see that she got married. There was always time by and by for a little pleasure. She would owe him, and she would know it. He would see to her as he had arranged for so many of his people to get what they really needed. Crystal walked back to the car with him, almost dancing.

"Mr. Lynch," she said softly, "you're like a father to me."

"And you're my good girl, Crystal. The one I count on. And I take care of my own. I always have."

JUDITH

It was the sort of weather tourists, summer people and motel owners liked, and regular residents and the keepers of shops and galleries hated. One sun-baked day followed another under an aluminum sky. Every day was a beach day. The grasses parched to brittle straw the color of rabbit fur. Little ponds dried up and bigger ponds were surrounded by a wide margin of heavily trampled beach. Judith had to water constantly. Her tomatoes were half their normal size. All afternoon Trey, the three-legged dog who preferred to be outside, moved from patch to patch of shade around the compound. The cats stretched in the deep cool under the porch, bellies to the earth, all except Io and Portnoy. Io, with long white fur, lay on the bathroom tile. Portnoy spent all of his time in Gordon's bed or on the porch with him, when Gordon could be helped out there. Portnoy had appointed himself a caretaker. He was careful not to sit on Gordon but was never more than a foot from his side. Portnoy was a solid gray cat with a dignified air, a little chubby and extremely affectionate. He had been hit by a car when still a kitten. Natasha had heard about him. Judith paid his bills and Natasha brought him home. His name was Thousand Dollar Bill until Gordon renamed him.

Judith was summoning all the family members and Gordon's closest friends now for Rosh Hashanah. It came early this year—the second week of September. It did not matter if the children were back in school, it did not matter what kind of arrangements each of them must make on the job. They were to come. Gordon was dying and this would be the final gathering. The doctor thought he would last that long but not much past September. So Judith was giving them six weeks notice to make their arrangements.

She suspected it would be her next to last public duty as Gordon's wife; after that would come only the funeral. She lived with death now in a daily, intimate way, something never entirely out of mind no matter what she was doing. She only hoped that the doctor was right and that Gordon would make it through mid-September. She urged him to stay in his room with the air conditioner, as that spared him the heat and filtered the air.

Gordon was sometimes entirely silly and seemed drunk from the painkillers. Sometimes he disappeared into himself and his eyes did not register her presence. Sometimes he was happy as a puppy. Sometimes he was nostalgic about friends long dismissed or dead, epic demonstrations, mythical parties, journeys to Kyoto and Budapest. Sometimes pain took him over and occupied him like a hostile army. Sometimes he was bitter with anger. He would be silent an entire day and then words and stories would bubble from him. Other days he slipped into heavy sleep or unconsciousness and was gone from her. His fever rose and fell. The doctors changed his drug regime constantly. They were just tinkering.

She copped a plea for Betty; she got a divorce for the woman who had been abused and hustled her off to a new life where she hoped the ex would not find her. Preliminary motions were occupying both her and the prosecution in her defense of the doctor who had assisted a suicide. The roof case kept being postponed: the least of her cases would drag on the longest from that batch. She had a new custody case, a drunk driving case, a tenant suing because lead paint poisoned his daughter. There was never an end to human troubles with the law or each other. She kept busy.

Natasha was down in Florida, learning to care for feral birds, pelicans fishermen had maimed out of hostility, tearing off half of their beaks; herons that had taken fish with hooks in them; a gull shot in the wing; a wood stork hit by a car. Judith wondered in trepidation what discarded pet or lame animal Natasha would bring home with her this time. But the animals were company for her this August of Gordon's slow departure. She lavished attention on all of them. Beppo the Crow was healed and ready to depart, and she let him go. He circled her on the dune once, twice, and then beat off steadily to rejoin his tribe. The next day he came back, but only to visit. Then he was gone again. She expected that she might see him in the winter, when rations were scarce. Would she recognize him, seen with his fellows like Hasids dressed all in black? It would be like seeing David in town and remembering intimacy.

They had less company this summer than ever, for she had made clear (without telling Gordon what she was doing) that people were to come for the holiday to say goodbye to Gordon, but not before then. All summer vacations on the compound were canceled. For the first time since she had visited that July fourth weekend when she had connected with her Bashert, her predestined husband, they were alone—except for his nurse, Mrs. Stranahan, and for Jana Baer, who came in to help and cook. The doctor asked if she would not prefer for Gordon to move into the local hospice. She did not even ask Gordon. Anything that could be done for him would be done right here, with her in attendance. Their marriage would end, but it would end with them together.

She spent all the time she could manage in the compound, even if it meant getting up in the middle of the night to beat the tide across the bridge when she had a court date in the morning. She would not lose any of their remaining time together. She would not waste it. She forgave herself for the time she had spent, yes, spent like mad money on David. She had honestly thought it might work for the three of them and later for her and David. She cut her losses, striving to forget him. At least she and Gordon had accomplished something politically—unless Crystal succeeded in subverting David to Johnny Lynch's will. That was a possible outcome, and it would be ironic indeed—but not irony she would appreciate. If David did betray the people who had elected him, she hoped he would wait until Gordon was gone, so her husband would not lose that sense of accomplishment that had so pleased him; the sense that he had finally changed the rules of politics in Saltash and opened up the government. If David took that away from Gordon, she would get even.

Mattie had shown her the letters in the papers from Crystal. By that point they were two weeks old. Mattie was embarrassed to explain how she had noticed them so late. "Well, it's just that I pile up old papers by the toilet . . ." Another month had passed since then. Basically Judith saw almost no one outside her office, except family.

The second week in August, David showed up at her office just as she was about to leave. He stood close to her, his eyes insisting she meet his gaze. She remembered that intensity of desire, from before Crystal. Searching for a way to keep her distance from him, she brought up the dike letters.

"When I confronted her, she said she felt sorry for the animals and birds, and she thought that area where the houses were going up was just beautiful and perfect for families. That's a quote."

"Did you think to point out to her that it is contradictory to save the land for herons and foxes, then destroy it by building houses there?"

He winced. "I asked her as long as she's living in my house please to show me any more letters she writes to the local papers."

"She's working for Mr. Politics and she's living with a selectman. . . . I hope this doesn't mean you've changed your stand on the dike."

"The more I try to understand the dike issue, the more complex it gets. Now the state's involved too."

"David . . ." She risked touching his cheek for a moment. "Don't turn against the people who worked so hard to elect you. Don't turn this town back to business as usual."

"You think Crystal can make me do that?"

"We haven't come to the end of what she can make you do, David Greene." She picked up her purse and her briefcase.

"Are you leaving? I thought we might have tonight."

"David, you're living with Crystal."

"I am at the moment. I'm working on that."

"I'm not someone you can have on the side. I didn't do that to you. I tried to be clear that this was a major commitment for me—not some fling. Would Crystal approve of your spending time with me?"

"She hates it. But she knows I won't give you up."

"David, you already have." She headed for the door and Gordon. If she drove quickly, she could just make it across the bridge before the 6:45 P.M. high tide covered it. When she pulled into the street, she could see him in the rearview mirror standing in the parking lot, handsome and forlorn. Heat touched the back of her eyes as if she would cry, but she had cried too much this summer. She squinted hard and regained control. As she crossed the rickety bridge, she felt safe. This island was where she belonged, with her only love, her husband.

DAVID

Letters from Florida addressed in Vicki's hand had a way of turning my stomach inside out. I usually tore them open immediately, right there in the post office, to get the bad news over with. But this one was from Terry.

Dear Dad,

Mom said to write you to tell you I'm a pitcher now. Not like you were but just in softball. I pitched for the color war in my camp (we were the Blue team) and I won the game. I miss you. I can't wait til November when you come to visit. I still have the books you bought me at Epcot last time. My cownslor's name is Ted and he says if my real father was a baseball pitcher then I have a strong arm in my jeans to be one too. Granpa Wynn died of a heart attack. We were all crying and stuff. Mom had to sell Valiant Prince. She says maybe I can visit with you if you want but school is starting soon and she says your probably busy but I miss you. If you want to write me back we're moving to an apartment. Mom says she doesn't know the address yet. The baby and Suzi cry a lot but mom says the new apartment will have a pool. Please write me back as soon as you can. I miss you and want you to teach me to be a pitcher like you.

Your son,
Terry

I didn't go back to the nursery from the post office. I went straight to my house. Crystal was working and Laramie was at the summer rec program until three. Vicki should have been at work, but I don't why, I had a feeling. I dialed her home number. "It's David," I said when I heard her voice, bracing myself as always for an unpleasant response.

"Oh," she said, more surprised than annoyed. "Hi. You got Terry's letter. That was fast."

"He said your father . . . Wynn . . . I'm sorry, Vic."

"Well, it was his second heart attack. Then he had a third one in the hospital."

"I didn't know."

Silence. How would I?

"Anyway, Terry sounds like he got through it okay."

"Oh, he's great. He told you about his baseball?"

"Is something wrong, Vicki? I don't want to pry into your life or any-thing." The truth is, I never had. The less I asked, the less I got hurt. As the conversation went on, however, Vicki's voice seemed to soften and almost die away. "The letter said you were moving?"

"Well, there's legal stuff. Some bullshit lawsuit. They were hounding Daddy. Anyway, yeah. We're moving. Me and the kids. Mom had to sell the house. She's moving in with my brother, Junior."

I don't know why it was so hard to ask. I thought I'd gotten over Vicki a long time ago. But pain sticks, I guess, like the question itself in my throat. "And your husband, Cesar. How's he taking all this?"

"Cesar and I split up in May." She sounded annoyed, as if I was in-deed interrogating her. "He moved up to Jacksonville."

"I'm sorry."

"Right."

"Listen. Terry said in the letter he might want to visit. That would be great with me. I'll pay the airfare. It wouldn't cost you a thing."

"Not right now. I think the little ones need him around. He's a really good big brother."

"I know he is," I said, but the truth is, I had no idea.

"I think we should make the move," Vicki said. "Get settled. Then we'll see."

"Is he there?"

"He's at camp. They're doing this overnight thing in the Everglades. Him and his cousin Justin are in the same group."

"I bet he loves it."

"I'll tell him you called, David. All right? He'll be excited."

"He can call me anytime."

"I'll tell him."

"Collect!" I said, but Vicki had already hung up.

I didn't go back to work right away. I did something I hadn't done in years: nothing. I simply sat there on the couch. No TV, no radio, no one arguing, no Laramie sprawled in the living room or Crystal rubbing my back. The quiet seemed to wrap around me like a blanket. I read the letter over and then over again. I even laughed: a strong arm in my jeans. I felt so full of hope I actually knocked wood the way my mother did—three knuckles against the coffee table to ward off the evil eye. Ju-dith had said she could help me bring him home. Part-time, vacations, summers, it didn't matter, it was a start. For years Wynn had built a wall around my son and there was no way through. I'd always hoped Terry would reach out to me; and now he had. I wouldn't hound Vicki, but I wanted some real time with my son, finally. But not here, not in this house. I thought I understood what kept me with Crystal: pity, guilt

about leaving Laramie, the complete submission of a woman and her
body. But I couldn't subject my son to my mistakes, to a woman who
used pleasure and pain as hard currency. Not if I ever hoped to have my
son with me. If I was going to make a move, it had to be now.

"Please, Crystal, put your clothes on. We have to get Laramie up. You
have to get to work."

"What do you care? You're leaving. You don't love me anymore. You
think I'm fat, is that it? I disgust you? That's why you don't want to
make love to me?"

"That's not true, any of it." It was impossible for me to speak my
mind. My eyes kept drifting over her breasts, the little gold rings in her
nipples, even her belly, which she hated, the delicate hill of soft flesh.
"Just please get dressed."

"Why should I? It's my bedroom. Oh. Sorry. *Your* bedroom. Which I
took away."

"No, it's still your bedroom. Our bedroom. I'm only moving over
to my mother's for a few nights a week. I'm trying to keep her off her
ankle. You know what the doctor said. Until it heals."

"She has help."

"Mrs. Falco is only part-time. She doesn't get there until after nine.
My mother wakes up early. Crystal, this is no big deal."

"No big deal? That you don't like to make love to me anymore?"

"I love to make love with you. We made love last night."

"With a condom, David. You could hardly feel me. We have to stop
everything to put it on. You think I'm trying to trick you? You think I
want a baby with a man who doesn't want it—or me?"

We'd fallen asleep last night after the same argument. This morning
I'd awakened at five A.M. in the midst of an erotic dream that turned out
to be a very real Crystal between my legs, sucking me. She sensed I was
about to come and began to mount me, when I rose and got out of bed.
I did not lie. "I want you so much." I did. Even now.

"Then why are you packing? Why are you leaving our home?"

"We talked about this. It's not right the way it is. You work for Johnny
Lynch. You write letters to the newspapers for him—"

"I'm too stupid to have my own opinions, so I do it just for him? Is
that what you're saying?"

"I'm saying I'm an elected official. I'm saying you are economically
dependent on a man who stands to gain by my vote. I need a place for
my notes, a private place to do my work."

"I've never looked at your stupid notes."

"What was your little Donkey Sparks speech about last night?"

Crystal covered her face, the way she did when buying time to think. When she dropped her hands, her eyes looked bloodshot and sore. "I said he had his faults, but was a good manager. That he could handle a rough bunch of guys because he'd earned their respect."

"Now where would you hear that?"

"I work in an office. People talk. Don't you come home and tell me what kind of trees you planted? Sorry, didn't you used to come home and tell me things? You don't anymore. You hardly talk." Crystal sighed, crossed the room and scooped a tee-shirt off the floor. Even as she stretched it over her head and shoulders, I glanced at the perfect shaven lips between her thighs.

"Crystal, I don't think you do it purposely, but Johnny's trying to get to me through you."

"I know that, David. I'm not stupid. But we can use him. Don't you see? Why can't you give me credit for anything?" Her voice broke. Tears collected in the corners of her eyes. "You're a good man. The best this town has ever had. You won't let yourself be fooled. So what if he offers us things?"

"Damn it, three-quarters of an acre is a huge bribe. He wants me to have a financial stake in an issue I'll have to vote on. Don't you see what he's doing?"

"You said you weren't sure about voting to open the dike. You said you had a lot of questions."

"Is that what you told Johnny?"

"This is really because of Judith, isn't it? She's the reason why you're leaving me. She tells you not to trust me. Do you honestly think I'm spying on you for Mr. Lynch?"

"I'm not leaving you," I said, even as I threw clothing and books into a cardboard box. "I'm setting up a space for myself with a desk and a mattress. . . . In case I want to work late. Or if my mother needs me. I'm not leaving you."

"You're not?" Crystal said, pulling the hem of her tee-shirt down to cover herself. "Then tell him."

Laramie stood in the doorway. When I lifted him in my arms and touched his cheek to mine, it was utterly cold.

JOHNNY

44

Johnny laid his hand on Donkey's shoulder. "Don't you worry. The kid isn't going to vote against you out of spite, just because you once had an argument. I'll call out the troops for you. Never doubt it."

Donkey still looked worried, his long face drooping. "I've done a good job, for you and the town, Johnny. I'm not ready to be hung out and dried. Jeez, who'd have expected the little kike to get in. I never did."

"Sit down, Donkey. Have a touch of scotch." He poured them each a shot and sank back in his BarcaLounger. "People like ex-sports heroes. They're heroes, one, and two, they've come down in the world. Makes people feel good. But you have friends here. And so do I." Johnny thought that Donkey always looked as if he had stayed in the sun too long: his face was permanently pink and his eyes popped. Donkey's father had suffered from high blood pressure, and so did Donkey. The whole Sparks family had it. Donkey's father had died of a sudden heart attack at fifty-two, dropping dead right in the middle of Main Street chasing a tourist who had walked out of his shop without paying. Donkey was forty-nine. "Don't get yourself hot under the collar. You'll keep your job."

"I've always come through for you, Johnny, you know I have. What's this town coming to? I grew up here, and so did my dad and my mother and my granddaddy before them. There's been Sparkses in this town since Adam and Eve. We come over from Devon almost two hunnert years and we been here ever since." Donkey was spread across the whole Naugahyde couch, his arms and legs splayed wide. He was not a big man but occupied a lot of space.

"You're a part of this town for sure," Johnny said soothingly. He would like Donkey to calm down and get off his back. He intended to fight for the man's reappointment, not only for Donkey's sake, but because controlling the Department of Roads, Bridges and Waterways was damned useful. Johnny had controlled it for thirty-five years, and he wasn't about to lose his grip on it now.

"This is good whiskey," Donkey said admiringly. "Smooth as a young girl's behind."

"I wouldn't give you less than my best," Johnny said.

When Donkey finally went home, Johnny tilted the BarcaLounger upright and sat with a big yellow legal pad on his lap planning his campaign. He had two selectmen but he needed a third. He would draw up a list of people willing to write a letter or make a phone call, put up a fight for a hardworking local boy. Shouldn't Davey Greene himself be owing him something? For that lot they'd be building on? Crystal hadn't got back to him about that. Just what did the boy say? Did he bite like a fish or was he coy? The latter, most likely, but he'd come around—once he realized how much his pride would cost him. Johnny would make sure there was enough public pressure to make it easy for David to vote for Donkey.

Johnny arrived at the office Monday morning with his lists. Maria was working on the books, so he had Tina and Crystal start putting in the calls. He'd take each one, of course, but they could run the people down first, leave messages, get whoever they could. By noon he had talked with eleven people. Then he had lunch with Ralph Petersen, but not at the Binnacle. He ordered up roast beef sandwiches and soup and a bit of salad—not that the Binnacle normally did takeout, but this was for him. He'd seen their expansion through the Zoning Board of Appeals; convinced the Board of Health to grant them a variance on their septic system. And why not? If you wanted an evening meal in this town after Labor Day, it was the Binnacle or pizza. They ran a necessary year-round business. Good for the town.

Johnny and Ralph had a private lunch in the office. Johnny liked to watch Ralph eat. Ralph was what they used to call a string bean, tall and skinny with a shiny dome and a white mustache, but he ate as daintily as a fastidious miss in lace gloves. It was his mustache. He was vain about it (the only hair he had left above his chin) and dreaded getting something caught in it. It had happened to him publicly maybe fifteen years ago. Palmer Compton, it was—the father of that one-armed idiot—stood up in a selectmen's meeting and said, "You have tomato sauce for suppah, Chairman Petersen? Or'd you get that punch in the mouth you deserve?" Ralph's skin was as thin as the finest silk. He never again appeared in public with a speck of food in his mustache.

"So how is our new kid selectman doing, Ralph?"

Ralph made a noise in his throat. "Going to be trouble."

"He grew up here, Ralph. Not like our ex-professor and Miss Nursery School. I think we can get to him."

"You gonna fight for Donkey?"

Johnny spoke slowly, because he was about to give Ralph his line: "Donkey Sparks knows the men and they trust him. By the way, we should call him Sparks from now on, not Donkey when we refer to him. Sure, Sparks may lack computer skills and the ability to go out and get grants from the state, but he keeps a firm hand on a difficult department. He's a hands-on manager of the old school."

"Hands-on manager of the old school," Ralph repeated with satisfaction. "That's one I can use."

"Sparks grew up here and he loves this place and is loyal to it, not some careerist passing through to a bigger town with a bigger budget."

Ralph put up another finger. "Not using us as a stepping-stone."

"A son of this town, Sparks knows the people and the land." Johnny paused for Ralph's full attention, "Yes, the people and the land of Saltash."

Ralph nodded sagely. "Remember the last big snowstorm, when the old people couldn't get out? Donkey Sparks plowed his way into the back woods with the meals-on-wheels right behind."

"That's it." Johnny nodded. Ralph was a good man if you gave him some direction. He didn't need everything spelled out, just the outline and he'd be ready to take on the foe. "Talk to Davey Greene. Try to get him on our side. Take him under your wing, Ralph. You can do it."

Ralph shrugged. "I'm not so sure of that."

"He's a local boy. What does he have in common with the Gordon Stone gang? He got recruited in bed. Now that's over and he's going to wake up and see where his true alliances are. We can get him to come over. I know it." Johnny opened his office door. "Crystal, dear, could you put on a pot of coffee for two old gentlemen?" He winked at Ralph.

"You've got his girlfriend in your pocket."

"Just about. And I suspect he'll be marrying her soon enough."

Ralph nodded, seeing which way the land lay.

"He doesn't want to build a house," Crystal said.

He had asked her to stay a little late for one more letter. "Why wouldn't he jump at the chance?"

"He said it was a bribe. And now he's moving out!" Crystal's face collapsed and two fat tears rolled down her cheek.

He was glad he had waited till the girls left to broach the subject. He patted her shoulder. "Moving out where?"

"He's staying half the time in that barn behind his mother's."

"Where his uncle Georgie used to live? It's barely an attic. Did he say why?"

"He said he can't keep his mother off her feet. You know, her ankle swelled all up. But I was taking care of her fine before he hired Mrs. Falco. He's moved his selectman papers there. I think he suspects I told you about the letter—before the election?—and other stuff. I just tell you what I think you need to know. I know you want what's best for all of us."

"But why does he suspect you? Has he ever tried to get you to quit?"

She shook her head no. "I think he's too glad I'm working to argue about where."

"Well, that's a blessing. You know how the girls and I depend on you in the office. There's not one of us knows those computers the way you do. Nothing would get done around here without you . . ."

She sniffed and he handed her a crisp white handkerchief, the sort he always carried, Irish linen and monogrammed. "You make me feel important. Nobody else does." Crystal rubbed at her eyes. "I just don't know what's happening with him or what he's feeling."

"What does your little boy think of all this?"

"He's scared. He doesn't say anything. But he watches and he listens and he knows that I'm in trouble."

"So Davey Greene doesn't want to build a house. There could be forty reasons for that, dear. Perhaps he doesn't want to go into debt right now with his mother injured and disabled. You mustn't panic."

She had the air of someone about to burst into hysterics, which he definitely did not want. He kept talking in a soothing voice. "He cares for your son, you've seen that, and obviously he cares about you. Give it time. Perhaps things moved too fast and you need to wait for him to settle down and settle in. Men often get balky, take my word for it, when things get serious. A man needs time to get himself around to thinking it's his idea, not the woman's."

"I just can't believe he moved into that drafty barn to get away from me! It's so unfair."

"Do you think something instigated this move? Something triggered it?"

She wiped her face in his handkerchief and sat down, frowning. She was in control again, a fragile patched-together control, but no longer verging on hysteria. "I know he's stewing about that head of the roads and bridges department."

"Donkey Sparks? Stewing about what, exactly?"

"I'm telling you, two things made him run for office. One was that bitch Judith Silver and the other was Donkey Sparks."

"So that's why he ran?"

"I think that had a lot to do with it. He said Donkey made him feel invisible." Crystal shook her head sadly. "He felt like they ran over him instead of just his fence."

Johnny needed time to think about this.

Crystal was still talking, slowly, her brows drawn together in thought. "He says that Judith Silver broke up with him, but I'm sure she has something to do with this. I know he's sneaking in some evenings to see her, I just know it. That's why he moved over there."

"She's a dangerous woman," Johnny said. "The first time I met her was in court. She lost, and I don't think she ever forgave me. That is one lady, if I can still call her that, who does not like to lose, Crystal. I'll keep my ears open. Nobody has any secrets around here, believe me. If he's seeing her, there's always someone who notices." He would do that for Crystal and for himself, to refine his strategy. When Stumpy came by for his monthly check, Johnny would quietly, indirectly, patiently question him.

As Stumpy rowed across the harbor to town, he brought more than an appetite for beer and sausage: he brought news. This would not be the first or the second or the third time Johnny had used Stumpy for intelligence on the doings of the Stones. Who had come by to visit with Gordon? Whose cars were parked overnight? Who came to a particular meeting? Stumpy noticed everything, but he didn't take sides. He would never understand that information had any value. Day after Labor Day, Stumpy would come in for his check. They'd have a nice long conversation.

DAVID

If Johnny Lynch no longer grabbed the headlines, there was no doubt about his ability to draw a crowd. The night of Donkey Sparks's reappointment hearing, Johnny stood at the door shaking hands, guiding people to their seats like a night club maitre d'. He sat Donkey's family in the first three rows, wife, children, grandchildren; Donkey's loyal crew and their families in the rows behind. All three local reporters had been alerted. The cable news people were setting up lights and cameras. When the seats were all taken, the aisles filled; late arrivals were peering through the doors. Since four of the five votes were set in stone, it appeared that Johnny went to all this trouble to influence me.

The hearing was scheduled to begin at seven-thirty, but at seven, during the open session, Johnny Lynch slowly lumbered to the microphone. "I want to know where we stand on the issue of home-based contractors and parking," he demanded. "You people are holding an ax over our heads." Some months ago the legality of local tradesmen working out of their garages had been questioned. It was an emotional issue for them; an equally excitable one for their neighbors, who didn't want their quiet streets turning into little industrial parks. Johnny knew perfectly well the board had no intention of changing the rules. But one after another, carpenters, plumbers, house painters, come directly from their day jobs or the bar at Penia's Pizza, stood up to warn the board not to mess with their rights. This was not the usual crew we saw at selectmen's meetings, not people accustomed to expressing themselves in a public forum. They were here because Johnny had started a rumor they were about to be screwed—and in so doing had filled the hearing room with people most likely to support Donkey Sparks.

Ralph Petersen called the hearing to order. Ralph had asked after my mother's health this evening; only last week he had begun to address me by my first name. Not a forceful chair, he used cold efficiency to bull his agenda through, announcing the issue in a dry monotone, calling for debate and as soon as possible thereafter, the vote. Fred Fischel not only made the motion to reappoint Donkey Sparks, he read a prepared speech. Fred waved his arms as he recounted the heroic exploits of Donkey leading an army of meals-on-wheels volunteers through the frozen tundra of the Saltash winter forests. I glanced over at the progressives on the board, Sandra Powell and Lyle Upham, who were wearing serene and confident smiles, certain we had the votes.

Petersen called on the audience to speak. The people and the land, they kept repeating, as if scripted. "If there's one thing Donkey knows better than the people of this town, it's the land itself." By my second month on the board, I'd perfected the art of looking fascinated while not listening, and the further ability to avoid the stares of those who were obviously contemplating my grisly death. It was clear that the room was packed with Donkey's supporters, and that the only ones who weren't here were those who had elected me to get rid of him. But Johnny Lynch understood that an X on a ballot is dead and gone, while influence lives in the anger of the people who show up.

One after another they made points I couldn't refute. Donkey Sparks did know every road in this town. He was available twenty-four hours a day. He belonged to the Fire Department, which often worked hand in hand with his own. Although he had never graduated college, he knew as much about highway construction as a civil engineer. Moreover, he knew his men. Knew how to keep them from goofing off (when he cared to), how to send them home when they came in drunk and get them to return sober the next day, how to keep them from filing endless petty grievances with the union.

"I'll hear three more speakers," Ralph said to a line that stretched from the microphone out to the lobby.

Nini Sparks, Donkey's wife, had sung in my mother's choir. She was a soft heavy woman who wore sweatpants and tee-shirts emblazoned with the names of places they'd gone on vacation. She stared at me, her jaw locked, doing her best to threaten, absently chewing her stringy brown hair. Everybody knew about Donkey's temper; everybody saw the bruises on her arms. When Donkey lost his job, how much of his anger would fall on her?

Although he never strayed from the square of space in front of his seat, Donkey made me think of an animal pacing his cage. What hair he had left was clipped close to the scalp, the same texture as the stubble on his cheek, so that his whole head looked to be cast in shadow. Inarticulate, uneducated, crude, as my mother had described him, he stared only at me, alternately offering me certain death and sugarcoated favors. What could I expect if I voted his way? Snow plowing up my mother's driveway to her door? A water view lot in Johnny Lynch's development? First dibs on all the hardwood his crews cut down?

Ralph called for the vote. "Fred?"

"I vote for Mr. Sparks and I hope all of you do the same."

"Lyle?"

"No."

"Sandra?"

"No."

Ralph would cast his vote last, but everyone knew what it would be. There wasn't a sound in the hall. "Davey?" The diminutive now; the guy was practically adopting me.

Harlan Bowman in the sixth row back was bent at the waist, appearing ready to sprint up the aisle. He looked to be coaxing me, eyes wide and hopeful and welcoming. If I came through for them this once, he was trying to tell me, I'd be one of them, as good as native born. And why not? I had to ask myself. Did I imagine I had more in common with retired college professors? With the people whose yards I maintained? Why not prove myself to the locals? Donkey wasn't even the problem. He was a puppet. He jumped when Johnny Lynch pulled the strings. How many department heads would I have to cut off before I killed the hydra? Would I have to retire Abel Smalley? And the town manager? And the health inspector? And the harbormaster? Would I have to knock off Johnny's minions one by one and in the process fire every native-born man and woman in town government? Bring in administrators with advanced degrees, people who at best had vacationed in Saltash, who saw the town as a step in their career path? Was that the only way to get to Johnny?

"Davey? The question on the floor is to reappoint Mr. Duncan Sparks as superintendent of Roads, Bridges and Waterways. How do you vote?"

If Gordon or Judith were here, I'd have a moral anchor. I'd know the way I was about to vote was right. So many things about this job reminded me of Judith. I missed her clarity, her tough legal mind. I had never felt so public and at the same time so alone. I looked from Nini Sparks to her husband's fists. From Harlan Bowman back to Johnny Lynch himself, arms folded, rocking back and forth in his seat. Join us. His smile was soothing. Our side is your side. Join us.

But Johnny read my vote in my eyes, and before the word *no* could leave my lips he was out of his seat, striding to the microphone. "Chairman Petersen!"

"We're voting, Mr. Lynch."

"As Mr. Sparks's attorney, sir, I'd like the opportunity to speak." He didn't wait for permission from the chair. "I believe there may be a conflict of interest here. I believe Mr. Greene has had a personal dispute with Mr. Sparks and I question whether he can be fair and impartial. . . ."

Sandra and Lyle looked at me with steely impatience. Didn't I know this was one of Johnny's tricks? Had I expected him to go down quietly?

Answer yes, of course you can be impartial, and then let's cut the bastard's legs off. What are you waiting for?

"Isn't it true, Mr. Greene, that on the afternoon of April six of this year you accused Mr. Sparks of covering over a scandal in his department? The town manager was in the room at the time, Mr. Greene. Isn't it true that you accused Mr. Sparks of impeding your landscape business? As you well know, this is not a court of law. You are not required to answer, but I suggest that if you do not recuse yourself, you are opening this town to legal action."

Before I could form an answer, Fischel's hand shot up. "Mr. Chairman, I move we indefinitely postpone the motion to reappoint."

"I'll second for the purpose of discussion," Petersen said. "The motion is open to debate."

"Mr. Chairman, we obviously need to talk to legal counsel." Fischel glared at Lyle Upham. "Anyone who doesn't support the motion is clearly exposing the town to risk."

Upham glared at me.

No one in the crowd was sure exactly what had transpired, except Johnny Lynch, who seemed to nod, Well done! to Selectman Fischel and to wink at Donkey Sparks.

JUDITH

Judith wondered sometimes if she shouldn't just take a leave of absence from her law practice so she could spend all her time with Gordon these last weeks of his life. But the bills not covered by insurance piled up and piled up. Her clients could not put their lives or their troubles on hold. So she went on, with half her attention always focused on Gordon. Not that he exactly kept track of when she was there and when she wasn't. She knew he drew comfort from her presence, but he drew almost as much from close friends. He was heavily drugged and high, kiting through internal skies on winds she could not perceive. Sometimes he was back in 1952 or 1967. Usually he recognized her, but now and then he confused her with some previous wife or girlfriend, wanting to reminisce with her about events that preceded her birth. She never corrected him; what would have been the point? Occasionally he realized what he had done, and then he told her he simply could not help imagining she had always been with him, that she was his real wife and the others had been mere preparations, false attempts, approximations.

Dr. Barrows told her that Gordon would last at most another month. He did not tell Gordon, but she suspected Gordon knew. It could happen at any time, was the way Dr. Barrows put it. Again the hospice was discussed and dismissed. She wanted Gordon to have the New Year's celebration he had requested. That week she was taking off as best she could, for she would have a full house of guests. His second oldest son, Dan, came with his family over Labor Day, since he could not come for Rosh Hashanah. They had left the day before. Now Judith was beginning preparations for the meals she would be providing the guests, but especially the dinner on the first night of Rosh Hashanah. Gordon scarcely ate, but he enjoyed the sight of food, and this feast was of enormous and terminal importance to him.

Gordon was lying in bed, gray against maroon sheets. "Did you invite David?"

"No, I did not. Have you forgotten I'm no longer seeing him?"

"Don't be bitter. I've made messes every bit as destructive as David has got himself into."

"I'm only bitter because I let myself count on him."

"I pushed you." Gordon fell silent, his eyes closed. After several minutes she thought he had fallen asleep, as he sometimes did in mid-conversation. But when she was halfway to the door she heard his hoarse whisper behind her. "I want him here. No matter how he may have disappointed us personally, politically he's vitally important. We have to stay in touch with him. We have to keep him on our side."

"You really want me to invite him? He probably goes to his sister's, the same as at Pesach."

"No." Gordon had a fit of coughing and they both waited until he could once again gasp out a sentence. "Marty told me he and Holly go to his parents then. Invite David. I want to see him one last time. After all, he's my project as much as yours."

"Your half of the project was far more successful . . . I'll ask him. Do we have to entertain his girlfriend too?"

"I think he would understand a request that he come alone."

David had left two messages for her, but she had not called him back. She knew what he had to tell her. According to Judith's sources, which included Mary and her daughter Jo, Mattie, Enid Corea, and Jana Baer, David had changed his address and phone and was living part-time in his mother's barn. However, he was still spending at least three nights a week with Crystal. Crystal was reported irked at this development and wanted him back living with her. Judith sighed. At least he was trying to disengage. One thing David had never understood was that while Gordon and she were always minor scandals, they were also deeply linked into the town. They had many friends and many supporters, people for whom one of them had done a favor, people she had represented or helped to services they needed. Like Johnny Lynch, they had multitudes of enemies and multitudes of friends. And like Johnny, they knew there were no secrets in this town. There was always an observer, a witness, a leak. If you wanted to know anything, you had only to wait and someone would come and tell it to you; if you were impatient, you just had to know who to ask. She knew, for instance, that Crystal had leaked David's election morning letter to Johnny Lynch and hence to Blossom. She had heard it from Mary who had overheard Johnny's secretary and his bookkeeper talking about it in the tea room. Nonetheless, she had never told David, but only suggested to him he might be wise to remember that Crystal was on Johnny's payroll. When he moved all his files to his mother's barn, Judith guessed he had figured out a few things.

She still wished him well. She had contempt for women who hated men they had been with for no further reason than that they were no longer lovers. It was undignified; it was petty. She had met the other Mrs. Stones; men had erratic tastes in women. She must pick up the phone and call David. She sat at her desk in her office by the harbor and made ugly doodles on a legal pad. Or could she run into him? That would be easier. She had to invite him at once, before the day was out, or he might make other plans and disappoint Gordon. She had never been capable of disappointing Gordon, even in minor things; but now it was passionately important not to fail him.

She picked up her purse, rushing past Mattie, who called after her, "Where are you going? You have an eleven o'clock."

"On an errand. I'll be back in less than half an hour."

She drove straight to the nursery. She would buy two bronze chrysan-themums. She would do it, that is, if she saw his red truck outside. If he was out on a job, she would make a new plan. But she saw the truck and then she saw him, helping Doris Fisher load a birdbath into her station wagon. Judith parked and caught him as he was walking back into the building. She didn't even have to buy the chrysanthemums.

"David, Gordon's dying. He wants to get all his family and friends to-gether for Rosh Hashanah dinner. He views you as a friend. I hope you won't let him down."

He mumbled an answer, caught by surprise, his head bowed, hardly looking at her. Then he finally raised his gaze. "Do you really want me to come?"

"By yourself. Or do you need to bring the family?"

"I'll come alone."

"Good," she said. "Gordon expects you. He really wants you. It's his goodbye."

His sister was standing at the plate-glass window glaring. Marty had detested Judith ever since he had tried to kiss her at a party years ago and she had given him a hard push. Holly should have appreciated Ju-dith's response, but who knows what she thought had happened? Judith turned on her heel to march back to her car.

"Judith!" David called after her. She swung back, waiting. "Is he really dying?"

"Yes. He knows what's happening. I think he's almost ready for it."

"Judith. I want to talk to you about my son. Once you said maybe you could do something about how things are. Well, I think this might be a good time."

"If you want to consult me as a lawyer, you need to make an appoint-ment at my office, David. I'm not taking on any new cases right now—for reasons I hope are obvious." She had given the invitation for Gordon. She would continue to be friendly, remote and untouchable. Her feel-ings were her own business.

Gordon had many bad nights now, when the pain was uncontrollable, when his fever rose and convulsions took him. Then the demon would withdraw a bit. He would slide into sleep or unconsciousness. It was hard for her to tell the difference.

Fern had come early from the ashram and settled herself into the shack she had painted pink years ago. She began spending afternoons in Gordon's room. "You seem almost ready to pass over."

Judith, standing in the hall, overheard Fern and came in at once, fearful that Fern would upset Gordon.

"I'm not ready to die . . . but it seems I have no choice . . . I'm game for it, but . . . I had so much else I wanted to do and see. I feel as if I'm . . . walking out on a very good show."

To talk with Gordon required great patience, because it could take him up to five minutes to finish a sentence. His mind was quick, but his breathing was labored and his strength failing. However, Fern was nothing if not patient. When she was not with Gordon or helping Judith, Fern would sit with her hands open in her lap. Judith assumed she was meditating. Sometimes she forgot Fern was in the room. She admired Fern for her patience. She herself sometimes finished Gordon's sentences for him, and then felt bitterly ashamed of herself.

"No, I'm not angry," Gordon was saying. "I've . . . lived the life I wanted . . . I've had so much . . . it would be gluttonous . . . not to . . . be satisfied."

But I'm not satisfied, Judith thought, lurking outside their conversation. I have not had enough of him. I will never have enough of him. How am I going to just keep on after he is gone from me? Suppose I was offered a bargain, you can't ever touch him but you can talk with him, you can sit with him just one hour every day. Even that would be something. Even that. I would pay for it in blood. But I am going to lose him altogether. Knowing the pain he suffers and the convulsions and the difficulty of simply surviving by now, how can I argue with death? No one wins that argument, not even a crack lawyer.

She came to the doorway but did not disturb them. Gordon lay back on his pillows with Fern sitting beside him in a straight chair, one hand on his. This was one of the moments when her beauty shone out. Judith stood there unseen and thought about how much Gordon had been loved and still was loved, yet that love was weak against the dissolution taking him.

DAVID

I was at my new place, what Crystal called the barn, when I heard Judith's voice on the answering machine. Ceilings, walls and floor: I had painted the whole place white so that it felt vast and clean and pure. And quiet. I fell in love with the quiet, the padding of my footsteps in socks across the floorboards, the chatter of squirrels in the locust branches, the rain on the high-pitched roof above the loft. My bed was a mattress on the floor. "Like your uncle Georgie," my mother said, when I helped her upstairs. I couldn't bear furniture clogging the place, blocking the light and my ability to glide across the glossy white floor like a skater. I often lay on that floor to read, to write, to do nothing but stare: at the spiders walking the rafters, at Georgie's old stereo speakers, at my life, which seemed as full of possibilities as this fresh wide-open room. I was listening to one of my handful of CDs and reading when I lunged for the phone. "Judith, wait!" I said. "I'm here."

"Oh, David. Good of you to pick up." This was her lawyer voice. I had sat across her desk and heard it. I had heard her switch it on in bed, when she used the telephone after sex. I had seen her features sharpen as she paced the floor naked, trailing the telephone wire behind her tight little buttocks like the tail of a Siamese cat. I had heard her discuss rape and disfigurement and medical malpractice in the same tone she used with me now.

"You'll never guess what I was reading," I said. "Robert's Rules of Order. Since I'm getting clobbered every week I thought I might as well figure out how they do it."

She ignored me. "It's about Rosh Hashanah, David. There's a problem."

"About you and me?"

"David, there is no 'you and me.'"

"Sorry."

"Rosh Hashanah falls on the new moon, one of the highest tides of the year. It's scheduled to peak at about eight-thirty that night."

"Which means trouble getting over the bridge."

"More complications: I just saw on the Weather Channel that they're predicting a cold front coming in tomorrow night, preceded by a big storm. Those will be winds from the west that tend to push the water in early and keep it in. I'm asking everyone to cross the bridge by six at the very latest. So if you're intending to come—"

"I told you. I'm coming."

"Then come early. I don't think the bridge will be passable after six."

"Judith, can I talk to you about something?"

"I really don't have time, David. I only caught the weather report two hours ago and I'm still calling relatives from out of town."

"Judith, I've missed you."

"Tomorrow night, then. Gordon will be happy to see you."

I told Ralph Petersen I'd be absent from the Monday night meeting. He said Fischel would be out of town too. With just three selectmen—meaning two others who would probably vote against him every time—he'd keep the agenda to a few housekeeping items. But if Judith had a storm to worry about, I still had Hurricane Crystal.

How could I announce I was going to Judith's? The mention of her name would cause a fight. I was apologizing all the time for insisting on condoms, for sleeping at my place four nights a week. Reading Crystal and Laramie the letter from Terry had only made things worse. Crystal asked if I was going to stay in my ex-wife's apartment when I went down to Florida. She was now deeply suspicious of Vicki, convincing herself that since Vicki was getting divorced, she would be interested in me. Laramie thought he was being replaced. He sat in the kitchen drawing pictures of houses burning. He slumped on the couch with his knees drawn up staring at the TV, his mouth slightly open. When I turned off the TV, he didn't move.

Crystal would throw a shit fit if she found out I was going to Squeer Island without her; no less for a Jewish holiday. Everything Jewish was associated with Judith. Crystal didn't like Laramie to question me about Jewish holidays, or even why I was circumcised when he wasn't. She got nervous if she heard him asking Holly's daughters what they learned in Hebrew school, or if they showed him how to write his name in Hebrew letters. My religion was a subject off limits, a battlefield on which she couldn't compete. It had been easy to avoid the issue over the summer. But I couldn't tell her I was going to celebrate the Jewish New Year with Gordon and Judith. Without her.

I waited until Sunday night. I told Crystal that after the regular selectmen's meeting there would be an executive session with the town counsel. I said I wanted to go out for a drink with him afterwards, to pick his brain. I'd sleep at my place Monday because it was going to be a late night.

"And Tuesday?" she said, as if she'd caught me holding something back. "Were you planning on staying away from us Tuesday too? Because I know what Tuesday is."

"Tuesday?"

"I'm not stupid, David. I have a calendar. Tuesday is Rosh Hashanah, isn't it?"

Her calendar was a free gift from the hardware store. It listed the Jewish holidays, but not that they began at sunset the night before. "If that's what the calendar says."

"I'm making a holiday dinner. Don't look so glum."

"Why do you say that?"

"Because we both remember Shabbat. But I've got a cookbook now and I'll do it right." She pulled out an old yellowing paperback, *The Art of Jewish Cooking* by Jennie Grossinger.

"Where'd you get that?"

"I found it at the thrift store. And you'd better be here. Tomorrow I'm seeing Mom and I'm going to invite her."

"Crystal, it's a weekday night. We have to get up so early. Let's put it off till the weekend. Maybe Friday? Mom won't mind. I'd enjoy it more."

She just smiled. "Just leave it up to me. I won't fuck up."

JUDITH

48 Judith had her lists. She had lists of foods to be purchased, food to be cooked ahead of time on Sunday. Food to be cooked on Monday. Lists of where each of the thirty guests would be lodged, for almost everyone at the dinner must sleep on the island. The September new moon brought very high tides, and the bridge would be underwater by the time the meal started. Most of Gordon's children had their own accustomed places in the compound, but Sarah had stopped visiting when her father married Judith. In fact, Sarah's old shack had been renovated into Judith's home office, so in recompense, Judith put Sarah and her daughter in her own bedroom in the big house. She would sleep in her office.

She had lists of what her lieutenants were each to do: Natasha, her right arm, her comfort and joy; Jana Baer, who would come back for the dinner. The Baers, like the Squeers, had lived on the island for generations. Mattie, her secretary, would be helping all day Monday but would leave before the tide rose.

Sunday had been a reasonably paced day. People were arriving and must be greeted and escorted to their housing, unless it was where they always stayed. A couple of tents were set up as a boys and a girls dormitory, one on the beach and one on the dune. Judith had the keys to the Bechaud house, where she could put two whole families of Gordon's friends. Then Judith discovered a storm was predicted for tomorrow. She cursed.

Monday began at dawn. Judith went flat out all day. Aside from eating her brief meals in his room, she scarcely saw Gordon. The nurse, Mrs. Stranahan, was with him, as was his oldest son, Ben. Others dropped by until sent on their way by Mrs. Stranahan, protective of Gordon's waning energy. This crowd was what he had wanted: she was providing him with a last gathering of those he cared for. She set Ben and Larry to taking down the tents before the wind did it for them; she figured she would put the kids in sleeping bags on the living room floor once the tables were removed. Ben was forty-nine, taller than his father and much broader. He was an academic, a family man, a little stolid, almost professionally dependable and easy to like. She hated pairing him off for chores with Larry, who at thirty-two was still boyish and liable to sulk.

In the afternoon they cleared the furniture from the living room (except for the baby grand they could only push aside) and set up a square of tables. Most were from the various structures in the compound, but she had also borrowed a big table from the Bechaud house and a card table from Stumpy. They were all covered in tablecloths of various colors. Sarah had gotten involved in creating pleasing color contrasts and choosing the napkins; she regarded herself as artistic. Every dish in the cupboards went out, plates dating all the way back to the first Mrs. Stone and each wife since. The Bechaud house was raided for cutlery. Mattie lent her more glasses. There was a kids' table for the five- to eleven-year-olds and an adolescents' table. By three-thirty it was all set up.

Larry was trying to be sardonic. "It's the funeral feast before the fact," he said in her ear. "So macabre. Like a Buñuel flick."

"This is the time of year to reconsider your faults and failures with other people, Larry. Don't you have something to reconsider?" She bared her teeth at him. But nothing could really touch her. She was efficient, she was busy, she was numb. She must hold it all together. There was no time for pain and the anticipation of worse pain. "Your mother and her husband should be here any moment. Why don't you go wait for them?" The sky was gray and low but the storm had not yet hit. The wind was curiously soft and vague, the bay almost glassy, the air heavy as a damp plush curtain.

At four she sent Natasha with two of the more reliable kids to round up all the animals. At 4:45 the dogs were fed and penned up for the evening. At five all the cats were overfed and then distributed where they would be safe and out of the way, all except Portnoy, the big gray who had spent the last six years never more than two feet from Gordon. She left Portnoy on Gordon's bed. She brought Io, Pretty Boy Floyd and Principessa to her shack. They could amuse themselves throwing her briefs around. They all got along and could sleep with her tonight. The two recovering birds in their cages Natasha moved into the garage. The wind had risen sharply. Now the surf was pounding the beach. When she climbed the dune for a moment's respite from the kitchen, the wind had whipped the surf into a lather the color and consistency of steamed milk. She could see the rain coming across the bay toward them. As she walked back into the house, the first drops stung her neck and back. The day was still sickly warm, but the wind felt chilly. Two of Ben's sons and Mark's stepson were shooting baskets in the rain. Sarah's seven-year-old daughter and Ben's youngest were playing fish on the porch, but the wind was beginning to tear the cards away. As she passed, Sarah and Mark were arguing in the living room.

They could not keep away from each other. Nothing had healed in six years of divorce.

First course, gefilte fish. That she had bought along with white and red horseradish. She did not relish making gefilte fish, although Yirina had done so every year. Judith hated the smell and the mess. Then came chopped chicken livers and newly baked round challah. Three enormous bowls of salad. Apples, being sliced by Jana and Mattie. She checked the clock. Mattie had to leave now. She kissed her and took over. Lemon juice to preserve color.

Sarah, curiously subdued, was ladling honey from a huge jar into little bowls for each section of table. Judith had only met Sarah once, when they had flown out to Phoenix—where Gordon was speaking— and visited her for an evening. Since then she had gotten divorced. Sarah had been distinctly unfriendly then and on the phone since, but not this time. She was blond and sharp-featured like her mother, Bev Caldwell, who had just arrived with her Texan husband, Buck. They had made reservations in Provincetown and announced they would leave when the tide went down, no matter what the time. Judith shrugged. Two less to bed down. She could move the teenage girls into that room.

It was the final assault on dinner for thirty-two. A turkey was in the oven at the Bechauds' with Ben's wife delegated to baste it. She had four chickens in her two ovens here. Another turkey and a chicken were at Jana's. There were huge potato kugels baking that should be crisp and brown on the surface and inside, moist and oniony. She had made baba genoush and hummus yesterday, by the vat. The eight vegetarians would have plenty to eat. For fruit, pomegranates and an apple and carrot tsimmes redolent of cinnamon and nutmeg. The tsimmes had been cooked in the morning and would be reheated on the stove. All the umbrellas were lined up by the door for the use of anyone needing to cross the compound. The rain was coming in hard, at a forty-five-degree angle. It drummed on the roof.

The honey cakes had been baked the day before and were laid out under towels on top of the piano. Almost every couple had brought wine, some kosher, some not. She was sure Gordon did not care. Natasha distributed the bottles along the tables. Ben's youngest boy laid the short ritual on every plate. Natasha and Judith had put it together on Friday and Mattie had photocopied it.

When everyone finally came to the table and was sorted out, she felt so taut she could scarcely sit. Natasha, beside her, whispered, "Relax. There's nothing can go wrong now. The food is all cooked. The guests are all here. Everyone's complained about the weather. Now let's get on with it."

David had arrived sometime in the last twenty minutes. She had been too busy to notice. He was sitting between Natasha and Stumpy. All Gordon's ex-wives were there except his first, who had died in an auto accident. His children were present, and his grandchildren, including those not of his blood (ex-husbands and ex-wives who had married and multiplied) but still of his mishpocheh. Only Dan and his family were missing, and they had come the weekend before. Colleagues, comrades from old battles, drinking companions. Only eight invited had failed to show, and five of those had come over Labor Day. Thus Gordon even at the end commanded loyalty and affection from those who had known him, who had put up with him, who had enjoyed him.

Judith and Natasha rose and lit the candles, blessed the wine and the challah, and almost everyone sang the Shechecheyanu, the Blessing for the New Season. She was amused to hear Stumpy's loud uncertain baritone raised in song. He had heard it so many times over the years, he had learned it. Everyone dipped slices of apple in honey for the new year to be abundant and sweet. Then the pomegranates. The younger kids began spitting the seeds at each other and painting themselves scarlet with the juice. Outside, the storm was an audible roar. Occasionally a branch broke with a thump, or something hit the side of the house. Please, please, please don't let the power go out, she prayed each time the lights flickered. There would be no water from the well, no functioning toilets, no way to wash dishes. Please, she begged, keep the power on until the last one of them leaves.

She stood at the midpoint on the table that was raised a little from the others and presided, as she had over so many feasts and rituals since she had come to this house. Gordon had not been observant, but had gone along with her, and then had gradually come to count on the holidays. At first there had been some resistance. Now his older children—older than she—asked her questions about preparing for their children's bar and bat mitzvahs, about how to put on their own holidays when they did not come to hers.

"Gordon wants me to tell you tonight that I will go on living here after he is gone from among us, and that you will always be as welcome in this house and on this land as you have been before I ever came here. We both want you to know that."

Gordon managed to nod.

"It's hard for him to speak now, so I have to speak for both of us."

Once she and Gordon had thought that when the time came to say goodbye to his family, David would stand beside her and they would all meet him as a family member. So they had dreamed, in their arrogant fantasies. She glanced briefly at him where he sat between Natasha and Stumpy. Several at the table were in tears. David was staring at her with his intense gray eyes in his tanned face. People helped themselves to the fish and the chicken livers, and the meal began.

Gordon was propped up in a big chair. He could speak little and simply watched and dozed off, watched and dozed off. He was skeletal by now. His head, too large for his body, lolled on his wasted neck. His skin was gray with a bluish tone. It was impossible to look at him and not think of death. Ben sat on his right side and Larry on his left. Larry looked extremely nervous. Ben was solicitous. His role of the good loyal son was one he had played with comfort for many years. She was grateful to Ben.

She and Natasha went out to the kitchen to start serving the main part of the meal. Gordon used to insist on carving every bird himself. Now Ben had been recruited. David pressed into the kitchen behind him. "I can help carve. I know how."

"Why not?" She was arranging platters that Natasha, Jana and Ben's wife were carrying out. The kugels would be served in their baking dishes and cut up at each table. Ben was carving one turkey as David attacked the other. Ben was faster. In the meantime, she cut up the roasted chickens and set out platters of vegetables that had been cooked with them, carrots and onions and heads of garlic, aromatic and almost caramelized. Sarah appeared, tentative, and Judith gave her the vegetarian dishes to lay out. Ben finished his turkey and went to serve it. At once, David paused in his carving and turned to her.

"Judith, I have to talk to you. You haven't answered my calls."

"Natasha! Take the last platter of chicken out. David, please finish carving. This is no time for talk. Let's get the food on the tables." She didn't feel particularly motivated to hear his explanations. What was, was. But Gordon wanted a friendship, so she would put up with some self-justification—after the meal was over, after all was done and done well.

For the most part, the dinner went smoothly. There was a screaming match between Sarah's daughter and her ex-husband's wife's son; there were wineglasses tipped over and unlikely flirtations. Ben's sixteen-year-old daughter was doting on Larry. Incest aside, their levels of emotional maturity were a match, she thought. Everyone ate too much and seemed relatively content. Gordon lay on the sofa where Ben and Larry had carried him and smiled vaguely around him. He drank some wine and ate a bite of turkey and of kugel. Then he lay back, exhausted. But he was still smiling.

After dinner, people sang around the piano Ben's son was playing while Larry beat congas ineptly. Some sat reminiscing or arguing or boasting. Ben and Mark put the living room back. Breakfast would be a more informal meal, and most of the guests would be leaving through-out the day tomorrow. Judith was overseeing clean-up. David helped, but whenever she let him catch her eye, he projected an urgency she could not manage to ignore much longer.

He finally caught her as she started the dishwasher with the first load. "Judith, I need to talk to you. There's no use saying there isn't any 'us.' For me, there is."

Ben's wife and his son's girlfriend were carrying in plates. "All right. Wait for me in my shack. I'll get away when I can. I don't know when that will be. We can talk *briefly*."

When she had cleaned up as much as she could (she had run the dish-washer through two cycles and would do more in the morning), Judith ran to make sure Gordon was all right. Ben and Stumpy had carried him to his bed. There he lay in the sleep of the heavily drugged. Portnoy was curled around his head like a gray fur cap. The cat blinked at her, but Gordon did not wake. He was exhausted. She hoped this last good-bye had been worth the drain on him.

She came back into the kitchen intending to head for her shack. Sarah was sobbing. Natasha, who had been comforting her, began to cry. Kids were rushing through the kitchen. Jana was looking for her roaster pan. Judith found it and then coaxed Sarah and Natasha into her bedroom and shut the door.

"He's really going to die!" Sarah moaned. "I can't stand it."

Judith stroked her back and held her, but she could think of little to say. For the last thirteen years, Sarah had seen her father exactly twice. She longed to disentangle from Sarah and go to Natasha, whose tears simply would not stop. Judith felt exhausted, but she had to summon the strength to comfort both women. It was her role. She did not know if she hoped David would wait for her or give up. She only wished there were someone who could hold her and comfort her as she was soothing Natasha and Sarah.

JOHNNY

Johnny saw her first in the drop of Ralph Petersen's jaw, the way he strained halfway across the table to get a better look. Johnny had been dozing through the meeting, thinking of leaving, not that he had anywhere to go but home alone. With barely a quorum present, the selectmen were slogging through a utility pole hearing when discussion stopped. Crystal stood in the open door with the boy pressed to her hip, tears mixed with raindrops streaming down her cheeks. Even before he'd followed Petersen's gaze, Johnny had caught the scent of her rose perfume, heard the clack of her boots on the gray tile floor. Crystal didn't see him wave her over, but stared at the table of three selectmen and two empty chairs. The boy saw Johnny and tugged at her, but she wouldn't move.

Johnny read the expression on her face. He'd caught glimpses of it in the office, when Crystal was upset, but he'd seen it in his wife every time she took ill. That's what scared him. That inability to move, the hopeless glaze, the lips forming sentences only the speaker herself could hear. All he needed was one of his girls going batty in the Town Hall assembly room.

"Ah, you made it, dear," Johnny said for the benefit of the curious. "You finished typing up that brief for me, then. Bless you for bringing it in a rain like this." He took her elbow and steered her to the door.

Although the boy was properly dressed in a yellow slicker with a hood, Crystal's denim jacket was soaked through. She hadn't even thought to wear a hat. Her hair dripped in pale strands down her face. He whispered, "What's going on? Do you mind telling me what you're doing here?"

It was the boy who answered. "Looking for David. But he's not here."

"I couldn't find him." She wasn't talking to Johnny or the boy but to herself. "He wasn't at work or the barn or his mother's house. He's not here."

"What's the fuss, dear? You know you can't be a millstone around a young man's neck."

"He's on the island," she said. "With her."

"Well, if that's true, I think there's a good reason for it."

"What do you mean?" she said, meeting his eyes for the first time.

The lobby was empty but voices carried in this old building. Years ago he'd had a conversation in the men's room that was all over Town Hall before he zipped up his fly. "Have you eaten?" Johnny asked, first Crystal, and when he got no response, the boy. "Have you had a good dinner, my friend?"

"French fries and a hamburger."

"Well, that's more than I've had. How about a little dessert? Would you and your mother be my guests?"

The boy shuffled his feet. He was unsure but sensible. Anything that might cheer up his mother. "Can we?"

"I've got some movie videos my grandchildren used to like. I think we can find something." The boy seemed eager. "Why don't you just follow me home. I'll pick up some ice cream. What's your favorite flavor? Let's have a little party."

"A party for what?" Crystal said.

"Just follow me home." Johnny smiled, eager to share the news.

In the past few years of living alone, Johnny made little use of his recreation room, spending his time in his living room between the TV and the mini bar. He'd stopped shooting pool and never looked at the autographed photos of his favorite baseball stars, the big model of the schooner, the basketballs signed by six Celtic championship teams. The little boy followed Johnny downstairs as if entering Santa's workshop. His eyes were wide as quarters as he turned around and around, stepping toward the trophy case and then the ship in full sail.

Johnny took him by the shoulder. "You like it, then?"

The boy nodded, shy but enthusiastic.

"How about I set you up with a bit of ice cream and a good movie while I talk to your mother upstairs?"

"What movie?" Laramie settled himself on the Naugahyde couch.

"Here's a good one," Johnny said. "*Star Wars*, would you like to see that?"

Laramie nodded and nodded. He kept looking around. "Do you have kids?"

"I have two boys and a girl, but they're all grown up and they don't live here any longer."

Laramie stared at him. "You live here by yourself?"

"That's the way it is, son."

He tucked a quilt around the boy's legs before starting back upstairs. The boy gazed at him as if he were an uncle, a family member, a trusted friend. Crystal was pacing before the big windows in the living room, staring at the whitecapped chop of the harbor where the lights from his outdoor floods illuminated the blackness.

"I was going to make a Jewish holiday dinner for him, from the stupid cookbook. But when I went to invite his mother today, she told me it was tonight, not tomorrow night. She said Holly had left already for her in-laws. That's why I asked you to let me off a little early today. I went straight to the nursery. But it was closed."

"Now sit down," he told Crystal. "You're soaked through. I'm going to give you a little something to calm you down."

"I'm sorry, I can't drink. What did you want to tell me?"

"This is fifteen-year-old single malt scotch. It's not a drink, it's an occasion. Now I'm not going to say a word until you sit down and take off that wet jacket and have a little sip." Given no choice, she obeyed. "That's better. Now I'm not happy about what I have to say, because it involves someone's bad fortune," yet he could feel the scotch rise up in his chest like victory. "Gordon Stone is dying. He hasn't got but a week or two to live."

Crystal's face went deadly still. The finger of scotch he'd given her was gone. When he poured another glass for each of them, she didn't resist. "So you see, if he is over there, there's no hanky-panky going on. The whole harem is there, his dozen wives, his children, his grand-children." At the thought of all Gordon's grandchildren surrounding him at his deathbed, Johnny felt a cold pang of jealousy. Where would his own grandchildren be when he was ready to pass on? His two sons and adopted daughter were all on the West Coast—but of course, he couldn't be jealous of Gordon. Gordon was about to die. Johnny had won.

"How do you know this?" Crystal said. Again her drink was gone; again he filled it.

"Gordon may be a socialist and satyr, but he's always been good to Stumpy Squeer. That may be the one thing the two of us have in common." One cold April night the idiot burned his own house down. Having gone through the two cords of wood Johnny had provided him, and too lazy to cut up more, Stumpy dragged an entire log into his living room, stuck the end of it into the fireplace and lit it as if it would just burn like a candle. That summer Johnny had provided the materials, Gordon the labor, and by late fall Stumpy had a new house. Johnny had to admit he'd enjoyed driving over to the island to see the progress of the house: the arguments with Gordon over the Vietnam war, still raging that summer; the beautiful women Gordon always had around the compound. He'd seen that ex-actress, then Gordon's wife, sunbathing once without her top on.

Crystal was on her feet.

"Now where are you going?"

"I don't know," she said, taking two steps forward, then back, clutching herself. "To see if Laramie's okay."

Johnny poured himself another drink. Waves of rain from the west struck the windows like buckshot. He had constructed the government of this little town as carefully as one of his ship's models; glued his people in place with loving care, the selectmen, the Board of Health, every member of every committee, with himself at the helm. He steered this town like the captain of a ship, through budget crises and state land grabs and unfunded mandates from on high that had sunk other towns this size. For thirty-five years he was the captain, until Gordon and his hippie riffraff and his intellectual pretenders rose up to challenge him. Now who was left standing?

When Crystal returned, she strode directly to the bottle and poured herself a glass. "Is he all right, dear?"

"He's asleep. He fell asleep smiling. He hasn't done that in weeks."

"My own children used to fall asleep on that old couch." He noticed her face, all puffy and red. She'd gone downstairs to cry. "What's the matter, dear? I thought you'd take heart in the news. No one's glad to hear of a man's death, but surely you understand why your man went over there. I dare say I'll pay a visit myself, if not before he passes, then certainly afterward. That's the way of politics."

"Don't you understand? Now she's free. Now he can go to her, he can live with her." Crystal's words were tumbling one on top of another. Too much to drink. "Now he doesn't even live with me, doesn't want to live with me, and he'll go to her."

"No, he will not go to her. Sit down, dear. Sit down and no more whiskey." She did sit. She hung her head, then lifted it as he spoke, looking at him as a little girl looks at her father. "You are a warm and beautiful woman."

"He doesn't think I'm beautiful."

"Then he's an idiot. Because you are. And you're young. Too young to have lost anyone close to you. Because when you do, the last thing on your mind is finding another. Believe me. As cold as Judith Silver is, it'll be months before she's ready to think of loving again. Maybe years. I know that because I went through it. During that time, you will have your chance to talk sense into David, and, I truly believe, you'll win him."

Crystal took his hand, dangling at his side, and kissed it, kissed it not like a daughter on the back of his wrist, although it began that way, but like something else. Slowly, lovingly, the way he'd only imagined in his most private thoughts, she touched the tip of her tongue between his fingers. Then she rose and pulled him close.

"No, dear," he said.

"Yes," she whispered, taking his hand and putting it on her breast.

"Yes, Mr. Lynch—Johnny. You've been so good to me. I want to be with you now. I want to be in your bedroom with you."

"But the boy—"

"He's fast asleep under the quilt you threw over him. Where's your bedroom, Johnny?" It was the woman, not the little girl, who spoke now, who led him upstairs and knelt at his feet and unbuckled him, who took him in her mouth, and then inside her body. "You're so good to me, so good to me." She locked her legs around his back and rocked. She cried into his shoulder. He couldn't believe what was happening, really happening, just like something he imagined when he couldn't sleep. Her body was smooth, lush. When he felt her down there, she was hairless. Maybe young women now shaved themselves? Both her nipples had little rings through them. It was all strange. It was as if she had taken him into a strange country, the country of the young where bodies were beautiful and fragrant, smelling of roses and sex, and exotic in ways unlike the bodies of women he had known, pierced and shaven.

"It's so nice to be with you," she murmured. "You make me feel safe. Your wife was a lucky woman. You make me feel beautiful."

He was half asleep when he heard her dressing. He stood at the window and watched her lift the boy like a sack of potatoes—the way he used to lift his own children—and carry him out to her car. Twice she stumbled but kept on going. Then he slipped back into his warm bed. By the clock, it was now only 9:45. If he was a younger man she might have stayed, but of course, she was not about to share his bed. He would not fool himself. This had happened once and would never happen again; or not for a long while, not until she was secure and married to Greene.

But this was more than satisfaction; this was a justice he could never have imagined. As his enemy lay dying across the roiling waters of the harbor, Johnny Lynch took a woman less than half his age. He slid easily into a deep and blissful sleep.

DAVID

I must have been dozing when I heard the horn, a long blare as if the driver had fallen into the steering wheel. Three cats leapt to the window. It must have taken me a few minutes to register all this, to shake off the wine and the heavy supper, to run from Judith's shack to the big house. I arrived as the car pulled up and Beverly climbed the stairs.

Rain ran down the woman's face, blurring her makeup, blue liner through rouged cheeks. "There's a car off that little bridge," she sputtered. "The headlights are on. It's just sitting there underwater."

She spoke to relatives grouped around the kitchen table. Judith was not there. "Call the rescue squad," I said, halfway out the door.

The angry son, Larry, ignored me and languidly stretched his neck in Beverly's direction. "A car underwater? Right, Mom. You drink a little too much Manischewitz tonight?"

"Call 911," I said. Gordon's second wife was a pretentious, overdressed woman who decked herself in gold, but she had summered on Squeer Island for a decade and knew the territory. "Now!" I directed the stupid boy. "You tell them there's a car off the Squeer Island bridge. Tell them Selectman Greene is down there. *Do it now.*"

All that night I'd been expecting trouble—a screaming phone call from Crystal or Gordon's deathbed curse. An accident didn't surprise me. My truck was blocked. I jumped in the waiting car. "Take me to the bridge."

"Where's my wife? Who are you?" His accent was thick west Texas. Buck, they called him. He was drawing the last puff of a cigarette and listening to a baseball game on the radio.

"A friend of the family."

There was sarcasm in the man's laughter. "Some damned family."

"Take me to the bridge." I was prepared to throw him out of the car and I believe he knew it.

The bridge to Squeer Island was a mile from Judith's house. The road was all sand up to the causeway, slow going in good weather, pocked with deep black puddles in tonight's storm. There was no moon. Wind pushed the rain up the windshield, swamping the wipers. I imagined Judith in that car, crouched in the seat well, rationing air. "Do you have to steer around every puddle?" I said.

"I do if I want to have brakes. For Christ's sake, I'm going as fast as I can."

What I knew as silver-green marsh in the daylight was a vast shifting surface, bottomless and black. Up ahead, in the high beams, I caught sight of the causeway, a thin asphalt ribbon just emerging from the sea.

"You know we could have just seen the accident and driven right on," he said, steering hard right to avoid a mudhole. "We could've looked for a phone booth on the other side and not turned back to the house at all."

"You're a model citizen."

The blacktop was slick as ice. It was six feet wide. Whitecaps lapped the tires. What looked ahead like an old gray raft broken free of its mooring was the Squeer Island bridge, the guardrails hanging in splinters off one side. "Stop the car," I told Buck and jumped out. The bridge seemed to ripple underfoot, thrumming with the force of the wind. As I leaned over the splintered rail, I saw two beams of light in black water. The car was upside down.

On the mainland side, vehicles sped down the hill, lights flashing: police cruisers, an ambulance. By my watch, the tide had peaked two hours ago. But even as the water receded, the rain whipped the shoreline, searing my skin with the force of shot. I couldn't open my eyes without squinting. I could barely hear above the wind. A parade of headlights snaked along the water's edge. Car doors slammed. Rescue workers poured out. The force of their boots shook the bridge.

I shouted, "We can get down there. It's not too late. We can get her out." Her. I don't know why I thought I knew, but I felt her down there, cold, alone. "We can," I insisted, tears and raindrops on my tongue.

Abel Smalley did not address me, but neither did he order me off the bridge. I'd be tolerated, I understood, as long as I stayed out of the way. Divers suited up in the mist. Hulks in orange slickers stood at the ready.

"What are we waiting for?"

"We can't do nothing in a current like this," Abel said. "No way in a wind this fierce."

"Bullshit," I said. "We have to move now. We have to do something."

He turned his back. "You know the procedure," was all he said.

The Rescue Squad was as close to a hospital as we had in this town. Their bravery was beyond question. But their first priority was safety. Risk versus benefit; I'd been apprised of their policies from the day I took office. They would be assessing a car off a bridge in a forty-five-mile-per-hour wind. No bodies visible; no one assumed to be alive.

A fire truck rolled slowly to the water line, its floodlights casting the bridge in a stark white light. I heard the crackle of orders over handheld transceivers. When the tide subsided and the current slowed, they'd have an hour before the creek gave way to mud. Black mayonnaise, they called it. Silt and water, a texture like pudding between the toes: a runny voracious mud known to swallow fishermen and suck a man up to his neck in seconds. All Saltash parents told the story of a little boy who wandered away from his family while chasing a crab and disappeared in front of his mother's eyes, simply slid into the mud quick as an oyster down a man's throat.

"We are not going to stand here and do nothing." I felt my throat burning as I imagined hers filling with saltwater. "I order you—" I screamed at the chief of police, just before he thrust me out of the way.

It was past one A.M. when I saw the first diver blow water from his mouthpiece, adjust his mask and plunge. He shifted the searchlight between his hands. I heard bubbles playing on the surface. By this time, the tires of the car were visible, like the paws of a dog on its back. I seemed to have lost the strength to stand. I leaned against what was left of the railing. Island people were huddled along the causeway. Finally the diver broke the surface. "The driver's side window is smashed," he said, swallowing. "No one in the driver's seat. One body in back. Looks to me like a kid."

DAVID

51

Crystal's body was discovered at daybreak the following morning and wrested from the mud by a small hovercraft. Using a canvas winch fastened beneath her arms, the vessel tugged until the vacuum was broken and she was lifted aboard. A Coast Guard helicopter circled above a small army of rescue personnel and their assembled vehicles, news vans and photographers and a hundred onlookers come to gawk behind a yellow cordon strung up by the police. I watched from the bridge. I heard a radio barking orders, trucks spinning tires in the sand, car doors slamming, and above it all voices asking, Who was she? Why did she climb out the window? Why did she leave the little boy?

I tried to call Crystal's mother that day, but I could not find her address or phone number. It was Johnny Lynch who called her father. Far from dead, as she had told me, he was living in New York outside Troy, remarried and raising Airedales. He drove down at once, a heavyset red-faced man with bulging pale blue eyes, a shambling walk and slightly slurred voice. He seemed overcome and kept wiping his forehead and then his eyes. "I gave her that Olds when she was on her way here. She stopped with us for a month. I had it fixed up for her. It's such a big car, I thought it was safe for her and the boy. I gave it to her because the wreck she was driving had bad brakes. I thought it was a safe car. . . ."

He said he would take the bodies back to Troy, after the autopsy was completed. He wrung my hand. "She thought she could get a better job here. We didn't have room for her to stay with us, but there were apartments. She thought she could do better for herself here. Now look what's happened!"

I meant to arrange some kind of memorial for Crystal and Laramie, but the day after the accident my mother informed me there would be a morning service in the Catholic church. Crystal was not Catholic. The service was not held in the sanctuary nor conducted by a priest. Johnny arranged for the basement hall. In Quaker style, all those whose lives had been touched by the deceased would rise and speak their minds.

Laramie's third-grade class attended, and one by one the students stood to say goodbye. The women in the office rose next and then my sister. Michelle sobbed through the entire service. Tommy sat a little apart from her, rubbing his nose as if it itched. Johnny Lynch wore a black pin-striped suit, a gray vest, and strode the stage like a bad Shake-spearean actor. "Lamentation" and "mortal flesh" and "heartache" left his lips.

Beside me, my mother cried. "If only you had told her the truth . . ."

"A tragedy?" he intoned. "Or a tragic allegory?" He brought his hand to his heart. "A young mother wandering in the darkness, searching for help for her child."

Why did I feel Johnny's hand in Crystal's death? Why had Johnny left with her that night? Ten people told me Crystal had gone off with him. Where did they go? What did he tell her? I had no concrete reason to suspect him. Maybe I just needed someone else to blame. But Johnny Lynch had sent her across that bridge.

I delayed dealing with my house for a week, until I could not put it off. An open cookbook on the kitchen counter; a stack of folded laundry. Everything seemed to wait for them to return: Laramie's marking pens, Crystal's clothes. Crystal had astonishingly few clothes. Four dresses in the closet, five skirts, five pairs of pants. One drawer of underpants and socks. Another of sweaters and shirts. Laramie's closet was crammed with jeans she had ironed, flannel-lined khakis, cor-duroys; plaid shirts and plain. There were two winter coats. A little blue blazer. He had one drawer for underwear, another for socks, one more for sweaters. I counted three pairs of sneakers, six pairs of shoes, a new pair of winter boots. I had never noticed how very well dressed she had kept him; how little she spent on herself. Really, the only thing she wanted was a father for her child.

I spent the weekend in the house, sitting mostly, walking from room to room. I wrote a letter to Crystal's mother, whose address her father gave me. I attempted to read: minutes of meetings; the *Baseball Al-manac*; Robert's Rules; a tide chart—anything that promised some sem-blance of order. Saturday night I wrote to Liam. Sunday morning I just stared at Laramie's drawings on the refrigerator. The faded ones showed three figures in a house; in the newer ones they were replaced by flames.

Crystal had dragged an old student desk from my garage to use as a vanity. There she sat every morning applying her eye makeup when she came in fresh from the shower, wrapped in a towel. Laramie would be calling for chocolate milk, the TV screaming cartoons, the dryer would buzz or a bowl would break, while Crystal outlined her eyes with the concentration of a master jeweler. Laramie and I lived all over the house. I had weights in the living room, books over the toilet, piles of mail and magazines on the kitchen table. Laramie's space rangers and action toys were on every shelf and chair. But Crystal had one yellow desk in front of a mirror. I never approached it until she was dead, and then, cautiously, as if she'd appear any minute, as if I was spying.

Twenty perfumes, all samples, all recalling the way she used her middle finger to daub a drop between her thighs. Lipsticks, liners, nail polish, deodorant, lotions, face creams, depilatory; boxes of pins; of tweezers. I was ashamed to think this: they're still half full. What a waste to throw them out. Of course I did, quickly into a plastic bag.

In the bottom drawer, blond hair dye and a hair dryer. Tampons and pads and birth control pills. A box of sewing supplies. Some prescription painkillers from Las Vegas. I emptied the drawer and moved on. The next drawer was full of photos and postcards. I recognized a very young Crystal in jeans and tee-shirt with, yes, Billy Lynch, Johnny's second son. I remembered him, all right. A bully, but once I started playing baseball, he left me alone. Crystal in a prom dress in front of a saguaro cactus, a grinning Mexican-looking guy with his arm around her. Crystal with a blond lady who must be her mother. I'm sure I never met her. The woman was wearing a suit a little too tight and a big corsage. Crystal was dressed as a bridesmaid and beside her mother stood the bride, also blond. On the back, Crystal had written "Didi's Wedding" and dated it eight years ago. There was nothing to suggest Crystal had ever seen her mother or her sister since. What had happened at that wedding?

One photo taken in an arcade showed Crystal and a redheaded guy mugging. Another showed pregnant Crystal with a bald biker. Crystal, a baby (Laramie?), and a middle-aged guy. An uncle? Crystal in Disneyland with Laramie, now three or four. Crystal in western gear posed in front of the Mirage volcano in Las Vegas, her boot up on the fence to show her leg. A studio portrait of Laramie looking serious and hopeful. Crystal with her arms around two guys, in a black bat-girl Halloween costume. A page from a magazine: "Six Ways to Firm Your Breasts." Crystal in a nightie, pouting for the camera. Crystal without a shirt on, palms across her nipples. Always her eyes seemed to be asking the camera, am I okay? Am I doing it right? Is this enough?

The one photo I kept was of Crystal holding Laramie, perhaps two, in her lap. For once, she was not looking at the camera at all, but at him with an expression so intense, it almost frightened me. The men in these photos, they appeared and disappeared, but at the center was her son.

A flattened sprig of lavender crumbled in my hand. A wine label. A black elastic garter wrapped around a matchbook: "Congratulations, Robert and Katherine Ann!" Were they good friends or relatives? Who had she gone to their wedding with? Were they still married? I had a hundred questions about every item in the drawer, an almost physical yearning to know her. I had been afraid to probe, to know too much, to be drawn too far in. Now I felt afraid even to turn around. Crystal was in that room with me; over my shoulder; touching my ear, whispering, "Why couldn't you love me enough to ask?"

I had no words to describe the turmoil I felt. Nor was anyone able to say a thing that made sense to me, except, oddly enough, Liam, whose response to my letter arrived with surprising speed.

I'd written him because I thought he should know; because I'd wish to know if a son of mine, however unwanted, had died. Liam was guilty; Liam was innocent. I felt I understood him in a way I never expected anyone to understand me.

Dear David,
I have to admit I was reluctant to reply. I never really knew the boy. I can't say I feel responsible, except for fooling around with his mother, but no one, least of all the innocent himself, deserves a fate such as this. I can't be sending you any money toward the funeral, if that's what you'd be wanting, only my sincere regrets. It was a tragedy for the mother and son, for us all. What you tell me happened doesn't make sense, but I guess there's no understanding something so sad. What can I say but that Crystal was a troubled girl and I was an idiot. May all my sins be forgiven.

At that I said, Amen.

I sat with Liam's note for almost an hour, reading it over and over in the post office parking lot. A single phrase repeated itself to me then and for hours after. "What you tell me happened doesn't make sense . . ."

Later that day, I called the chief of police and asked to see the autopsy report.

JUDITH

52 Gordon died in her arms exactly two weeks after Rosh Hashanah at 3:35 A.M. The last forty-eight hours had been very bad. He went into convulsions, then slipped into unconsciousness. Occasionally he came to, briefly. His breathing was hoarse and loud, then almost inaudible. He moaned and gasped out nonsense. She sat behind him in bed holding him and stroking him, sometimes singing to him, sometimes just talking in a soothing voice about how much she loved him. His agony was protracted and she was torn between wanting him to stay with her and recognizing he could not endure more and must let go. The strength of his will was keeping him alive by the barest thread. Then she felt it snap. His eyes flew open and his body grew rigid, then limp. His eyes were glazed. She could find no pulse.

It was a quiet night and she could hear the surf after she could no longer hear his halting breath. The surf was up because a tropical storm had passed far out to sea, only the waves and the occasional lost pelagic bird marking its power. Almost at once his body began to cool. Entropy. The end of her life as she had known it. Portnoy remained on the bed, and she allowed him to sniff Gordon's face. He knew. He jumped off the bed, his fur on edge, and went straight to the door demanding to go out. She was afraid he would somehow commit feline suicide, get caught by a coyote, fall in the marsh mud. "No," she said quietly. She would keep him in all week, until he had adjusted to Gordon's absence. She was alone here with the animals, and they would need her. And she would need them.

She told everyone she called they did not have to come. Gordon had insisted on cremation, which she regretted. She would be buried, and she had hoped they would have side-by-side graves. She had not been raised to believe in cremation and could not suddenly embrace it. But Gordon had been insistent, and she would honor his wishes. It had all been arranged. It would be done immediately. There would be a brief Jewish service. She would dig the ashes into the patio of the compound, as he had requested, and in spring she would plant a low growing tree the winds would not injure. A dwarf conifer, perhaps. They had discussed everything, endlessly. Nonetheless she experienced a deep shock as the two undertaker's men carried him out to their hearse in a body bag.

There would be a memorial in the spring, but as she told people, Gordon's goodbye had been the dinner. Nonetheless, Ben and his family came and, of course, Natasha. She made the calls, she made the arrangements, she went through with the cremation and brought the ashes home, half dead herself. She put food on the table and prepared to sit shiva. Natasha took Ben and his family to the plane the next day and remained with her for the next three days.

It was not until she woke on the fifth day after the funeral, alone in the house, that she began to weep uncontrollably. She wept on and off all day. She had canceled her appointments, of course, pulled the phone from the wall. Now she wandered the house, lost, without will or hope. It was a large house and a huge compound around her. Never had it felt so big and so desolate, like an abandoned village. She was out to sea, isolated amidst the wind and the rising surf, alone and desperately lonely. If it had not been for the animals in her care, she would have fled anyplace, into Boston, to New York. Portnoy was miserable and mourned with her, looking for Gordon and then asking to go out, then lying with his head on his paws, eyes half closed, not sleeping and not moving. He seemed her grief clad in gray fur.

She thought that in Gordon's long dying, she had practiced at missing him. She had grown used to being celibate over the last few months. She had grown used to not bothering him with problems and details. She had taken over fixing things he had always done, ordering wood and stacking it or getting help with what she could not manage alone. She had thought she was almost prepared for widowhood, but she had been wrong. His presence, however diminished, was nothing like his total absence.

She did not think she could endure it, but there was nothing to do but endure it. It would not go away; she could not go away. She continued. The following Monday she returned to work. She had Mattie reschedule appointments she had canceled and began working a ten-hour day. She could not sleep. She ate little. But she could work. She could write briefs, she could make deals on the phone, she could probe, she could litigate. While she was engaged in the law, her pain was distant: never gone but no longer overwhelming. However, like a visitor hanging around outside the door waiting to catch her alone, the moment she put down her work or turned aside, pain was back with her. At night she could not escape it. She fell asleep after midnight and woke at three. She was always exhausted, her nerves abraded raw, her eyes sore.

The second Friday in October, Natasha came home for the weekend. She drove straight through from Cornell, arriving just after midnight.

They had omelets and the last garden tomatoes. They drank Beaujolais, and Natasha told her stories of her fellow students, her professors and the animals they were learning to treat. That night, Judith slept. She slept and slept. When she woke, it was nine-fifteen—she, who always was up by six. She felt groggy but well. If only she could keep a piece of Natasha with her. They picked grasses and sea lavender in the marsh to make arrangements with chrysanthemums, golden and bronze and musky pink, from her garden. They dug the potatoes she had forgotten.

"I'm so glad you're here." She tried to tell Natasha how she felt, but words were feeble. "I've been lost, except for work."

"Maybe you need a roommate."

"Oh, Natasha, I'm too bossy. Who could I stand to live with?"

They walked by the bay past closed-up houses, some boarded against winter storms. The tide was receding and bits of seaweed, scallop and slipper shells washed up at their feet, rocks and pebbles vivid in color because they were still wet: gold, greenish, slate-gray, pink, shiny black. They saw footprints of a man and a dog, but no people except far, far in the distance two figures like themselves walked. Across the curve of the bay, a distant town glittered in the afternoon sun like a mirage of paradise. Terns were diving into the gentle ebbing waves. An emerging sandbar was studded with gulls resting.

"So, did anyone give you trouble about that woman drowning?"

"Mattie tells me there was talk in town that she committed suicide. Or that David or I plotted her death. It just seems so long ago. Everything before Gordon's death feels that way."

"But why did she have her kid with her? That's so tragic."

"What was she supposed to do with him at nine-thirty at night? Leave him home alone? That's neglect. When she decided to drive out to the island and confront David, she had to bring the boy. It's too bad she didn't get through. She would have found thirty-two people cleaning up a big meal and singing off key. Hardly cause for a jealous rage. I didn't exchange twenty words with David all night. It was desperation pure and simple, the desperation that drives so many women. That's one reason I bailed out."

"David had already moved out on her, right? And you weren't seeing him. So how can anybody blame you?"

"People can always blame a woman who's seen as strong. No matter how weak as a rag I feel. Anyhow, it was a two-week wonder. Then they had Gordon's death to talk about. Now there's a new scandal. Michelle, Crystal's friend, is accusing Tommy Shalhoub of molesting her daughter. Tommy has been calling me, so I have to decide if I'm willing to take on his case."

"It might keep you busy."

"I'm busy already, Natasha. It doesn't seem to help much. I'm alone, and I'm not used to it. The worst thing about a good marriage is after it ends." She sighed.

"I miss him terribly. I keep thinking of things I want to tell him, stories he'd enjoy." Natasha threw up her hands in a gesture of scattering. "Then I realize I can't tell him. I'll never be able to share anything with him again. He's gone, and I can never, never talk to him."

"I think that's what I miss most too. Talking with him. Our life was so examined, Natasha, examined together. It feels incomplete now. Nothing seems important to me. I don't really care about the gossip and it's hard to make myself care about town at all. I feel too sorry for myself. I'm no role model these days."

"Oh, you think you were my role model? Nonsense, Judith. Dr. Doolittle was. The man who talked to the animals."

"Well, you better get busy talking to them. They're like me, they're all lonely and a little crazy."

DAVID

53

Abel Smalley didn't have to say where, just when. Noon always meant the Binnacle. As I approached his table, I noticed his hand drop over a thin manila envelope. "You sure you want to see this?"

"It's more a question of need, to tell you the truth."

He sighed, "It was a terrible accident. There was marsh grass on the bridge. The surface was slippery, the visibility poor—"

"I was there."

"Suit yourself." He pushed the envelope across the table.

He wasn't required by law to provide me with an autopsy report. I could have made a written request of the medical examiner. But since I'd been elected, Abel had offered me any number of courtesies I'd never dreamed of receiving from the police. A license to carry firearms; a permit to park anywhere in town. If I wanted the autopsy of some dead girl I'd been screwing, his practical smile said, Sure. No problem. You sick fuck.

Commonwealth of Massachusetts
Office of the Chief Medical Examiner
Autopsy Report

CAUSE OF DEATH: *Drowning*

MANNER OF DEATH: __ *Natural Causes*
                      _x_ *Accident*
                      __ *Suicide*
                      __ *Homicide*
                      __ *Undetermined*

HISTORY OF TERMINAL EVENT:

The history as known at the time was provided by the Medical Examiner.

Crystal Lee Sinclair was a thirty-two-year-old white female, living in Saltash, Massachusetts. On the evening of September 22 the car in which she was the driver veered off the Squeer Island bridge, overturned, and sank below the surface of the water. The driver's side window smashed on impact. It is presumed Ms. Sinclair climbed out of the window and in a disoriented state wandered in search of help. On Sept. 23 her body was found by State Police helicopter and recovered from the inner breakwater of Squeer Island

Cove. Body was removed and taken to the Josiah Squeer landing in Saltash where it was viewed by this M.E. at 7:10 A.M. She was pronounced dead at 7:13 A.M. on Sept. 23.

AUTOPSY:

The autopsy was performed in the Medical Examiner's Office between the hours of 10:00 A.M. and 1:00 P.M.

Present at Autopsy: Medical Examiner and Office Technician.

Clothing: The clothing is wet and consists of a denim jacket, brown western boots, brown belt, blue jeans, a white blouse, black socks, black bra, black underpants.

EXTERNAL EXAMINATION:

The nude body is that of a white female who is five feet six inches and weighs approximately 140 pounds. Scalp shows silver-blond hair about nine inches in length. In the center of the scalp in the parietal region there is a red contusion measuring up to one inch in greatest dimension. The eyes are blue-hazel. The pupils are equal. The conjunctivae are injected. The teeth of both upper and lower jaws are in excellent repair.

I suddenly found myself smiling. "The daughter of a dentist," I said. Abel, stirring his coffee, looked up and shrugged.

The lips reveal no injury. Facial abrasions and signs of feeding activity of crustaceans and marine life are consistent with superficial trauma from waves and contact with ocean bottom and force of breakwater on body. The right and left earlobes show signs of cosmetic piercing.

Chest: The abdomen is slightly protuberant with a nine-inch curved linear scar in the right lower quadrant. There is an absence of hair in the pubic area. Right and left nipples show scar tissue consistent with cosmetic piercing (rings were found in each nipple).

Again, I glanced at Abel, embarrassed. At some point the waitress had delivered his meat loaf with mashed potatoes, a side of overboiled green peas in a little dish next to the salad. He hummed as he ate and never looked up from his newspaper.

Arms: The arms are muscular. The hands reveal evidence of injury on the right palm consistent with slashes due to beach grass. There is a one-inch abrasion beneath the right armpit consistent with the feeding activity of an eel.

Ever since I'd been a boy, I'd heard of bodies washed up in Saltash harbor, crabs that colonized the skull as comfortably as curling into a

paper cup; eels that ate their way through human intestines. For the
first time in years, I thought of Corkie Pugh and his morbid stories.

> *Upper arms reveal striated abrasions and evidence of injury due to auto-*
> *mobile window glass. One shard of glass, approximately one centimeter in*
> *diameter, found in upper arm.*
>
> Legs: *There is scar tissue on the right inner thigh, approximately 4.5*
> *centimeters in diameter, consistent with the surgical removal of a tattoo.*

"It was a butterfly," Crystal told me. A biker boyfriend liked to brag
that he didn't eat his women because it was boring, so she got herself
tattooed. "As a joke," she insisted. "To give him something to watch.
Like TV." I didn't laugh.

"I was drunk," she had said and looked away, ashamed.

> ### INTERNAL EXAMINATION:
> Heart: *The heart weighs 450 grams. The cardiac valves are normal.*
>
> Stomach: *The stomach contains approximately one ounce of opaque*
> *gray liquid. The small bowel contains semiliquid to semisolid fecal material,*
> *and in the rectum there are areas of purple-red streaking and dilated inter-*
> *nal hemorrhoids, but no primary nor metatastic tumor is identified.*

"Put it in my ass," she had told me. "Come on, I bet you're a virgin. I
want to be your first time." When I did, I felt her back muscles con-
strict. She clenched her jaw. When I removed myself, I saw a tear roll
across her cheek. "Did you like that?" She sat up with difficulty. "Did
you? You can do anything you want to me. Anything."

> Brain: *The brain weighs 1290 grams.*
>
> Body Cavities: *The body cavities are open in the usual manner. There is*
> *no evidence of blunt force or penetrating injury to the chest or abdominal*
> *cavities. The lungs are expanded and the organs are in their usual anatomic*
> *locations. Evidence of semen found in the vagina.*

A sound I made, a gasp, attracted Abel's attention. I had not seen
Crystal since the Sunday night before she died. I'd used a condom.
"Where was she before the accident?" I asked him.

I was sure he expected the question. He drew back his shoulders.
He leveled his voice. "I don't have that information."

I didn't need it. I knew. Why had Johnny left Town Hall with her that
night? Where did they go? Crystal was Johnny Lynch's lover. Why hadn't
I seen it? Because he was an old man? Because the thought of his
nakedness was beyond my imagination? I'd expected Crystal to make

me pay for Judith. I was certain the price was Tommy. But Johnny Lynch? Did they meet at my house when I was with Judith? How long had it been going on?

The Commonwealth of Massachusetts
Department of Public Safety
Chemical Laboratory

NAME OF VICTIM: *Crystal Lee Sinclair*
RESULTS: *Blood Alcohol: .11% (MKL)*
Urine Barbiturate Screen: negative (WGH)
Cocaine Metabolite Screen: negative (WGH)

"Abel, what does this mean? Blood Alcohol, point-eleven percent. Is that a lot? Does it mean she was drunk?"

"For a girl her size, I'd say so. Legal limit is point oh-eight."

"So you think that explains it?"

"Why she drove off a bridge? Wandered around disoriented? Sounds like drunk to me."

"Abel, she didn't drink."

"All the more reason, if she wasn't used to it."

"I mean she didn't touch it, Abel. Ever. She gave up drinking years ago. I lived with her. I know."

He said, "Believe anything you want."

"What if somebody got her drunk?"

Abel brought his napkin to his lips. His voice was official. "Due process has been followed, Mr. Greene. I suggest you try to put this unfortunate accident out of your mind."

As if that were possible. As if I would ever forget.

"I'm sorry but I've done the best I can. For you and the girl and her family. The law is satisfied."

I was not.

JOHNNY

Johnny dialed his daughter's telephone number, slightly ashamed that he had to rely on his address book. What kind of a father didn't memorize his children's phone numbers? What kind of a world was this, in which their numbers were crossed out and replaced, each one farther away than the last? He had no idea where Novato was (a suburb of San Francisco, she'd said), only that it was seven o'clock out there and Mary Rose should be home. He desperately wanted her to pick up. He needed to tell her how much he loved her, and that if there was anything she needed, anything at all, he was here. He needed to hear her talk about the good times—before her mother took ill; before she'd moved in with that bartender twice her age. He needed to hear from her lips that she loved him.

"Hello and have a nice day!" The damn answering machine spoke in the voice of the new husband, the idiot who sold insurance. "If you have called for Rodney, Mary Rose, Emily, Rebecca, or John . . ." Jesus help us, Johnny thought, Rebecca was four years old and John eleven months. Who in blazes was going to leave a message for them on the answering machine? He'd try later.

He'd tried all day after the memorial service and three times today. Seeing Crystal's father confirmed in his heart his love for his own children: whatever the imagined slights between them, whatever their youthful sins. The Lord worked in mysterious ways. He closed one door and opened another. Johnny had never been a religious man; that had been his wife's department. But he'd begun to see patterns now as he entered his old age; he'd begun to wonder if there was a hidden purpose in things.

Perhaps the Lord in His wisdom had brought Crystal into his life for just this reason, to unite him with his children; to soften his heart toward those he loved and to sharpen his resolve. For who were the rightful owners of the land above the dike? "Who stood to gain or lose?" as Gordon Stone used to proclaim at town meetings. Surely not himself, for he was an old man. Surely it was the rightful inheritance of his children and grandchildren he was fighting for.

Little Laramie and Crystal were messengers, he saw that now. A girl like Crystal had been with a hundred men; rough men, hoods, Las Vegas gamblers, men who used her like David Greene. So why had she ended up in Johnny's care except to show him the way back to his own children? He'd provided everything he could for Crystal, a good job and fatherly advice and, God rest her soul, a fitting memorial service. But he was weaker than the forces of evil, weaker than David Greene and Gordon Stone, who had lured her across that bridge to her death. Had David done his part by her, had he married her and cared for his boy, the door would not have been closed on Crystal, nor opened, to show Johnny the way back.

He tried his daughter's number again. Ten o'clock on the West Coast. They had three children: where the hell could they be?

"Yeah, hello?"

"Hello, Rodney? Is that you? I'd nearly given up. I've been trying to get you for hours."

"Uh, yeah. We went out to eat. Who is this?"

The idiot. "It's Johnny. Mary Rose's father. In Massachusetts."

"Right, she's puttin' the kids to sleep. Can you call back?"

"Well, it's one A.M. here. Can you ask her to come to the phone?"

Johnny thought he heard him mumble, "Shit," before the receiver dropped hard.

"Hello, Dad? Is something wrong? I was in with the baby."

"No, no, dear. I was just wanting to hear your voice. Wanting to tell you I love you, that—"

"Hold on, Dad. Okay? Goddamn it, Rodney. Just wait a minute and I'll be right there. Hello, Dad? I'm glad you called."

"You are?"

"The stove is dying. The old gas stove that came with the house."

"Oh, no, dear. Is it dangerous?"

"No, but I'm down to two burners here, for the five of us."

"Do you need something, dear? Would five hundred dollars be of help?"

"A big help."

"I know what a simple thing like a good kitchen stove can mean. The kitchen is the center of a family." He remembered winter evenings, when he came home after work to find his family at the table, the older ones doing their homework, Emily Ann at the stove.

"Hello, John. Rodney, here."

"Where's Mary Rose?"

"With the baby. Listen, thanks for the kind assistance with the stove. I feel like I want to do something for you in return."

"I'm sure that's not necessary."

"John. Tell me something. What kind of a health care plan do you have in your office, John? Because I think I can really help you with your insurance needs—"

"Thank you, we can talk about that next time. Now it's bedtime for me. I'll send the check off tomorrow." Johnny hung up without waiting for a response. One sleazy husband after another; no wonder Mary Rose didn't have a minute for her dad. Rodney was number three. Mary Rose had been adopted after his wife had lost two babies. Poor Mary Rose was always searching for love. What she needed was security; more than he could send her in dribs and drabs, a real nest egg for herself and her babies. Nothing less than their rightful inheritance.

When the summer crowds were finally gone and the rental business slowed, he had another series of meetings with the dolts from the bank. Roger told him that until the question of the dike was settled, and settled favorably, they could not forward him money on his land. "It will be settled," Johnny said. "It'll be settled soon."

"What do you mean, you want the dike on the agenda?" Ralph Petersen said. "I'd think that's the last thing you'd want."

"No, no, it's time," Johnny insisted. There was a buttery softness to the light in late October, a kind of gentle haze that cast the browning marsh grass in a golden glow. He could have been staring through his office window at a field of wheat. The streets were empty of tourists. Neighbors stopped to chat in the long blue shadows of afternoon. When he was a younger man he was up at four A.M. this time of year, duck hunting in the river valley, arriving at the office on a good day with five or six mallards for the girls. God help him if he brought them home to Emily Ann; she didn't even like his shotguns in the house.

"But the vote won't go your way, Johnny. You know that our young friend asked Abel for an autopsy report."

"And I advised Abel to give it to him. Why not? The girl is dead and buried, Lord rest her soul. It's time to move on, Ralph. I suggest you put it to the board this way: the Capital Improvement Plan is due to be updated in December. If there needs to be any work on the dike, it should be discussed now."

"There shouldn't have to be any work to speak of. It'll either be opened or left closed."

"Well, I'm asking you to call for a vote on that, Ralph."

"Put it off, Johnny. You won't get the votes. Sandra and Fred come up for reelection in May. We can win both seats. We can have the majority back if we work for it. I don't see any new David Greenes in the picture."

"Put the dike on the agenda, Ralph. Do this for me."

David Greene. Six months ago the name was no more than the memory of a small intense boy who played high school baseball. Now he'd joined Judith Silver, Palmer Compton and the attorney general himself on Johnny's list of enemies. Davey Greene, the Pitching Machine. Johnny turned away from the marsh. He opened his office door to walk among his staff. Crystal's desk stood in the corner like a shrine. David Greene. The idea that the amoral little prick should judge Johnny Lynch, when the entire town knew why the dear girl crossed that bridge—to confront him and his dirty little triangle, to demand he act like a proper father to her child, to bring the wayward man home.

He felt David Greene's hatred whenever their paths crossed; he could sense those hard gray eyes across a room. Twice Johnny had attempted to approach him—and why not? They'd both lost a dear presence in their lives; why grieve alone when the natural business of this town drew them together? Both times David Greene simply stared at him with silent accusation, as if he himself had anything to feel guilty about.

All this was unfortunate. Johnny had honestly thought he'd won David over to his thinking about the dike. No, David hadn't accepted a water-view lot; he wasn't greedy and he wasn't stupid. But through his observations over time and his conversations with Crystal, Johnny had come to think of David as a realist rather than a knee-jerk environmentalist. Now it seemed the boy's hatred would hold sway. So be it. If David voted to keep the dike closed, the bank would come on board Johnny's project like a shot. If David's vote swayed the majority to open the dike, well then, he was depriving Johnny of the fair use of his land and opening the town to a sizable lawsuit for recompense. Either way, Johnny would win.

Maria had come to him, closing the door behind her. "We have to replace Crystal," she said bluntly. "None of us can work those programs the way she did. We need someone young. And her empty desk is depressing the girls. Everytime they stop and look at it, one of them starts blubbering."

She put on his desk an ad she had drawn up for the local papers, "Wanted, Secretary for Legal Office, Good Benefits, Must Have Computer Skills."

Now, two weeks later, the ad still sat on his desk. Why hadn't he put it in? He was waiting, superstitiously waiting, until the vote on the dike came up. After that, he would fill the position. It would be nice to have another young face around the office, but this one would be more stable, calmer. Pretty but stolid, that was his recipe for peace in the office.

The hearing on the dike was finally scheduled for the week after Thanksgiving. Sandra Powell and Lyle Upham seemed delighted to take up the issue. They were friendly and full of chat before the meeting began, exactly as Johnny would be if he was about to cut someone down with his vote. Ralph and Fred Fischel were uneasy. Fischel hadn't been convinced the hearing was Johnny's idea. Fred called him when the agenda was announced to hear it from Johnny's own lips. David was Mr. Hatchet Face—had been since the girl went off the bridge. Nobody expected so much as a how-do-you-do from Selectman Greene these days.

All the usual nuts filled the seats. Palmer Compton had his boy by his side. Johnny smiled. "Hello, Palmer," he said, and got a grunt in return. There were all the other conspirators from Gordon Stone's group; Dr. Garvey in his natty bow tie and even Judith Silver, looking, he had to say it, delightful in her gray wool coatdress. Word had it David had not been over on the island since Gordon's death; you had to give him that. So what if the opposition far outnumbered Johnny's own troops tonight? He hadn't bothered sounding the alarm. He felt almost serene as he watched the drama unfold, as if he was a visitor from far away, come to observe the curious behavior of the natives. Let them rail against the dike—and rail they did—a full two hours, as Ralph and Fred seemed to shrink in their seats. Johnny yawned.

It was a quarter past ten when Ralph gaveled discussion to a halt, looking at Johnny in the back row as if to say, This wasn't my idea. Johnny responded with a simple smile.

"Mr. Chairman."

"Mrs. Powell."

"I move that this Board of Selectmen do what we rightly should have done many years ago, that is to open the Tamar River dike."

"Second." Lyle Upham beamed at the applauding crowd.

Ralph looked pale and tired. His voice was pure defeat. "The motion on the floor is to open the dike."

"Mr. Chairman, I move to refer the motion to a committee," David Greene said.

Johnny thought he hadn't quite heard him at first. Refer to committee? What was Greene trying to do? Where did he pick that up? "Mr. Chairman," Johnny shouted. "I rise to a point of order!"

"Excuse me, Mr. Chairman." David Greene again. "Mr. Lynch is not a member of this board . . . any longer. He can't call for a point of order." The little prick smiled straight at Johnny.

Above the noise in the hall, Fred Fischel glanced from Petersen to Greene, obviously confused. "I second the motion to refer."

The fool. What did he think he was doing? A referral to committee would delay action either way, the one thing that could hurt Johnny. He couldn't believe where this was going.

"Debate on the motion is allowed." Ralph's voice was lighter, infused with hope. "Mr. Greene."

"I believe this is one of the most controversial issues in the history of the town," David Greene said. "I think it's only prudent to study the matter further. We have approximately $25,000 left in the consultancy line of the budget. I move we form a committee to draw up a request for a proposal to seek an engineering study that might tell us the effects of either opening or closing the dike."

Johnny was on his feet. "That'll take years!" he heard himself shouting.

Ralph banged his gavel. "I believe the floor is Mr. Greene's."

"As Mr. Lynch himself has pointed out many times, Mr. Chairman, the dike has been in place for over twenty years. It would be imprudent and rash of us to eliminate it without study."

"You're stalling, you little bastard!" Johnny felt sweat under his collar. "You think I can't see through your cheap parliamentary tricks." The bank would not wait for a study; studies took years. He'd be stuck with the property until he died. He'd never cash out. "Yes or no, up or down. It's time to decide. We can't have this hanging over us."

"Mr. Lynch!" Petersen was shouting now, glancing worriedly at the reporters in the front row. "Mr. Lynch, sit down."

David Greene continued, "If we make the wrong decision, as Mr. Lynch, an esteemed attorney and former town counsel knows, we could open the town up to a significant lawsuit."

Before Johnny could shoot his hand up to answer the patronizing bastard, a hundred people were clamoring to speak. He couldn't see Ralph through the waving arms, but debate was cut off. They were already voting as he lumbered to the aisle.

"All those in favor of referring the motion to a committee . . ." Three hands flew up. "Those opposed . . ." Two. "The motion passes."

Palmer Compton leapt on a chair and called them all cowards for not opening the dike once and for all. Joe Pound cornered Upham and Palmer. Fischel huddled with Ralph Petersen and a hundred conversations echoed in the room. Johnny couldn't believe what he'd witnessed, what had slipped through his hands. The reality of his situation weighed like sand in his arms and legs. He could not move. Two reporters stood at his shoulder, asking questions. Ralph Petersen said as he brushed past that he would call the office in the morning. But they were all a blur to Johnny. He saw one thing and one thing only: Judith Silver smiling at him. As another lawyer, she understood as well as Johnny did how thoroughly he had just been skewered.

JUDITH

55 It was a late February day of tentative sunshine and low scudding clouds when Judith buried Portnoy under the Sargent's weeping hemlock, where Gordon's ashes were. The gray cat had always been Gordon's. He had died gradually, like Gordon. The vet said kidney failure, but she knew it was a failure of the will to live. The other deserter was Trey, the three-legged dog, who had attached himself to Stumpy. He needed a male pack leader, and Stumpy seemed flattered and willing to take him in. The other cats and the remaining dog, Silkie, were hers.

It was a quiet winter. Only Natasha came to visit. Judith spoke frequently to Hannah, had supper twice a week with Barbara. She spent more time with all her women friends and made herself go to Boston to see an evening of dance or music every month. She did not read much, because she found herself thinking of Gordon instead of paying attention. On television, sitcoms were too concerned with love and domesticity, medical shows were lethal, so she watched cops, science fiction, documentaries about anything—Antarctica, gerbils, any war, the homeless, coal mining. She took to bringing home videos. She played music loudly, to fill the silences in the house. The house was too big for her, but she could scarcely tear down half of it. She simply closed up the rooms she was not using.

At first she spent an occasional hour in Gordon's room, to conjure him up. Natasha put a stop to that. "It's morbid, keeping the room that way. Besides, it stinks. You have to clear it out. It doesn't make me think of how Daddy was. Only how he died. It's just a sickroom."

Together they bundled up Gordon's clothes and took them to Goodwill. "Somebody will like the warm sweaters and good coats and jackets," Judith said, weeping as she put them into boxes. But she would not let Natasha clear out his office. Two of his colleagues had promised to go through his papers next July and decide if there was anything publishable, what should be kept or archived.

Finally she took out his videos from several television appearances, a taped lecture from Capetown, and spent an evening watching them. That night she did not sleep. In the morning she put them away in his office, where she would not be tempted to look at them again for a long,

long time. She felt as if the tentative skin that had grown over her
wound had been torn off.

So the winter passed into March. Now the ground was thawed and
the first migrating birds were passing overhead, sometimes settling in
the compound. Ducks rested overnight in the pitch pines, one roosting
over Gordon's grave. She accepted an invitation to dinner from a lawyer
who lived two towns farther up the Cape. It was a pleasant enough eve-
ning. Timothy was even taller than Gordon had been and thin as a
rapier. His hair had receded, leaving the top of his head quite bald, al-
though it was still thick and brown on the sides. His forehead seemed
to go on and on, marked only by slight eyebrows perpetually surprised.
Timothy had a deep baritone that he could use to fine effect in the
courtroom. His skin was tanned even in late March, for he was an avid
boater and always took off a couple of weeks during the winter to sail
around the Caribbean. He sailed all winter, keeping his boat in a harbor
that usually stayed free of ice on the Sound. He offered to take her out,
but she said she'd wait for spring. She saw Timothy again the next
week. And the next.

She was not immediately drawn to him as she had been to David,
but perhaps this was a more intelligent attraction: he was in her field, a
professional, divorced with a daughter he seemed reasonably attentive
to. He saw his daughter weekends, which slowed down the progress of
their relationship. That was good, for she was in no hurry. She knew she
had to see men now, to resume her life. At twenty, dating had felt natu-
ral; at forty-one, it seemed a foolish and tedious game. The thought of
starting from zero with someone and having to explain exactly who she
was, to explain her life, exhausted her in anticipation. She was pleased
to have found a sensible man with obligations and standing in the com-
munity. Since they were both part of the same collegiality of lawyers
practicing in the same courts, they knew a certain amount about each
other.

She went out with a recently divorced therapist once and once only.
He had a condescending attitude she found abrasive. Mattie intro-
duced her to a somewhat younger man, David's age, who had just
moved to the Cape and opened a chiropractic office. He was full of di-
dactic advice on what to eat and what she must not eat, to the degree
that supper with him was a duel. No, Timothy was the best man she
had interviewed, as it were, and if she was in no hurry to rush into an
affair, he seemed equally cautious. They settled into a pattern of eating
supper together every Thursday and afterward taking in a movie or
a play. The first Saturday in April, he introduced her to his ten-year-
old daughter, Amy, and they spent the afternoon at an ice-skating rink.

Timothy was astonished that Judith had never before put on a pair of skates. She did her best to remain upright, but the next day she was sore. Her back felt out. If it stayed this way, she might have to see that didactic chiropractor. She had begun tomato and pepper seedlings inside, half her usual number. Natasha came home every three weeks or so. She had a new boyfriend she was considering bringing on spring break. Judith hoped she would like him, but knew herself hard to win over as far as Natasha's boyfriends went. None seemed worthy. She would try to be more tolerant.

"Do you ever see David?" Natasha asked as they were turning over the garden, about to start planting the hardiest crops.

"I've gone to the selectmen's meetings a few times. But you'd be surprised how long you can go without running into someone, even in a town this small. I get my mail delivered. He picks his up at the post office. I shop on Saturdays. I use the Shell station. A few small changes of pattern, and you can avoid almost anyone."

Natasha leaned on her shovel. "Why do you need to avoid him?"

"Why do I need to see him?"

"You don't ever think about getting together with him?"

"Do you think we should plant the bok choi in the row next to the lettuce? Or should we put the leeks there?"

DAVID

During Christmas school vacation I flew down to Florida. Since Terry's first letter, we'd exchanged a couple more and talked most Sunday nights on the phone. But a lifetime apart was hard to make up in two weeks, in spite of our best intentions. The weather didn't help. A cold snap froze half the state's citrus crop. We canceled our camping trip and spent two weeks shuttling between theme parks, Epcot, MGM, Busch Gardens, sleeping late, eating pizza, watching TV, playing catch in the parking lots and arguing about all the things I made him do that his mother didn't. Any notions I'd had about him were nothing more than that—notions. He was a sweet and energetic kid and headstrong just like my sister at his age, but Wynn's death and Cesar's departure had left him bitter and scared.

Our arguments spun full-blown out of nothing. Sometimes Terry flailed at me; sometimes he sulked and wouldn't speak. He was pushing, testing my limits. Who was this son of a bitch who showed up and called himself Father Number Three? I'd been a sentimental idiot to imagine Terry would have welcomed Laramie. He was fiercely jealous of his half siblings. He would have torn Laramie apart. I didn't blame myself for Terry's problems, but I wondered what the hell I had thought I was doing: sacrificing my life to one lost little boy, while my own son didn't know who to call Daddy—his grandfather or a stable hand who passed himself off as a trainer.

The night before I left, Terry called me a fucking asshole, then fell asleep in my arms. I knew that I wanted him to start visiting me, but when I brought that up with Vicki, she put me off as always. She was living with the three kids in a garden apartment in West Palm Beach. She was defensive about her plans. I could not get her to talk seriously with me about Terry or anything else.

The winter back home continued to break all records, which seemed to fit my needs. When I ventured out, it was for breakfast or long walks with my new dog. Work was mostly snow plowing. I occupied myself with crises. The pipes freezing in Town Hall. The roof collapsing in the fire station. An age discrimination suit. What I lacked in intimacy, I made up for in meetings.

* * *

"I see you got yourself a dog," Judith said. It was early April and three days of rain had all but washed away the last of the winter's ice. She was standing on the Squeer Island bridge, shielding her eyes from the sun. She looked neither happy nor annoyed to see me, but amused, if not at the mud all over my clothes then at Flubber, who kept leaping up the slippery embankment and sliding back down on his belly.

He was a golden retriever puppy, the kind that wiggles all over and runs for a stick before you throw it. "Stay!" she said firmly when he clopped up the embankment, and stay he did in his way, chasing his tail in circles. Her own dog, the shaggy black one, was upon us in seconds. Both of them slid into the muddy creek bottom, sniffing, running toward each other and away, leaving us alone on the bridge to accomplish much the same thing.

I'd seen Gordon's three-legged dog sitting up in the prow of Stumpy's dinghy, following him into town for his beer and sausages, and now a bag of kibble. "Did Judith give him away?" I asked.

"Didn't give nothing away. This 'un picked me out," Stumpy said proudly. "Moved in on me."

I'd watched for Judith at meetings, at the post office, the tea room; collected stray facts and rumors as if amassing a scrapbook. The stories had her moving to New York, sleeping with another lawyer, selling the house, becoming a lesbian, buying a boat, starting a shelter for wounded seabirds. I'd avoided the island for seven months since Crystal's death, but lately I began walking the dog here in hopes of crossing Judith's path. If she still had Silkie, she had to walk her. Her favorite walks were around the island or from her house to the bridge and back.

She looked even thinner, tired around the eyes. I wasn't surprised that she didn't smile at me the way she once had; encouraging, expectant. If anything she seemed to look through me. I'd practiced a hundred different opening lines and promptly forgot every one. "Did you hear about the new candidate Johnny's running for selectman?" I said. "Bernice Cady."

"Are you serious?" Judith stepped toward me, then stopped. "That sweet little girl who used to be a teller at the bank?"

"Loan officer now. Very bright. Native born. Makes perfect sense, if you think about it. Not abrasive, unassuming. Absolutely one hundred percent loyal to Johnny. People miss the old favor machine."

"Sure, the people who got the favors."

"Well, she's very convincing. Didn't you read about last Monday's meeting?"

Judith hugged herself as if against the cold, shaking her head. "Must have missed it."

"She gave a speech about the way Saltash used to be. Neighbors who used to build each other's houses. Flags in every window for the Fourth of July parade. Respect for our elders."

"Sounds like it got to you."

"Might have, if it was anything like the town I grew up in."

"Sorry I wasn't there."

"People loved it. She may win."

Judith looked in my eyes for a moment, then back up the road, as if someone were calling. "It sounds as if you have your hands full," she said. "Come on, Silkie," she walked back the way she had come.

I was surprised to be invited to the *alter kockers'* meeting because none of them had spoken to me since the hearing on the dike. But if we were to keep the wolf at bay, if we were to defeat Johnny Lynch again, we had to do it together. I was sitting behind the glass-topped liquor cart when I met Judith for the second time. She was wearing a cashmere turtleneck, ribbed, blue; silver half-moon earrings and a perfume that brought me back to the day she led me to her shack, let her coat slip to the floor, and slid her cold hands under my shirt.

In the middle of the meeting she turned suddenly and murmured, "Is there something you want?"

"No. Why do you ask?"

"Because you're staring at me."

"Well, there is something."

"Go on," she said. She didn't sound pleased.

"Do you remember that broom crowberry I got for you last year? Is it still alive or did it die over the winter? It's been a very cold winter."

"It's alive. I had a mulch of pine needles on it."

"Because if it's still alive . . . I think I could get some more and we could make a very nice area for it. If you want to."

"I'll think about it." Her eyes took me in.

"Well, if you do want it . . ."

"I know how to get in touch with you," she said. "If I do."

You can go without seeing somebody for months in this town, then suddenly cross paths every day. Or maybe I was trying to bump into Judith, and she stopped avoiding me. I caught sight of her at the grocery, in the street, her car flashing past, her suede jacket disappearing into the library. She was chatting in front of Town Hall. She was buying a Sunday paper at Barstow's Convenience. She had resumed coming to the selectmen's meetings occasionally.

I brought Kara and Allison to a Disney movie. I was taking them to the four o'clock show with a hundred other parents or surrogates and two hundred overexcited kids, then out for pizza. There was Judith with her lawyer, Timothy Worth. I'd seen him argue a case before our zoning board. Bow tie and Brooks Brothers suit; deep voice and little content. With them was a girl about ten. Before I figured out what to do, Kara bounded over. "Judith!" she screeched. "When is Natasha coming to our school again?"

"When she comes home for Passover, maybe then."

"Will she bring a hawk?"

"I never know what Natasha will bring," Judith said with a rueful smile.

Timothy paid little attention to me. Because they were sleeping together? Or because they weren't? I tried to see how she looked at him, to gauge the electricity.

"Who's Natasha?" his daughter asked. If she didn't know, they probably weren't involved. Yet.

I cleared my throat and butted in. "Did you think about that broom crowberry?"

"All the time," she said, and let Timothy Worth draw her away. What did that mean, all the time? Was she being sarcastic? Did she mean she missed me? Judith always meant something.

I should have called first. But I couldn't bring myself to ask. If Timothy Worth's car was in the drive, I would leave. Judith and I would be friends, nothing more; I owed her that much. It was ten-thirty on a Saturday morning—time enough to be up and dressed. I didn't want to embarrass anybody. I hit the horn when I turned up the drive. I could see that about a third of the garden had been planted. The peas were up and rows of tiny seedlings. Something was growing under plastic milk cartons. Judith's was the only car in sight.

Silkie started barking. Flubber spun around in the front seat, whimpering to be let out. Two cats were sunning themselves on the porch railings, one of them the one-eyed Io and the other Principessa, the huge silver tabby who took one look at me and dove under the porch. "Stay!" I said to the dog. I felt enough of an intruder myself.

I was carrying one pot of the broom crowberry with me, as an excuse, an offering, a talisman. Bring me luck. You did before. Judith peered out the window and then disappeared. For a while nothing happened. Finally the door opened.

I held out the pot.

"But I didn't say I wanted it."

"It's yours anyhow."

"For how long?"

"To live and die here."

She studied my face, my eyes, and then finally she smiled and stood aside, letting me in. "That seems a satisfactory guarantee. I guess I'll take it. Welcome back, David. Welcome home."

I put the pot down carefully and took her in my arms.

DAVID

I couldn't say I'd ever moved back into my house after Crystal and Laramie died; but now I was moving out. I sold the house quickly. The new owners wanted the couch, the rugs and kitchen appliances, even the sagging queen bed in my room, utensils, plates, the works. They intended to close the place up winters and rent it by the week in the summer. The couple bargained to the last nickel on every item down to the shower curtain, leading me from room to room, taking turns like interrogating cops. If they hadn't made me feel like a mark, I would have given it all away. I didn't want to look at this old stuff. I had to get out of here.

Although I told Judith there was nothing left to move but my clothing—what little wasn't already at her house—she insisted there were objects I'd overlooked. She loaded three boxes with Laramie's toys alone. There were things of Crystal's that I had ignored or simply could not bring myself to touch. The suitcase that had served as a bedside table next to Michelle's old couch. A black silk kimono on a hook behind the bathroom door. Judith arrived with me at seven A.M. on a Saturday morning and packed boxes furiously until noon. It saddened me to see the house with everything pulled out. A stray button under a dresser, a tiny lost horse behind a door. When Judith's car was loaded and each box labeled—Goodwill, Salvation Army, Day Care Center, Church—she touched my shoulder. "Are you all right?"

"Why not? What do you mean?"

She was looking at Crystal's exercise bike, which I'd discovered behind the couch and begun dismantling. Six bolts, twice that many screws. But my palms were moist and the screwdriver kept slipping from my grip. It had taken me the better part of an hour. "Is it hard to leave?" she said.

"This house? With all the work it needs?"

"But I can't help feeling it's what you wanted." She unbuttoned her coat and made a place for herself, not next to me but on the floor, where the apparatus lay between us like Crystal's dismantled life. "A little house. A little family. There's nothing wrong with that, David."

"But it was a life with you that I wanted. I just thought I couldn't have it. Because you loved Gordon. Because you were so much more than I was."

"David."

"I did the same thing I did when I played baseball. I turned my back on what took work and patience, what I couldn't have right away, and did the next easiest thing. What you and Gordon offered was beyond anything I could imagine possible. Living with Crystal felt familiar. Mother. Father. Child. A little house in town. People wanted me to be that person, don't you see? My mom. My sister. They couldn't understand what I was doing with you. But with Crystal, I was just like them. Even people in town. I was one of the guys out with the woman and kids at Penia's on Friday night. I was one of *them*. Finally. Maybe Crystal is what I felt I deserved."

Judith frowned. "Don't imagine you'll be one of them if you're living with me, David. I'm not the kind of woman nice people like. I say what I mean. That's considered bitchy. I never had children. That's considered weird. Your own sister calls me cold. You'll be living in a ten-acre waterfront compound worth well over a million dollars on the market. Don't imagine people aren't counting. That won't make you one of the guys."

"Why would I care?"

"Because you always did. You were an outsider from the day your folks moved here. You married into a family that used you. You were always looking for a way inside."

"Not anymore. I killed a woman and her son doing that. Maybe I can finally be what I choose, no matter how different it is."

Judith kicked aside the tools and piping between us. She touched her fingers to my lips. "You didn't kill anyone."

"Whatever I did or didn't, it's over. You're the one I want."

"I wish I could believe that."

"You will. Over time, you will."

JUDITH

58 Judith was using her shack again to get away from the construction noise. David was having a greenhouse added onto the south side of the house. It would be part working greenhouse and part breakfast room. It was necessary for David to feel it was his house also, and his needs and his aesthetic did not always coincide with what Gordon had built. Her bedroom was to become their bedroom, with some space borrowed from the room where Gordon had spent the last years of his illness and where he had died. What remained of that room would become an additional bath and a hallway to the new greenhouse. The construction was not the most peaceful way to begin and to work out their relationship, but it was essential.

After selling his house, David used the loft in his mother's barn for his office and occasional bedroom in town. They needed to save money. She had taken a mortgage to finance the renovations. On her advice, David had used the money from selling his house to buy into the nursery. Judith had gone over the books with her accountant and set up the deal. She thought it was important that David actually be a partner instead of an employee—for his position in town, his self-esteem, and as an argument when the custody agreement was reopened.

Sometimes it took all her skill as a negotiator to work out their problems. It would not be easy. David was not as verbal as Gordon, nor as confident in setting forth his needs. He kept his thoughts to himself, and a simple discussion could feel like prying. There were compensations.

In the evening after the construction crew left and they had supper, often they went out into the dunes together. It was June, the perfect month before hordes of tourists and summer people clogged town, before the black and greenhead flies came swarming. It was picnic weather. It was beach blanket weather. It was love with the sun setting across his shoulder, the clouds barred orange and fuchsia. Their bodies fit together even better than they had.

The first summer would be ragged, with Gordon's children and grandchildren having to adjust to a new proprietor, a new boss, a new possessor—of her and the land. David had to work out his roles with each of them. Except for Natasha, all Gordon's offspring were perturbed by David's presence. His mother and sister were not overjoyed with her. She had not succeeded in charming them yet, but she had not given up trying. It would be hard for David to feel he was not an impostor assuming Gordon's clothes; but he would find his own way gradually, she was convinced.

She watched his confidence grow with her in bed, in conversation, in meetings with her more established friends and his inherited family; in dealing with the contractors as if this truly was his house. She knew what he wanted. He needed to have a clear position. That was how it was with David. Patiently she waited for him to bring the matter up: sometime this summer they would marry. She could feel it approaching them like a season, something coming into view. If they were married, it would be easier to renegotiate the custody settlement so that David could have his son part of the summer, half the school vacations. She would make the arrangements so she could plead on a *pro hac vice* motion before a Florida court, along with his new lawyer down there. She had spoken to the lawyer a couple of times and they had exchanged more formal letters. David would pay more child support in return for having his son with him part of the year. They would manage.

The sun slipped into the bay and the sky turned to greenish-violet. A breeze played over their bare skin. It was time to get up and go into their changing house.

Afterword

We're talkers. We talk things over endlessly. Not only dinner, often the first subject broached over coffee every morning at dawn, but the garden, the cats, when to paint the bathroom and fix the car, meetings, families, friends, and, of course, our work. In the car, in the living room, in the supermarket, in bed, we discuss. On long walks through the quiet Cape Cod woods, it is not uncommon to hear our voices shouting through the underbrush, each arguing to get a point across. We've ruined the pensive walks of nature-seeking tourists and sent hunters away sputtering. There's a sense in which our life—like that of many tight couples—is a constant collaboration.

The first time we worked together was shortly after we met, when we wrote a play *The Last White Class*. About the busing crisis in Boston, it was written for community theaters, went through a number of productions and was published. Collaborating was a strain, but we survived it.

We did not think of writing together again for twenty years, when Ira had the idea for a novel that Marge found intriguing but felt needed more strands to complete. We began talking about it, just as a fantasy at first. We thought we might invent a whole new persona to author the novel, and even gave our creation a name and a biography. It was still simply a pastime, but as we discussed the novel, we began to be involved imaginatively in it and finally we simply decided to proceed without telling anybody (agents, editors, friends) what we were doing— so that no one could talk us out of it.

We had a rough idea of the shape of the story. Ira began writing David, and Marge began writing Judith and Johnny. We noticed immediately that David was in the first person (which is often how Ira likes to write) and Judith and Johnny were in the third person (which is how Marge usually writes). The logic was clear: the story begins in David's mind. From then on we alternated characters at various points.

When we had completed the first draft, we switched off for long periods, each of us having input into what the other had written throughout the second draft. We argued a lot in that process. What, you want to change that masterful delicious scene? How dare you! But we galloped along, rewriting and cutting and adding and moving scenes around.

Third and fourth drafts we did together, occasionally taking difficult parts off to be chewed on and worked over separately. Always we put it back together, both sitting in the same room, Marge at the computer (she is by far the faster typist) and Ira looking quite literally over her right shoulder. There were a few technical problems in switching from computer to computer, because although they are the same make and have the same software, we configure them differently. But those were minor glitches. We haggled a lot about the shading of the characters, we fought over sentences and paragraphs, we laughed and carried on and finished up. Then we sent off what we had written to New York.

Eventually we decided to scrap our pseudonym and be ourselves. We had learned something since working on the *The Last White Class*. Collaboration requires respect and good communication. It requires being able to detach from your own preconceptions and actually listen to the other person's notions. That means a fair amount of flexibility in an arena where the writer is usually in complete and godlike control of the story and the characters. It means relinquishing that control or at least easing up on it considerably.

Writing together is easier than writing alone. It isn't exactly half the work, but it is about two-thirds of the work of writing a novel by oneself. It is also more fun. Writing is usually a lonely activity, months and years of labor without much feedback. But collaborating is far from lonely. And when you are in a couple, it can be sexy and satisfying. Although there were times when we each wanted to strangle the other for stubborn resistance to our own precious ideas and our own irreplaceable brilliant words, nonetheless most of the time it was highly enjoyable. Marge enjoys the act of writing (usually), but for Ira it was more of a surprise to find writing pleasurable. We have both begun individual projects since completing *Storm Tide*, but some years down the pike, we may well work together again.

ACKNOWLEDGMENTS

A few acknowledgments: in researching minor league baseball, we found *Good Enough to Dream* by Roger Kahn; *False Spring* by Pat Jordan; and *The Boys Who Would Be Cubs* by Joseph Bosco helpful to us. *Women, Animals and Vegetables* by Maxine Kumin put to rest any fantasies we might have had about keeping horses instead of cats as pets; while *The Whole Horse Catalogue*, edited by Steven D. Price, told us more than we ever wanted to know about the sport of dressage. For information on topics as diverse as nipple piercing, lung cancer and land sale scams in Florida, various sites on the World Wide Web were indispensable. Closer to home, the Wellfleet library once again has our deepest thanks for numerous interlibrary loans. Ruthann Robson, terrific novelist and poet and a fine lawyer too, answered some legal questions that came up via Judith's career. *The Fundamentals of Surgical Oncology* edited by Robert J. McKenna and Gerald P. Murphy was invaluable, as was *Understanding Cancer* by Mark Renneker, in dealing with Gordon's illness.

ABOUT THE AUTHORS

MARGE PIERCY is the author of thirteen previous novels, including *City of Darkness, City of Light*; *The Longings of Women*; *He, She and It* (winner of the prestigious Arthur C. Clarke Award in Great Britain); *Braided Lives*; *Gone to Soldiers*; and *Woman on the Edge of Time*. She has also written thirteen collections of poetry, including *Mars and Her Children* and *What Are Big Girls Made Of?* She lives on Cape Cod with her husband, the novelist Ira Wood. Her work has been translated into sixteen languages. Her website address is http://www.capecod.net/~tmpiercy.

IRA WOOD is the author of two novels, *The Kitchen Man* and *Going Public*, as well as plays and screenplays. His workshops have inspired students all over the country to dig more deeply into their personal lives, to face the barriers of hopelessness and their fear of writing in order to overcome the inner censor. Recently, he and Marge Piercy started a small independent publishing company. Visit them at http://www.leapfrogpress.com.